D1637492

Dixie After the War

A Da Capo Press Reprint Series

THE AMERICAN SCENE
Comments and Commentators

GENERAL EDITOR: WALLACE D. FARNHAM
University of Illinois

F
216
.A94
1970

Dixie After the War

An Exposition of Social Conditions Existing
In the South, During the Twelve Years
Succeeding the Fall of Richmond

By Myrta Lockett Avary

THE LIBRARY
INDIANA STATE UNIVERSITY
EVANSVILLE CAMPUS

WITHDRAWN

DA CAPO PRESS · NEW YORK · 1970

038723

A Da Capo Press Reprint Edition

This Da Capo Press edition of *Dixie After the War* is an unabridged republication of the first edition published in New York in 1906.

Library of Congress Catalog Card Number 79-77701

SBN 306-71339-X

Copyright, 1906, by Doubleday, Page & Company

Published by Da Capo Press
A Division of Plenum Publishing Corporation
227 West 17th Street, New York, N.Y. 10011
All rights reserved

Manufactured in the United States of America

Dixie After the War

An Exposition of Social Conditions Existing
in the South, During the Twelve Years
Succeeding the Fall of Richmond.

By

Myrta Lockett Avary

Author of "A Virginia Girl in the Civil War"

With an Introduction by
General Clement A. Evans

Illustrated from old paintings, daguerreotypes
and rare photographs

New York
Doubleday, Page & Company
1906

Copyright, 1906, by Doubleday, Page & Company
Published September, 1906

All rights reserved,
including that of translation into foreign languages,
including the Scandinavian

To

THE MEMORY OF MY BROTHER,

PHILIP LOCKETT,

(First Lieutenant, Company G, 14th Virginia Infantry, Armistead's Brigade,
Pickett's Division, C. S. A.)

Entering the Confederate Army, when hardly more
than a lad, he followed General Robert E.
Lee for four years, surrendering at Appo-
mattox. He was in Pickett's immortal
charge at Gettysburg, and with
Armistead when Armistead
fell on Cemetery Hill

The faces I see before me are those of young men. Had you not been this I would not have appeared alone as the defender of my southland, but for love of her I break my silence and speak to you. Before you lies the future — a future full of golden promise, full of recompense for noble endeavor, full of national glory before which the world will stand amazed. Let me beseech you to lay aside all rancor, and all bitter sectional feeling, and take your place in the rank of those who will bring about a conciliation out of which will issue a reunited country. — *From an address by Jefferson Davis in his last years, to the young men of the South*

INTRODUCTION

THIS book may be called a revelation. It seems to me a body of discoveries that should not be kept from the public—discoveries which have origin in many sources but are here brought together in one book for the first time.

No book hitherto published portrays so fully and graphically the social conditions existing in the South for the twelve years following the fall of Richmond, none so vividly presents race problems. It is the kind of history a witness gives. The author received from observers and participants the larger part of the incidents and anecdotes which she employs. Those who lived during reconstruction are passing away so rapidly that data, unless gathered now, can never be had thus at first hand; every year increases the difficulty. Mrs. Avary's experience as author, editor and journalist, her command of shorthand and her social connections have opened up opportunities not usually accessible to one person; added to this is the balance of sympathy which she is able to strike as a Southern woman who has sojourned much at the North. In these pages she renders a public service. She aids the American to better understanding of his country's past and clearer concept of its present.

In connection with the book's genesis, it may be said that the author grew up after the war on a large Virginia plantation where her parents kept open house in the true Southern fashion. Two public roads which united at their gates, were thoroughfares linking county-towns in Virginia and North Carolina, and were much traveled by jurists, lawyers and politicians on their way to and from various court sittings; these gentlemen often found it both convenient and pleasant to stop for supper and over night at Lombardy Grove, particularly as a son of the house was of their guild. Perhaps few of the company thus gathered realised what an earnest listener they had in the little girl, Myrta, who sat intent at her father's or brother's knee, drinking in eagerly the discussions and stories. To impressions and information so acquired much was added through family correspondence with relatives and friends in Petersburg, Richmond, Atlanta, the Carolinas; also, in experiences related by these friends and relatives when hospitalities were exchanged; interesting and eventful diaries, too, were at the author's disposal. Such was her unconscious preparation for the writing of this book. Her conscious preparation was a tour of several Southern States recently undertaken for the purpose of collecting fresh data and substantiating information already possessed.

While engaged, for a season, in journalism in New York, she put out her first Southern book, "A Virginia Girl in the Civil War" (1903). This met with such warm welcome that she was promptly called upon for a second dealing with post-bellum life from a woman's viewpoint. The result was the Southern journey mentioned, the accidental discovery and presentment (1905) of the war journal of Mrs. James Chestnut ("A Diary From Dixie"), and the writing of the present volume which, I think, exceeds her commission, inasmuch as it is not only what is known as a "woman's book" but is a "man's book" also, exhibiting a masculine grasp, explained by its origin, of political situations, and an intimate personal tone in dealing with the lighter social side of things, possible only to a woman's pen. It is a very unusual book. All readers may not accept the author's conclusions, but I think that all must be interested in what she says and impressed with her spirit of fairness and her painstaking effort to present a truthful picture of an extraordinary social and political period in our national life. Her work stimulates interest in Southern history. A safe prophecy is that this book will be the precursor of as many post-bellum memoirs of feminine authorship as was "A Virginia Girl" of memoirs of war-time.

No successor can be more comprehensive, as a glance at the table of contents will show. The tragedy, pathos, corruption, humour, and absurdities of the military dictatorship and of reconstruction, the topsy-turvy conditions generally, domestic upheaval, negroes voting, Black and Tan Conventions and Legislatures, disorder on plantations, Loyal Leagues and Freedmen's Bureaus, Ku Klux and Red Shirts, are presented with a vividness akin to the camera's. A wide interest is appealed to in the earlier chapters narrating incidents connected with Mr. Lincoln's visit to Richmond, Mr. Davis' journeyings, capture and imprisonment, the arrest of Vice-President Stephens and the effort to capture General Toombs. Those which deal with the Federal occupation of Columbia and Richmond at once rivet attention. The most full and graphic description of the situation in the latter city just after the war, that has yet been produced, is given, and I think the interpretation of Mr. Davis' course in leaving Richmond instead of remaining and trying to enter into peace negotiations, is a point not hitherto so clearly taken.

As a bird's-eye view of the South after the war, the book is expositive of its title, every salient feature of the time and territory being brought under observation. The States upon which attention is chiefly focussed, however, are Virginia and South Carolina, two showing reconstruction at its best and worst. The reader does not need assurance that this volume cost the author years of well-directed labour; hasty effort could not have produced a work of such depth, breadth and variety. It will meet with prompt welcome, I am sure, and its value will not diminish with years.

CLEMENT A. EVANS.

Atlanta, Ga.

CONTENTS

CONTENTS—*Continued*

LIST OF ILLUSTRATIONS

THE FALLING CROSS

CHAPTER I

THE FALLING CROSS

"THE SOUTHERN CROSS" and a cross that fell during the burning of Columbia occur to my mind in unison.

With the Confederate Army gone and Richmond open to the Federal Army, her people remembered New Orleans, Atlanta, Columbia. New Orleans, where "Beast Butler" issued orders giving his soldiers license to treat ladies offending them as "women of the town." Atlanta, whose citizens were ordered to leave; General Hood had protested and Mayor Calhoun had plead the cause of the old and feeble, of women that were with child; and of them that turned out of their houses had nowhere to go, and without money, food, or shelter, must perish in woods and waysides. General Sherman had replied: "I give full credit to your statements of the distress that will be occasioned, yet shall not revoke my orders, because they were not designed to meet the humanities of the case. You cannot qualify war in harsher terms than I will. War is cruelty, and you cannot refine it." "The order to depopulate Atlanta was obeyed amid agonies and sorrows indescribable," Colonel J. H. Keatley, U. S. A., has affirmed.

There are some who hold with General Sherman that the most merciful way to conduct war is to make it as merciless and horrible as possible, and so end it the quicker. One objection to this is that it creates in a subjugated people such hatred and distrust of the conquering army and government that a generation or two must die out before this passes away; and therefore, in a very real sense, the method does not make quick end of conflict.

Richmond remembered how Mayor Goodwin went to meet General Sherman and surrendered Columbia, praying for it his pity and protection. General Sherman had said: "Go home and sleep in peace, Mr. Mayor. Your city shall be safe." Mayor Goodwin returned, praising General Sherman. By next morning, the City of Gardens was almost swept from the face of the earth. The rabble ("my bummers," General Sherman laughingly called his men set apart for such work), pouring into the town, had invaded and sacked homes, driving inmates—among these mothers with new-born babes—into the streets; they had demolished furniture, fired dwellings.

Houses of worship were not spared. The Methodist Church, at whose altar the Sabbath before Rev. William Martin had administered the Sacrament to over four hundred negroes, was burned. So was the Ursuline Convent. This institution was a branch of the order in Ohio; it sheltered nuns and students of both sections; Protestant and Catholic alike were there in sanctuary. One Northern Sister had lost two brothers in the Federal Army. Another was joyously hoping to find in Sherman's ranks one or more of her five Yankee brothers. The shock of that night killed her. A Western girl was "hoping yet fearing" to see her kinsmen. Guards, appointed for protection, aided in destruction. Rooms were invaded, trunks rifled. Drunken soldiers blew smoke in nuns' faces, saying:

"Holy! holy! O yes, we are holy as you!" And: "What do you think of God now? Is not Sherman greater?" Because of the sacred character of the establishment, because General Sherman was a Catholic, and because he had sent assurances of protection to the Mother Superior, they had felt safe. But they had to go.

"I marched in the procession through the blazing streets," wrote the Western girl, "venerable Father O'Connell at the head holding high the crucifix, the black-robed Mother Superior and the *religieuses* following with their charges, the white-faced, frightened girls and children, all in line and in perfect order. They sought the Catholic church for safety, and the Sisters put the little ones to sleep on the cushioned pews; then the children, driven out by roystering soldiers, ran stumbling and terror-stricken into the graveyard and crouched behind gravestones."

One soldier said he was sorry for the women and children of South Carolina, but the hotbed of secession must be destroyed. "But I am not a South Carolinian," retorted the Western girl, "I am from Ohio. Our Mother Superior was in the same Convent in Ohio with General Sherman's sister and daughter." "The General ought to know that," he responded quickly. "If you are from Ohio—that's my state—I'll help you." For answer, she pointed to the Convent; the cross above it was falling.

They recur to my mind in unison—that cross, sacred alike to North and South, falling above a burning city, and the falling Southern Cross, Dixie's beautiful battle-flag.

Two nuns, conferring apart if it would not be well to take the children into the woods, heard a deep, sad voice saying: "Your position distresses me greatly!" Startled, they turned to perceive a Federal officer beside a tombstone just behind them. "Are you a Catholic," they asked, "that you pity us?" "No; simply a man and a soldier." Dawn came, and with it some Irish soldiers to early Mass. Appalled, they cried: "O, this will never do! Send for the General! The General would never permit it!"

At reveille all arson, looting and violence had ceased as by magic, even as conflagration had started as by magic in the early hours of the night when four signal rockets went up from as many corners of the town. But the look of the desolated city in the glare of daylight was indescribable. Around the church were broken and empty trunks and boxes; in the entrance stood a harp with broken strings.

General Sherman came riding by; the Mother Superior summoned him; calmly facing the Attila of his day, she said in her clear, sweet voice: "General, this is how you keep your promise to me, a cloistered nun, and these my sacred charges." General Sherman answered: "Madame, it is all the fault of your negroes, who gave my soldiers liquor to drink."

General Sherman, in official report, charged the burning of Columbia to General Hampton, and in his "Memoirs" gives his reason: "I confess that I did so to shake the faith of his people in him"; and asserts that his "right wing," "having utterly ruined Columbia," passed on to Winnsboro.

Living witnesses tell how that firing was done. A party of soldiers would enter a dwelling, search and rifle; and in departing throw wads of burning paper into closets, corners, under beds, into cellars. Another party would repeat the process. Family and servants would follow after, removing wads and extinguishing flames until ready to drop. Devastation for secession, that was what was made plain in South Carolina; if the hotbed of "heresy" had to be destroyed for her sins, what of the Confederate Capital, Richmond, the long-desired, the "heart of the Rebellion"?

THE RUINS OF MILLWOOD

Millwood was the ancestral home of General Hampton, and was burned by Sherman's orders
The property is now owned by General Hampton's sisters.

"WHEN THIS CRUEL WAR IS OVER"

CHAPTER II

"When This Cruel War is Over"

"When this cruel war is over" was the name of one of our war songs. So many things we planned to do when the war should be over. With the fall of the Southern Capital the war was over, though we did not know it at once.

Again and again has the story been told of Sunday, April 2, in Richmond. The message brought into St. Paul's Church from Lee to Davis, saying Richmond could no longer be defended; the quiet departure of the President; the noble bearing of the beloved rector, Rev. Dr. Minnegerode; the self-control of the troubled people remaining; the solemn Communion Service; these are all a part now of American history of that sad time when brother strove with brother; a time whose memories should never be revived for the purpose of keeping rancor alive, but that should be unfalteringly remembered, and every phase of it diligently studied, that our common country may in no wise lose the lesson for which we of the North and South paid so tremendous a price.

Into Dr. Hoge's church a hurried messenger came. The pastor read the note handed up to him, bowed his head in silent prayer, and then said: "Brethren, trying scenes are before us; General Lee has suffered reverses. But remember that God is with us in the storm as well as in the calm. Go quietly to your homes, and whatever may be in store for us, let us not forget that we are Christian men and women. The blessing of the

9

Father, the Son, and the Holy Ghost be with us all. Amen." So other pastors commended their people.

None who lived through that Sabbath could forget it. Our Government, our soldiers, hurrying off; women saying goodbye to husband, lover, brother, or friend, and urging haste; everybody who could go, going, when means of transportation were insufficient for Government uses, and "a kingdom for a horse" could not buy one—horses brought that day $1,000 apiece in gold; handsome houses full of beautiful furniture left open and deserted; people of all sexes, colors and classes running hither and yon; boxes and barrels dragged about the streets from open commissary stores; explosions as of earthquakes; houses aflame; the sick and dying brought out; streets running liquid fire where liquor had been emptied into gutters, that it might not be available for invading troops; bibulous wretches in the midst of the terror, brooding over such waste; drunken roughs and looters, white and black, abroad; the penitentiary disgorging striped hordes; the ribald songs, the anguish, the fears, the tumult; the noble calm of brave souls, the patient endurance of sweet women and gentle children—these are all a part of American history, making thereon a page blistered with tears for some; and for others, illumined with symbols of triumph and glory.

And yet, we are of one blood, and the triumph and glory of one is the triumph and glory of the other; the anguish and tears of one the anguish and tears of the other; and the shame of one is the shame of both.

The fire was largely due to accident. In obedience to law, Confederate forces, in evacuating the city, fired tobacco warehouses, ordnance and other Government stores, gunboats in the James and bridges spanning the river. A wind, it is said, carried sparks towards the town, igniting first one building and then another; incen-

MRS. JEFFERSON DAVIS

diarism lent aid that pilfering might go on in greater security through public disorder and distress.

During the night detonations of exploding gunboats could be heard for miles, the noise and shock and lurid lights adding to the wretchedness of those within the city, and the anxieties of those who beheld its burnings from afar; among these, the advancing enemy, who was not without uneasy speculations lest he find Richmond, as Napoleon found Moscow, in ashes. General Shepley, U. S. A., has described the scene witnessed from his position near Petersburg, as a most beautiful and awful display of fireworks, the heavens at three o'clock being suddenly filled with bursting shells, red lights, Roman candles, fiery serpents, golden fountains, falling stars.

Nearly all the young men were gone; the fire department, without a full force of operatives, without horses, without hose, was unable to cope with the situation. Old men, women and children, and negro servants fought the flames as well as they could.

Friends and relatives who were living in Richmond then have told me about their experiences until I seem to have shared them. One who appears in these pages as Matoaca, gives me this little word-picture of the morning after the evacuation:

"I went early to the War Department, where I had been employed, to get letters out of my desk. The desk was open. Everything was open. Our President, our Government, our soldiers were gone. The papers were found and I started homeward. We saw rolls of smoke ahead, and trod carefully the fiery streets. Suddenly my companion caught my arm, crying: 'Is not that the sound of cavalry?' We hurried, almost running. Soon after we entered the house, some one exclaimed:

"'God help us! The United States flag is flying over our Capitol!'

"I laid my head on Uncle Randolph's knee and shivered. He placed his hand lightly on my head and said: 'Trust in God, my child. They can not be cruel to us. We are defenseless.' He had fought for that flag in Mexico. He had stood by Virginia, but he had always been a Unionist. I thought of New Orleans, Atlanta, Columbia."

An impression obtained that to negro troops was assigned the honor of first entering Richmond, hauling down the Southern Cross and hoisting in its place the Stars and Stripes. "Harper's Weekly" said: "It was fitting that the old flag should be restored by soldiers of the race to secure whose eternal degradation that flag had been pulled down." Whether the assignment was made or not, I am unable to say; if it was, it was not very graceful or wise on the part of our conquerors, and had it been carried out, would have been prophetic of what came after—the subversion.

White troops first entered Richmond, and a white man ran up the flag of the Union over our Capitol. General Shepley says that to his aide, Lieutenant de Peyster, he accorded the privilege as a reward for caring for his old flag that had floated over City Hall in New Orleans. On the other hand, it is asserted that Major Stevens performed the historic office, running up the two small guidons of the Fourth Massachusetts Cavalry, which were presently displaced by the large flag Lieutenant de Peyster had been carrying in the holster at his saddle-bow for many a day, that it might be in readiness for the use to which he now put it.

THE ARMY OF THE UNION

CHAPTER III

THE ARMY OF THE UNION: THE CHILDREN AND THE FLAG

THE Army of the Union entered Richmond with almost the solemnity of a processional entering church. It was occasion for solemn procession, that entrance into our burning city where a stricken people, flesh of their flesh and bone of their bone, watched in terror for their coming.

Our broken-hearted people closed their windows and doors and shut out as far as they could all sights and sounds. Yet through closed lattice there came that night to those living near Military Headquarters echoes of rejoicings.

Early that fateful morning, Mayor Mayo, Judge Meredith and Judge Lyons went out to meet the incoming foe and deliver up the keys of the city. Their coach of state was a dilapidated equipage, the horses being but raw-boned shadows of better days when there were corn and oats in the land. They carried a piece of wallpaper, on the unflowered side of which articles of surrender were inscribed in dignified terms setting forth that "it is proper to formally surrender the City of Richmond, hitherto Capital of the Confederate States of America." Had the words been engraved on satin in letters of gold, Judge Lyons (who had once represented the United States at the Court of St. James) could not have performed the honours of introduction between the municipal party and the Federal officers with statelier grace, nor could the latter have received the instrument of submission with profounder courtesy. "We went out not knowing what we would encounter," Mayor Mayo reported, "and we met a group of Chesterfields." Major Atherton H. Stevens, of General Weitzel's staff, was the immediate recipient of the wall-paper document.

General Weitzel and his associates were merciful to the stricken city; they aided her people in extinguishing the flames; restored order and gave protection. Guards were posted wherever needed, with instructions to repress lawlessness, and they did it. To this day, Richmond people rise up in the gates and praise that Army of the Occupation as Columbia's people can never praise General Sherman's. Good effect on popular sentiment was immediate.

Among many similar incidents of the times is this, as related by a prominent physician:

"When I returned from my rounds at Chimborazo I found a Yankee soldier sitting on my stoop with my little boy, Walter, playing with the tassels and buttons on his uniform. He arose and saluted courteously, and told me he was there to guard my property. 'I am under orders,' he said, 'to comply with any wish you may express.'"

Dr. Gildersleeve, in an address (June, 1904) before the Association of Medical Officers of the Army and Navy, C. S. A., referred to Chimborazo Hospital as "the most noted and largest military hospital in the annals of history, ancient or modern." With its many white buildings and tents on Chimborazo Hill, it looked like a town and a military post, which latter it was, with Dr. James B. McCaw for Commandant. General Weitzel and his staff visited the hospital promptly. Dr. McCaw and his corps in full uniform received them. Dr. Mott, General Weitzel's Chief Medical Director, exclaimed: "Ain't that old Jim McCaw?" "Yes," said "Jim McCaw," "and don't you want a drink?" "Invite the General, too," answered Dr. Mott. General Weitzel issued passes to Dr. McCaw and his corps, and gave verbal orders that Chimborazo Confederates should be taken care of under all circumstances. He proposed to take Dr. McCaw and his corps into the Federal service, thus arming him with power to make requisition for supplies, medicines, etc., which offer the doctor, as a loyal Confederate, was unable to accept.

Others of our physicians and surgeons found friends in Federal ranks. To how many poor Boys in Blue, longing for home and kindred, had not they and our women ministered! The orders of the Confederate Government were that the sick and wounded of both armies should be treated alike. True, nobody had the best of fare, for we had it not to give. We were without medicines; it was almost impossible to get morphia, quinine, and other remedies. Quinine was $400 an ounce, when it could be bought at all, even in the earlier years of the war. Our women became experts in manufacturing substitutes out of native herbs and roots. We ran wofully short of dressings and bandages, and bundles of old rags became treasures priceless. But the most cruel shortage was in food. Bitter words in Northern papers and by Northern speakers—after our defeat intensified, multiplied, and illustrated—about our treatment of prisoners exasperated us. "Will they never learn," we asked, "that on such rations as we gave our prisoners, our men were fighting in the field? We had not food for ourselves; the North blockaded us so we could not bring food from outside, and refused to exchange prisoners with us. What could we do?"

I wonder how many men now living remember certain loaves of wheaten bread which the women of Richmond collected with difficulty in the last days of the war and sent to Miss Emily V. Mason, our "Florence Nightingale," for our own boys. "Boys," Miss Emily announced—sick soldiers, if graybeards, were "boys" to "Cap'n," as they all called Miss Emily—"I have some flour-bread which the ladies of Richmond have sent you." Cheers, and other expressions of thankfulness. "The poor, sick Yankees," Miss Emily went on falteringly—uneasy countenances in the ward—*"can't* eat corn-bread—" "Give the flour-bread to the poor, sick Yankees, Cap'n!" came in cheerful, if quavering chorus from the cots. *"We* can eat corn-bread. Gruel is good for us. We *like* mush. Oughtn't to have flour-bread nohow." "Poor fellows!" "Cap'n" said proudly of their self-denial, "they were tired to death of corn-bread in all forms, and it was not good for them, for nearly all had intestinal disorders."

Along with this corn-bread story, I recall how Dr. Minnegerode, Protestant, and Bishop Magill, Catholic, used to meet each other on the street, and the one would say: "Doctor, lend me a dollar for a sick Yankee." And the other: "Bishop, I was about to ask *you* for a dollar for a sick Yankee." And how Annie E. Johns, of North Carolina, said she had seen Confederate soldiers take provisions from their own haversacks and give them to Federal prisoners *en route* to Salisbury. As matron, she served in hospitals for the sick and wounded of both armies. She said: "When I was in a hospital for Federals, I felt as if these men would defend me as promptly as our own."

In spite of the pillage, vandalism and violence they suffered, Southern women were not so biassed as to think that the gentle and brave could be found only among the wearers of the gray. Even in Sherman's Army were the gentle and brave upon whom fell obloquy due the "bummers" only. I have heard many stories like that of the boyish guard who, tramping on his beat around a house he was detailed to protect, asked of a young mother: "Why does your baby cry so?" She lifted her pale face, saying: "My baby is hungry. I have had no food—and so—I have no nourishment for him." Tears sprang into his eyes, and he said: "I will be relieved soon; I will draw my rations and bring them to you." He brought her his hands full of all good things he could find—sugar, tea, and coffee. And like that of two young Philadelphians who left grateful hearts behind them along the line of Sherman's march because they made a business of seeing how many women and children they could relieve and protect. In Columbia, during the burning, men in blue sought to stay ravages wrought by other men in blue. I hate to say hard things of men in blue, and I must say all the good things I can; because many were unworthy to wear the blue, many who were worthy have carried reproach.

On that morning of the occupation, our women sat behind closed windows, unable to consider the new path stretching before them. The way seemed to end at a wall. Could they have looked over and seen what lay ahead, they would have lost what little heart of hope they had; could vision have extended far enough, they might have won it back; they would have beheld some things unbelievable. For instance, they would have seen the little boy who played with the buttons and tassels, grown to manhood and wearing the uniform of an officer of the United States; they would have seen Southern men walking the streets of Richmond and other Southern cities with "U. S. A." on their haversacks; and Southern men and Northern men fighting side by side in Cuba and the Philippines, and answering alike to the name, " Yankees."

On the day of the occupation, Miss Mason and Mrs. Rhett went out to meet General Weitzel and stated that Mrs. Lee was an invalid, unable to walk, and that her house, like that of General Chilton and others, was in danger of fire. "What!" he exclaimed, "Mrs. Lee in danger? General Fitz Lee's mother, who nursed me so tenderly when I was sick at West Point! What can I do for her? Command me!" "We mean Mrs. Robert E. Lee," they said. "We want ambulances to move Mrs. Lee and other invalids and children to places of safety." Using his knee as a writing-table, he wrote an order for five ambulances; and the ladies rode off. Miss Emily's driver became suddenly and mysteriously tipsy and she had to put an arm around him and back up the vehicle herself to General Chilton's door, where his children, her nieces, were waiting, their dollies close clasped.

"Come along, Virginia aristocracy!" hiccoughed the befuddled Jehu. "I won't bite you! Come along, Virginia aristocracy!"

A passing officer came to the rescue, and the party were soon safely housed in the beautiful Rutherford home.

The Federals filled Libby Prison with Confederates, many of whom were paroled prisoners found in the city. Distressed women surrounded the prison, begging to know if loved ones were there; others plead to take food inside. Some called, while watching windows: "Let down your tin cup and I will put something in it." Others cried: "Is my husband in there? O, William, answer me if you are!" "Is my son, Johnny, here?" "O, please somebody tell me if my boy is in the prison!" Miss Emily passed quietly through the crowd, her hospital reputation securing admission to the prison; she was able to render much relief to those within, and to subdue the anxiety of those without.

"Heigho, Johnny Reb! in there now where we used to be!" yelled one Yankee complacently. "Been in there myself. D——d sorry for you, Johnnies!" called up another.

A serio-comic incident of the grim period reveals the small boy in an attitude different from that of him who was dandled on the Federal knee. Some tiny lads mounted guard on the steps of a house opposite Military Headquarters, and, being intensely "rebel" and having no other means of expressing defiance to invaders, made faces at the distinguished occupants of the establishment across the way. General Patrick, Provost-Marshal General, sent a courteously worded note to their father, calling his attention to these juvenile demonstrations. He explained that while he was not personally disturbed by the exhibition, members of his staff were, and that the children might get into trouble. The proper guardians of the wee insurgents, acting upon this information, their first of the battery unlimbered on their door-step, saw that the artillery was retired in good order, and peace and normal countenances reigned over the scene of the late engagements.

I open a desultory diary Matoaca kept, and read:

"If the United States flag were my flag—if I loved it—I would not try to make people pass under it who do not want to. I would not let them. It is natural that we should go out of our way to avoid walking under it, a banner that has brought us so much pain and woe and want—that has desolated our whole land.

"Some Yankees stretched a flag on a cord from tree to tree across the way our children had to come into

Richmond. The children saw it and cried out; and the driver was instructed to go another way. A Federal soldier standing near—a guard, sentinel or picket— ordered the driver to turn back and drive under that flag. He obeyed, and the children were weeping and wailing as the carriage rolled under it."

In Raymond, Mississippi, negro troops strung a flag across the street and drove the white children under it. In Atlanta, two society belles were arrested because they made a detour rather than walk under the flag. Such desecration of the symbol of liberty and union was committed in many places by those in power.

The Union flag is my flag and I love it, and, there- fore, I trust that no one may ever again pass under it weeping. Those little children were not traitors. They were simply human. If in the sixties situations had been reversed, and the people of New York, Bos- ton and Chicago had seen the Union flag flying over guns that shelled these cities, their children would have passed under it weeping and wailing. Perhaps, too, some would have sat on doorsteps and "unbeknownst" to their elders have made faces at commanding generals across the way; while others climbing upon the enemy's knees would have played with gold tassels and brass buttons.

Our newspapers, with the exception of the "Whig" and the "Sentinel," shared in the general wreckage. A Northern gentleman brought out a tiny edition of the former in which appeared two military orders promul- gating the policy General Weitzel intended to pursue. One paragraph read: "The people of Richmond are assured that we come to restore to them the blessings of peace and prosperity under the flag of the Union."

General Shepley, Military Governor by Weitzel's ap- pointment, repeated this in substance, adding: "The soldiers of the command will abstain from any offensive or insulting words or gestures towards the citizens." With less tact and generosity, he proceeded: "The Armies of the Rebellion having abandoned their efforts to enslave the people of Virginia, have endeavoured to destroy by fire their Capital. . . . The first duty of the Army of the Union will be to save the city doomed to destruction by the Armies of the Rebellion." That fling at our devoted army would have served as a clarion call to us—had any been needed—to remember the absent.

"It will be a blunder in us not to overlook that blunder of General Shepley's," urged Uncle Randolph.* "The important point is that the policy of conciliation is to be pursued." With the "Whig" in his hand, Uncle Randolph told Matoaca that the Thursday before Virginia seceded a procession of prominent Virginians marched up Franklin Street, carrying the flag of the Union and singing "Columbia," and that he was with them.

The family questioned if his mind were wandering, when he went on: "The breach can be healed—in spite of the bloodshed—if only the Government will pursue the right course now. Both sides are tired of hating and being hated, killing and being killed—this war between brothers—if Weitzel's orders reflect the mind of Lincoln and Grant—and they must—all may be well—before so very long."

---

* Gentlemen of the old regime would say: "A woman's name should appear in print but twice—when she marries and when she dies"; the "Society" page of to-day was unknown to them. They objected to newspaper notoriety for themselves, and were prone to sign pseudonyms to their newspaper articles. Matoaca, loyal to her uncle's prejudices, requires that I print him only by the name she gives him and the title, one which was affectionately applied to him by many who were not his kin. To give his real name in full would be to give hers.

These were the men of the Union Army who saved Richmond: The First Brigade, Third Division (Deven's Division), Twenty-fourth Army Corps, Army of the James, Brevet-Brigadier-General Edward H. Ripley commanding. This brigade was composed of the Eleventh Connecticut, Thirteenth New Hampshire, Nineteenth Wisconsin, Eighty-first New York, Ninety-eighth New York, One Hundredth and Thirty-ninth New York, Convalescent detachment from the second and third divisions of Sheridan's reinforcements.

"This Brigade led the column in the formal entry, and at the City Hall halted while I reported to Major-General Weitzel," says General Ripley. "General Weitzel had taken up his position on the platform of the high steps at the east front of the Confederate Capitol, and there, looking down into a gigantic crater of fire, suffocated and blinded with the vast volumes of smoke and cinders which rolled up over and enveloped us, he assigned me and my brigade to the apparently hopeless task of stopping the conflagration, and suppressing the mob of stragglers, released criminals, and negroes, who had far advanced in pillaging the city. He had no suggestions to make, no orders to give, except to strain every nerve to save the city, crowded as it was with women and children, and the sick and wounded of the Army of Northern Virginia.

"After requesting Major-General Weitzel to have all the other troops marched out of the city, I took the Hon. Joseph Mayo, then Mayor of Richmond, with me to the City Hall, where I established my headquarters. With the help of the city officials, I distributed my regiment quickly in different sections. The danger to the troops engaged in this terrific fire-fighting was infinitely enhanced by the vast quantities of powder and shells stored in the section burning. Into this sea of fire, with no less courage and self-devotion than as though fighting for their own firesides and families, stripped and plunged the brave men of the First Brigade.

" Meanwhile, detachments scoured the city, warning every one from the streets to their houses. . . . Every one carrying plunder was arrested. . . . The ladies of Richmond thronged my headquarters, imploring protection. They were sent to their homes under the escort of guards, who were afterwards posted in the center house of each block, and made responsible for the safety of the neighborhood. . . . Many painful cases of destitution were brought to light by the presence of these safeguards in private houses, and the soldiers divided rations with their temporary wards, in many cases, until a general system of relief was organised."*

---

* General Ripley, in "Confederate Column" of the "Times-Dispatch," Richmond, Virginia, May 29, 1904.

THE COMING OF LINCOLN

CHAPTER IV

THE COMING OF LINCOLN

THE South did not know that she had a friend in Abraham Lincoln, and the announcement of his presence in Richmond was not calculated to give comfort or assurance.

"Abraham Lincoln came unheralded. No bells rang, no guns boomed in salute. He held no levee. There was no formal jubilee. He must have been heartless as Nero to have chosen that moment for a festival of triumph. He was not heartless." So a citizen of Richmond, who was a boy at the time, and out doors and everywhere, seeing everything, remembers the coming of Lincoln.

One of the women who sat behind closed windows says: "If there was any kind of rejoicing, it must have been of a very somber kind; the sounds of it did not reach me." Another who looked through her shutters, said: "I saw him in a carriage, the horses galloping through the streets at a break-neck speed, his escort clearing the way. The negroes had to be cleared out of the way, they impeded his progress so." He was in Richmond April 4 and 5, and visited the Davis Mansion, the Capitol, Libby Prison, Castle Thunder and other places.

His coming was as simple, business-like, and unpretentious as the man himself. Anybody who happened to be in the neighbourhood on the afternoon of April 4, might have seen a boat manned by ten or twelve sailors pull ashore at a landing above Rockett's, and a tall, lank man step forth, "leading a little boy." By resemblance to pictures that had been scattered broadcast, this man could have been easily recognized as Abraham Lincoln. The little boy was Tad, his son. Major Penrose, who commanded the escort, says Tad was not with the President; Admiral Porter, General Shepley and others say he was.

Accompanied by Admiral Porter and several other officers and escorted by ten sailors, President Lincoln, "holding Tad's hand," walked through the city, which was in part a waste of ashes, and the smoke of whose burning buildings was still ascending. From remains of smouldering bridges, from wreckage of gunboats, from Manchester on the other side of the James, and from the city's streets smoke rose as from a sacrifice to greet the President.

A Northern newspaper man (who related this story of himself) recognizing that it was his business to make news as well as dispense it, saw some negroes at work near the landing where an officer was having débris removed, and other negroes idling. He said to this one and to that: "Do you know that man?" pointing to the tall, lank man who had just stepped ashore.

"Who *is* dat man, marster?"

"Call no man marster. That man set you free. That is Abraham Lincoln. Now is your time to shout. Can't you sing, 'God bless you, Father Abraham!'"

That started the ball rolling. The news spread like wild-fire. Mercurial blacks, already excited to fever-heat, collected about Mr. Lincoln, impeding his progress, kneeling to him, hailing him as "Saviour!" and "My Jesus!" They sang, shouted, danced. One woman jumped up and down, shrieking: "I'm free! I'm free! I'm free till I'm fool!" Some went into the regular Voodoo ecstasy, leaping, whirling, stamping, until their clothes were half torn off. Mr. Lincoln made a speech, in which he said:

"My poor friends, you are free—free as air. But you must try to deserve this priceless boon. Let the world see that you merit it by your good works. Don't let your joy carry you into excesses. Obey God's commandments and thank Him for giving you liberty, for to Him you owe all things. There, now, let me pass on. I have little time here and much to do. I want to go to the Capitol. Let me pass on."

Henry J. Raymond speaks of the President as taking his hat off and bowing to an old negro man who knelt and kissed his hand, and adds: "That bow upset the forms, laws and customs of centuries; it was a death-shock to chivalry, a mortal wound to caste. Recognize a nigger? Faugh!" Which proves that Mr. Raymond did not know or wilfully misrepresented a people who could not make reply. Northern visitors to the South may yet see refutation in old sections where new ways have not corrupted ancient courtesy, and where whites and blacks interchange cordial and respectful salutations, though they may be perfect strangers to each other, when passing on the road. If they are not strangers, greeting is usually more than respectful and cordial; it is full of neighbourly and affectionate interest in each other and each other's folks.

The memories of the living, even of Federal officers near President Lincoln, bear varied versions of his visit. General Shepley relates that he was greatly surprised when he saw the crowd in the middle of the street, President Lincoln and little Tad leading, and that Mr. Lincoln called out:

"Hullo, General! Is that you? I'm walking around looking for Military Headquarters."

General Shepley conducted him to our White House, where President Lincoln wearily sank into a chair, which happened to be that President Davis was wont to occupy while writing his letters, a task suffering frequent interruption from some one or other of his children, who had a way of stealing in upon him at any and all times to claim a caress.

Upon Mr. Lincoln's arrival, or possibly in advance, when it was understood that he would come up from City Point, there was discussion among our citizens as to how he should be received—that is, so far as our attitude toward him was concerned. There were several ways of looking at the problem. Our armies were still in the field, and all sorts of rumors were afloat, some accrediting them with victories.

A called meeting was held under the leadership of Judge Campbell and Judge Thomas, who, later, with General Joseph Anderson and others, waited on Mr. Lincoln, to whom they made peace propositions involving disbandment of our armies; withdrawal of our soldiers from the field, and reëstablishment of state governments under the Union, Virginia inaugurating this course by example and influence.

Mr. Lincoln had said in proclamation, the Southern States "can have peace any time by simply laying down their arms and submitting to the authority of the Union." It was inconceivable to many how we could ever want to be in the Union again. But wise ones said: "Our position is to be that of conquered provinces voiceless in the administration of our own affairs, or of States with some power, at least, of self-government." Then, there was the dread spectre of confiscation, proscription, the scaffold.

Judge Campbell and Judge Thomas reported: "The movement for the restoration of the Union is highly

THE WHITE HOUSE OF THE CONFEDERACY, RICHMOND, VA.

Presented to Mr. Davis, who refused it as a gift, but occupied it as the Executive residence. Now known as the Confederate Museum.

gratifying to Mr. Lincoln; he will give it full sympathy and coöperation."

"You people will all come back now," Mr. Lincoln had said to Judge Thomas, "and we shall have old Virginia home again."

Many had small faith in these professions of amity, and said so. "Lincoln is the man who called out the troops and precipitated war," was bitterly objected, "and we do not forget Hampton Roads."

A few built hopes on belief that Mr. Lincoln had long been eager to harmonize the sections. Leader of these was Judge John A. Campbell, ex-Associate Justice of the Supreme Court of the United States, and ex-Assistant Secretary of War of the expiring Confederacy. He had served with Mr. Hunter and Mr. Stephens on the Hampton Roads Peace Commission, knew Mr. Lincoln well, had high regard for him and faith in his earnest desire for genuine reconciliation between North and South. When the Confederate Government left the city, he remained, meaning to try to make peace, Mr. Davis, it is said, knowing his purpose and consenting, but having no hope of its success.

Only the Christmas before, when peace sentiments that led to the Hampton Roads Conference were in the air, striking illustrations in Northern journals reflected Northern sentiment. One big cartoon of a Christmas dinner in the Capitol at Washington, revealed Mr. Lincoln holding wide the doors, and the seceded States returning to the family love feast. Olive branches, the "Prodigal's Return," and nice little mottoes like "Come Home, Our Erring Sisters, Come!" were neatly displayed around the margin. Fatted calves were not to be despised by a starving people; but the less said about the pious influences of the "Prodigal's Return" the better. That Hampton Roads Conference (February,

1865) has always been a sore spot. In spite of the commissioners' statements that Mr. Lincoln's only terms were "unconditional surrender," many people blamed Mr. Davis for the failure of the peace movement; others said he was pusillanimous and a traitor for sanctioning overtures that had to be made, by Lincoln's requirements, "informally," and, as it were, by stealth.

"We must forget dead issues," our pacificators urged. "We have to face the present. The stand Mr. Lincoln has taken all along, that the Union is indissoluble and that a State can not get out of it however much she tries, is as fortunate for us now as it was unlucky once."

"In or out, what matters it if Yankees rule over us!" others declared.

"Mr. Lincoln is not in favor of outsiders holding official reins in the South," comforters responded. "He has committed himself on that point to Governor Hahn in Louisiana. When Judge Thomas suggested that he establish Governor Pierpont here, Mr. Lincoln asked straightway, 'Where is Extra Billy?' He struck the table with his fist, exclaiming, 'By Jove! I want that old game-cock back here!'"

When in 1862-3 West Virginia seceded from Virginia and was received into the bosom of the Union, a few "loyal" counties which did not go with her, elected Francis H. Pierpont Governor of the old State. At the head of sixteen legislators, he posed at Alexandria as Virginia's Executive, Mr. Lincoln and the Federal Congress recognizing him. Our real governor was the doughty warrior, William Smith, nick-named "Extra Billy" before the war, when he was always asking Congress for extra appropriations for an ever-lengthening stage-coach and mail-route line, which was a great Government enterprise under his fostering hand.

Governor Smith had left with the Confederate Government, going towards Lynchburg. He had been greatly concerned for his family, but his wife had said: "I may feel as a woman, but I can act like a man. Attend to your public affairs and I will arrange our family matters." The Mansion had barely escaped destruction by fire. The Smith family had vacated it to the Federals, had been invited to return and then ordered to vacate again for Federal occupation.

Mr. Lincoln said that the legislature that took Virginia out of the Union and Governor Letcher, who had been in office then, with Governor Smith, his successor, and Governor Smith's legislature, must be convened. "The Government that took Virginia out of the Union is the Government to bring her back. No other can effect it. They must come to the Capitol yonder where they voted her out and vote her back."

Uncle Randolph was one of those who had formally called upon Mr. Lincoln at the Davis Mansion. Feeble as he was, he was so eager to do some good that he had gone out in spite of his niece to talk about the "policy" he thought would be best. "I did not say much," he reported wistfully. "There were a great many people waiting on him. Things look strange at the Capitol. Federal soldiers all about, and campfires on the Square. Judge Campbell introduced me. President Lincoln turned from him to me, and said: 'You fought for the Union in Mexico.' I said, 'Mr. Lincoln, if the Union will be fair to Virginia, I will fight for the Union again.' I forgot, you see, that I am too old and feeble to fight. Then I said quickly, 'Younger men than I, Mr. President, will give you that pledge.' What did he say? He looked at me hard—and shook my hand—and there wasn't any need for him to say anything."

Mr. Lincoln's attitude towards Judge Campbell was one of confidence and cordiality. He knew the Judge's purity and singleness of purpose in seeking leniency for the conquered South, and genuine reunion between the sections. The Federal commanders understood his devotion and integrity. The newspaper men, in their reports, paid respect to his venerable, dignified figure, stamped with feebleness, poverty, and a noble sorrow, waiting patiently in one of the rooms at the Davis Mansion for audience with Mr. Lincoln.

None who saw Mr. Lincoln during that visit to Richmond observed in him any trace of exultation. Walking the streets with the negroes crowding about him, in the Davis Mansion with the Federal officers paying him court and our citizens calling on him, in the carriage with General Weitzel or General Shepley, a motley horde following—he was the same, only, as those who watched him declared, paler and wearier-looking each time they saw him. Uncle Randolph reported:

"There was something like misgiving in his eyes as he sat in the carriage with Shepley, gazing upon smoking ruins on all sides, and a rabble of crazy negroes hailing him as 'Saviour!' Truly, I never saw a sadder or wearier face in all my life than Lincoln's!"

He had terrible problems ahead, and he knew it. His emancipation proclamation in 1863 was a war measure. His letter to Greeley in 1862, said: "If there be those who would not save the Union unless they could at the same time save slavery, I do not agree with them. If I could preserve the Union without freeing any slaves, I would do it; if I could preserve the Union by freeing all the slaves, I would do it. . . . What I do about the coloured race, I do because I think it helps to save the Union."

GOVERNOR'S MANSION, RICHMOND, VA.

Erected 1811-13, to succeed a plain wooden structure called the "Governor's Palace."

To a committee of negroes waiting on him in the White House, August 14, 1862, Mr. Lincoln named colonisation as the one remedy for the race trouble, proposing Government aid out of an appropriation which Congress had voted him. He said: "White men in this country are cutting each other's throats about you. But for your race among us, there would be no war, although many men on either side do not care for you one way or the other. . . . Your race suffers from living among us, ours from your presence." He applied $25,000 to the venture, but it failed; New Grenada objected to negro colonisation.

Two months before his visit to Richmond, some official (Colonel Kaye, as I remember) was describing to him the extravagancies of South Carolina negroes when Sherman's army announced freedom to them, and Mr. Lincoln walked his floor, pale and distressed, saying: "It is a momentous thing—this liberation of the negro race."

He left a paper in his own handwriting with Judge Campbell, setting forth the terms upon which any seceded State could be restored to the Union; these were, unqualified submission, withdrawal of soldiers from the field, and acceptance of his position on the slavery question, as defined in his proclamations. The movement gained ground. A committee in Petersburg, headed by Anthony Keiley, asked permits to come to Richmond that they might coöperate with the committee there.

"Unconditional surrender," some commented. "Mr. Lincoln is not disposed to humiliate us unnecessarily," was the reassurance. "He promised Judge Campbell that irritating exactions and oaths against their consciences are not to be imposed upon our people; they are to be encouraged, not coerced, into taking vows of allegiance to the United States Government; Lincoln's idea is to make allegiance a coveted privilege; there are to be no confiscations; amnesty to include our officers, civil and military, is to be granted—that is, the power of pardon resting with the President, he pledges himself to liberal use of it. Lincoln is long-headed and kind-hearted. He knows the best thing all around is a real peace. He wishes to restore confidence in and affection for the Union. That is plain. He said: 'I would gladly pardon Jeff Davis himself if he would ask it.'"

I have heard one very pretty story about Mr. Lincoln's visit to Richmond. General Pickett, of the famous charge at Gettysburg, had been well known in early life to Mr. Lincoln when Mr. Lincoln and Mr. Johnson, General Pickett's uncle, were law partners in Illinois. Mr. Lincoln had taken warm interest in young George Pickett as a cadet at West Point, and had written him kindly, jovial letters of advice. During that hurried sojourn in Richmond, Abraham Lincoln took time for looking up Mr. Johnson. His carriage and armed retinue drew up in front of the old Pickett mansion. The General's beautiful young wife, trembling with alarm, heard a strange voice asking first for Mr. Johnson and then about General Pickett, and finally: "Is General Pickett's wife here?" She came forward, her baby in her arms. "I am General Pickett's wife." "Madam, I am George's old friend, Abraham Lincoln." "The President of the United States!" "No," with a kindly, half-quizzical smile, "only Abraham Lincoln, George's old friend. And this is George's baby?" Abraham Lincoln bent his kindly, half-sad, half-smiling glance upon the child. Baby George stretched out his hands; Lincoln took him, and the little one, in the pretty fashion babies have, opened his mouth and kissed the President.

"Tell your father," said Lincoln, "that I will grant him a special amnesty—if he wants it—for the sake of your mother's bright eyes and your good manners." A short while after that—when Lincoln was dead—that mother was flying, terror-stricken, with her baby to Canada, where General Pickett, in fear of his life, had taken refuge.

Mr. Lincoln left instructions for General Weitzel to issue passes to the legislators and State officials who were to come to Richmond for the purpose of restoring Virginia to the Union. The "Whig" had sympathetic articles on "Reconstruction," and announced in due order the meeting of citizens called "to consider President Lincoln's proposition for reassembling the Legislature to take Virginia back into the Union." It printed the formal call for reassembling, signed by the committee and many citizens, and countersigned by General Weitzel; handbills so signed were printed for distribution.

General Shepley, whose cordial acquiescence in the conciliation plan had been pronounced, said in after years that he suffered serious misgivings. When General Weitzel directed him to issue the passes for the returning legislators, he inquired: "Have you the President's written order for this?" "No. Why?" "For your own security you should have it, General. When the President reaches Washington and the Cabinet are informed of what has been done and what is contemplated, this order will be rescinded, and the Cabinet will deny that it has ever been issued."

"I have the President's commands. I am a soldier and obey orders."

"Right, General. Command me and I obey."

Mr. Lincoln's written order reiterating oral instructions came, however.

Admiral Porter, according to his own account, took President Lincoln to task for his concessions, and told him in so many words that he was acting outside of his rights; Richmond, being under military rule, was subject to General Grant's jurisdiction. The Admiral has claimed the distinction of working a change in the President's mind and of recovering immediately the obnoxious order from Weitzel, killing, or trying to kill, a horse or so in the undertaking. He characterised the efforts of Judges Campbell and Thomas to serve their country and avert more bloodshed as "a clever dodge to soothe the wounded feelings of the people of the South." The Admiral adds: "But what a howl it would have raised in the North!"

Admiral Porter says the lectured President exclaimed: "Well, I came near knocking all the fat in the fire, didn't I? Let us go. I seem to be putting my foot into it here all the time. Bless my soul! how Seward would have preached if he had heard me give Campbell permission to call the Legislature! Seward is an encyclopedia of international law, and laughs at my horse sense on which I pride myself. Admiral, if I were you, I would not repeat that joke yet awhile. People might laugh at you for knowing so much more than the President."

He was acting, he said, in conjunction with military authorities. General Weitzel was acting under General Grant's instructions. The conciliatory plan was being followed in Petersburg, where General Grant himself had led the formal entry.

"General Weitzel warmly approves the plan."

"He and Campbell are personal friends," the Admiral remarked significantly.

Whatever became of those horses driven out by Admiral Porter's instructions to be killed, if need be, in the effort to recover that order, is a conundrum. Ac-

cording to Admiral Porter the order had been written
and given to General Weitzel while Mr. Lincoln was
in the city. According to Judge Campbell and General
Shepley, and the original now on file in Washington, it
was written from City Point.

Dated, "Headquarters Department of Virginia, Richmond, April 13, 1865," this appeared in the "Whig"
on the last afternoon of Mr. Lincoln's life:

"Permission for the reassembling of the gentlemen
recently acting as the Legislature is rescinded. Should
any of the gentlemen come to the city under the notice
of reassembling already published, they will be furnished passports to return to their homes. Any of the
persons named in the call signed by J. A. Campbell
and others, who are found in the city twelve hours after
the publication of this notice will be subject to arrest,
unless they are residents. (Signed) E. O. C. Ord,
General Commanding the Department."

General Weitzel was removed. Upon him was
thrown the blame of the President's "blunder." He
was charged with the crime of pity and sympathy for
"rebels" and "traitors." When Lincoln was dead, a
high official in Washington said: "No man more than
Mr. Lincoln condemned the course General Weitzel and
his officers pursued in Richmond."

In more ways than one General Weitzel had done
that which was not pleasing in the sight of Mr. Stanton.
Assistant Secretary of War Dana had let Stanton know
post-haste that General Weitzel was distributing "vict-
uals" to "rebels." Stanton wired to know of General
Weitzel if he was "acting under authority in giving
food supplies to the people of Richmond, and if so,
whose?" General Weitzel answered, "Major-General
Ord's orders approved by General Grant."

Mr. Dana wrote Mr. Stanton, "Weitzel is to pay for

rations by selling captured property." General Weitzel apologised for magnanimity by explaining that the instructions of General Ord, his superior, were "to sell all the tobacco I find here and feed those in distress. A great many persons, black and white, are on the point of starvation, and I have relieved the most pressing wants by the issue of a few abandoned rebel stores and some damaged stores of my own." "All receivers of rations must take the oath," Mr. Stanton wrote back.

In Northern magazines left by Federal soldiers visiting negroes in Matoaca's yard, black Cato saw caricatures of Southern ladies mixing in with negroes and white roughs and toughs, begging food at Yankee bureaus. "Miss Mato'ca," he plead earnestly, "don' go whar dem folks is no mo'. It will disgrace de fam'ly." She had put pride and conscience in her pocket, drawn rations and brought home her pork and codfish.

Revocation of permission for the reassembling of the Virginia Legislature was one of Mr. Lincoln's last, if not his last, act in the War Department. Stanton gave him no peace till it was written; he handed the paper to Mr. Stanton, saying: "There! I think that will suit you!" "No," said the Iron Chancellor of the Union. "It is not strong enough. It merely revokes your permission for the assembling of the rebel legislators. Some of these men will come to Richmond—are doubtless there now—in response to the call. You should prohibit the meeting." Which was done. Hence, the prohibitory order in the "Whig."

Mr. Lincoln wrote, April 14, to General Van Alen, of New York: "Thank you for the assurance you give me that I shall be supported by conservative men like yourself in the efforts I may use to restore the Union, so as to make it, to use your own language, a Union of hearts as well as of hands." General Van Alen had warned him against exposing himself in the South as he had done by visiting Richmond; and for this Mr. Lincoln thanked him briefly without admitting that there had been any peril. Laconically, he had thanked Stanton for concern expressed in a dispatch warning him to be careful about visiting Petersburg, adding, " I have already been there."

When serenaded the Tuesday before his death, he said, in speaking of the bringing of the Southern States into practical relations with the Union: " I believe it is not only possible, but easier to do this, without deciding, or even considering, whether these States have ever been out of the Union. Finding themselves safely at home, it would be utterly immaterial whether they had ever been abroad."

His last joke—the story-tellers say it was his last— was about " Dixie." General Lee's surrender had been announced; Washington was ablaze with excitement. Delirious multitudes surged to the White House, calling the President out for a speech. It was a moment for easy betrayal into words that might widen the breach between sections. He said in his quaint way that he had no speech ready, and concluded humorously: " I have always thought ' Dixie' one of the best tunes I ever heard. I insisted yesterday that we had fairly captured it. I presented the question to the Attorney-General and he gave his opinion that it is our lawful prize. I ask the band to give us a good turn upon it." In that little speech, he claimed of the South by right of conquest a song—and nothing more.

THE LAST CAPITAL

CHAPTER V

THE LAST CAPITAL OF THE CONFEDERACY

FROM Richmond, Mr. Davis went to Danville. Major Sutherlin, the Commandant, met him at the station and carried him and members of his Cabinet to the Sutherlin Mansion, which then became practically the Southern Capitol.

The President was busy night and day, examining and improving defenses and fortifications and planning the junction of Lee's and Johnston's forces. Men were seeking his presence at all hours; couriers coming and going; telegrams flying hither and thither.

"In the midst of turmoil, and with such fearful cares and responsibilities upon him, he did not forget to be thoughtful and considerate of others," I have heard Mrs. Sutherlin say. "He was concerned for me. 'I cannot have you troubled with so many interruptions,' he said. 'We must seek other quarters.' But I would not have it so. 'All that you call a burden is my privilege,' I replied. 'I will not let you go.' He had other quarters secured for the Departments, but he and members of his Cabinet remained my guests."

In that hospitable home the table was set all the time for the coming and the going. The board was spread with the best the bountiful host and hostess could supply. Mrs. Sutherlin brought out all her treasured reserves of pickles, sweetmeats and preserves. This might be her last opportunity for serving the Confederacy and its Chieftain.

The Sutherlins knew that the President's residence

47

in their home was a perilous honour. In case the Confederacy failed—and hope to the contrary could not run high—their dwelling would be a marked spot. Major Sutherlin had been a strong Union man. Mrs. Sutherlin has told me how her husband voted against secession in the first convention to which he was a delegate, and for it in the second, with deep regret. "I saw in that convention," he told his wife, "strong, reserved men, men of years and dignity, sign the Secession Ordinance while tears coursed down their cheeks."

It is just to rehearse such things of men who were called "traitors" and "rebels." It is just to remember how Jefferson Davis tried to prevent secession. His letters to New England societies, his speeches in New England and in Congress, testified to his deep and fervent desire for the "preservation of the bond between the States," the "love of the Union in our hearts," and "the landmarks of our fathers."

But he believed in States' Rights as fervently as in Union of States; he believed absorption of State sovereignty into central sovereignty a violation of the Constitution. Long before secession (1847) he declined appointment of Brigadier General of Mississippi Volunteers from President Polk on the ground that the central government was not vested by the Constitution with power to commission officers of State Militia, the State having this authority.*

Americans should not forget that this man entered the service of the Union when a lad; that his father and uncles fought in the Revolution, his brothers in the War of 1812. West Point holds trophies of his skill

---

*In 1793, 1803, 1812-14, 1844-50, Northern States threatened to secede. Of Massachusetts' last movement Mr. Davis said in Congress: "It is her right." Nov. 1, Dec. 17, Feb. 23, 1860-61, the "New York Tribune" said: "We insist on letting the Cotton States go in peace . . . the right to secede exists."

ST. PAUL'S CHURCH, RICHMOND, VA.

It was to this church that the message was brought from Lee to Davis
announcing the necessity of evacuating Richmond.

as a commander and of his superb gallantry on the fields of Mexico. That splendid charge without bayonets through the streets of Monterey almost to the Plaza, and the charge at Buena Vista, are themes to make American blood tingle! Their leader was not a man to believe in defeat as long as a ray of hope was left.

As Secretary of War of the United States, Mr. Davis strengthened the power that crushed the South; in every branch of the War Department, his genius and faithful and untiring service wrought improvements. In the days of giants like Webster, Clay and Calhoun, the brilliant Mississippian drew upon himself many eyes and his course had been watched as that of a bright particular star of great promise. The candidacy of Vice-President of the United States had been tendered him— he had been mentioned for the Presidency, and it is no wild speculation that had he abjured his convictions on the States' Rights' issue, he would have found himself some day in the seat Lincoln occupied. He has been accused of overweening ambition. The charge is not well sustained. He did not desire the Presidency of the Confederacy.

In 1861, "Harper's Weekly" said: "Personally, Senator Davis is the Bayard of Congress, *sans peur et sans reproche;* a high-minded gentleman; a devoted father; a true friend . . . emphatially one of those born to command, and is doubtless destined to occupy a high position either in the Southern Confederacy or in the United States." He was "gloriously linked with the United States service in the field, the forum, and the Cabinet." The Southern Confederacy failed, and he was "Davis, the Arch-Traitor."

"He wrote his last proclamation on this table," said Mrs. Sutherlin to me, her hand on the Egyptian marble

where the President's fingers had traversed that final
paper of state which expressed a confidence he could
not have felt, but that he must have believed it duty to
affirm. He had tried to make peace and had failed.
Our armies were still in the field. A bold front on his
part, if it could do no more, might enable our generals
to secure better terms than unconditional surrender.
At least, no worse could be tendered. That final message was the utterance of a brave soul, itself disheart-
ened, trying to put heart into others. All along the
way to Danville, people had flocked to the railroad to
hear him, and he had spoken as he wrote.

He was an ill man, unutterably weary. He had borne
the burden and heat of the day for four terrible years;
he had been a target for the criticism even of his own
people; all failures were laid at the door of this one man
who was trying to run a government and conduct a war
on an empty treasury. It must have cost him something to keep up an unwavering front.

Lieutenant Wise, son of General Henry A. Wise,
brought news that Lee's surrender was imminent; on
learning of it, he had taken to horse and run through
the enemy's cavalry, to warn the President. Starvation had brought Lee's army to bay. Men were living
off grains of parched corn carried in their pockets.
Sheridan's cavalry had captured the wagon-trains of
food supplies. Also, the President was called from
the dinner-table to see an old citizen, who repeated a
story from some one who had seen General Lee in General Grant's tent. Other information followed.

Scouts came to say that Federal cavalry were advancing. There was danger that the President's way to the
South might be cut off, danger that he might be captured. All were in haste to get him away; a special
train was made up. The Sutherlin carriage drove hur-

riedly to the Mansion, the President and Major Sutherlin got out and entered the house.

"I am to bid you goodbye," said he to Mrs. Sutherlin, "and to thank you for your kindness. I shall
ever remember it."

"O, but it is a privilege—an honour—something for
me to remember!"

As explanations were being made and preparations
hastened, the President said: "Speak low, lest we excite Mr. Memminger or distress his wife more than
need be."

Mr. Memminger, ex-Secretary of the Treasury, was
upstairs, very ill; the physician had just left after giving
him a hypodermic of morphine and ordering absolute
quiet. Friends decided that the sick man and his wife
ran less risk in remaining than in following the President. But Mrs. Memminger, leaning over the balus-
trade, heard; and she and her husband came down and
went after the President in a rude farm wagon, the only
vehicle Mrs. Sutherlin could impress.

"Mr. Davis kept up a cheerful countenance the whole
time he was here," his hostess has borne witness, "but
I was sure that deep down in his heart he was not cheerful—I felt it. He was brave, self-possessed. Only
once did he betray evidence of break-down. When he
was leaving, I knew that he had no money in his pockets
except Confederate notes—and these would buy next
to nothing. We had some gold, and I offered it to him,
pressed it upon him. He shook his head. Tears came
into his eyes. 'No, no, my child,' he said, 'you and
your husband are much younger than I am. You will
need it. I will not.' Mr. Davis did not expect to live
long. He was sure he would be killed."

When General Sherman was accused by Stanton of
treachery because he was not hotter on the scent of " Jeff

Davis and his $13,000,000 treasure-trains," he retorted indignantly that those "treasure-trains dwindled down to the contents of a hand-valise" found on Mr. Davis when captured.

Mrs. Sutherlin pointed out to me the President's sleeping-room, an upper chamber overlooking the lawn with its noble trees, in whose branches mocking-birds lodge. At his first breakfast with her, Mr. Davis told Mrs. Sutherlin how the songs of the mocking-birds refreshed him.

Another thing that cheered him in Danville was the enthusiasm of the school-girls of the Southern Female College; when these young ladies, in their best homespun gowns, went out on dress parade and beheld Mr. Davis riding by in Major Sutherlin's carriage, they drew themselves up in line, waved handkerchiefs and cheered to their hearts' content; he gave them his best bow and smile—that dignified, grave bow and smile his people knew so well. I have always been thankful for that bright bit in Mr. Davis' life during those supremely trying hours—for the songs of the mocking-birds and the cheers of the school-girls.

Some weeks after his departure, General Wright, U. S. A., in formal possession of Danville, pitched his tent opposite the Sutherlin Mansion. The next Mrs. Sutherlin knew, an orderly was bearing in a large pitcher, another a big bowl, and between them General Wright's compliments and his hopes "that you may find this lemonade refreshing" and "be pleased to accept this white cut sugar, as the drink may not be sweet enough for your taste." Another day, an orderly appeared with a large, juicy steak; every short while orderlies came making presentation.

The Sutherlins accepted and returned courtesies. "We had as well be polite," said Major Sutherlin.

Photograph by Eutsler Bros., Danville, Va.

LAST CAPITOL OF THE CONFEDERACY

The Sutherlin Mansion, Danville, Va., which, for a short time after the evacuation of Richmond, was the head-quarters of the Confederate Government. President Davis and the members of his Cabinet were guests of Major Sutherlin at that time.

"There's no use quarrelling with them because they have whipped us." When they came to him for official information as to where Confederate Government ice-houses were, he responded: "It is not my business to give you this information. Your commanders can find out for themselves. Meanwhile, General Wright and his staff are welcome to ice out of my own ice-houses." They found out for themselves with little delay.

On the verandah where the Confederate President and his advisers had lately gathered, Federal officers sat at ease, smoking sociably and conversing with the master of the house. If a meal-hour arrived, Major Sutherlin would say: "Gentlemen, will you join us?" Usually, invitation was accepted. Social recognition was the one thing the Northern soldier could not conquer in the South by main strength and awkwardness; he coveted and appreciated it.

All were listening for tidings of Johnston's surrender. At last the news came. Around the Sutherlin board one day sat six guests: three Federal officers in fine cloth and gold lace, three Confederate officers in shabby raiment. A noise as of a terrific explosion shook the house. "Throw up the windows!" said the mistress to her servants, an ordinary command when shattering of glass by concussion was an every-day occurrence in artillery-ridden Dixie. Save for this sentence, there was complete silence at the table. The officers laid down their knives and forks and said not one word. They knew that those guns announced the surrender of Johnston's army. I suppose it was the salute of 200—the same that had been ordered at every post as glorification of Lee's surrender.

Some time after this, Mayor Walker came to Major Sutherlin with a telegram announcing that General

Meade and his staff would stop in Danville over night. They had been or were going to South Carolina on a mission of relief to whites who were in peril from blacks. At the Mayor's request, Major Sutherlin met the officers at the train.

"General," was his cordial greeting to General Meade, a splendid-looking officer at that day, "I am here to claim you and your staff as my guests." General Meade, accepting, said: "I will have my ambulance bring us up." "O, no, General! You come in my carriage, if you will do me that honour. It is waiting."

At breakfast, General Meade said to his hostess: "Madam, Southern hospitality has not been praised too highly. I trust some day to see you North that I may have opportunity to match your courtesy." Another time: "Madam, I trust that no misfortune will come to you because of the troubled state of our country. But if there should, I may be of service to you. You have only to command me, and I ask it as a favour that you will."

A Northern friend had warned her: "Mrs. Sutherlin, I fear your property may be confiscated because of the uses to which it has been put in the service of the Confederate Government. You should take advantage of General Wright's good will and of the good will of other Federal officers towards Major Sutherlin to make your title secure." Did she ask General Meade now to save her home to her?

"General, hospitality is our privilege and you owe us no debt. But I beg you to extend the kindly feelings you express toward Major Sutherlin and myself to one who lately sat where you now sit, at my right hand. I would ask you to use your influence to secure more gracious hospitality to our President who is in prison."

Dead silence. One could have heard a pin fall.

Wholesale confiscation of Greensboro was threatened because of Mr. Davis' stop there. Major Sutherlin strove with tact and diligence to prevent it. He lost no opportunity to cultivate kindly relations with Northerners of influence, and to inaugurate a reign of good-will generally. Receiving a telegram saying that Colonel Buford, a Northern officer, and his party, would pass through Danville, the Major went to his wife and said: "I am going to invite those Yankees here. I want you to get up the finest dinner you can for them." Feeling was high and sore; she did not smile. The day of their arrival he appeared in trepidation. "I have another telegram," he said. "To my surprise, there are ladies in the party."

This was too much for the honest "rebel" soul of her. Men she could avoid seeing except at table; but with ladies for her guests, more olive branches must be exchanged than genuine feeling between late enemies could possibly warrant. But her guests found her a perfect hostess, grave, sincere, hospitable.

There was a young married pair. When her faithful coloured man went up to their rooms to render service, they were afraid of him, were careful he should not enter, seemed to fear that of himself or as the instrument of his former owners he might do them injury.

Such queer, contradictory ideas Yankees had of us and our black people. A Northern girl visiting the niece of Alexander H. Stephens at a plantation where there were many negroes, asked: "Where are the blood-hounds?" "The blood-hounds! We haven't any." "How do you manage the negroes without them? I thought all Southerners kept blood-hounds—that only blood-hounds could keep negroes from running away." "I never saw a blood-hound in my life," Miss Stephens replied. "I don't know what one is like. None of our friends keep blood-hounds."

But to the Sutherlin Mansion. The bride asked: "Mrs. Sutherlin, what room did Mr. Davis occupy?" "That in which you sleep." The bride was silent. Then: "It is a pleasant room. The mocking-birds are singing when we wake in the morning. Sometimes, I hear them in the night."

A shadow fell on the hostess' face. The words recalled the thought of Mr. Davis, now shut out from the sight of the sky and the voice of the birds.

It has been said of this or that place at which Mr. Davis, moving southward from Danville, stopped, that it was the "Last Capital of the Confederacy." He held a Cabinet meeting in Colonel Wood's house in Greensboro; was in Charlotte several days; held a Cabinet meeting or council of war in the Armistead Burt House, Abbeville, S. C.; and in the Old Bank, Washington, Ga. He said in council at Abbeville: "I will listen to no proposition for my safety. I appeal to you for our country."

He stopped one night at Salisbury, with the Episcopal minister, whose little daughter ran in while all were at the breakfast-table, and standing between her father and Mr. Davis, cried out in childish terror and distress: "O, Papa, old Lincoln's coming and is going to kill us all!" President Davis laid down his knife and fork, lifted her face, and said reassuringly: "No, no, my little lady! Mr. Lincoln is not such a bad man, and I am sure he would not harm a little girl like you."

While the President was at Charlotte, there was another memorable peace effort, Sherman and Johnston arranging terms. Johnston's overture was dated April 13; Sherman's reply, "I am fully empowered to arrange with you any terms for the suspension of hostilities,"

Photographed in 1899

THE OLD BANK BUILDING, WASHINGTON, GA.

The last meeting place of the Confederate Cabinet when that body was reduced to two or three members.

April 14, the last day of Lincoln's life. Mr. Davis wrote General Johnston: "Your course is approved." Mr. Stanton nearly branded Sherman as a traitor. Sherman gave Johnston notice that he must renew hostilities. Mr. Davis left Charlotte, thinking war still on.

In Washington, Ga., the first town in America named for the Father of his Country, the Confederate Government breathed its last. A quiet, picturesque, little place, out of track of the armies, it was suddenly shaken with excitement, when Mr. Davis, attended by his personal staff, several distinguished officers, besides a small cavalry escort, rode in.

Mrs. Davis had left the day before. As long as her wagons and ambulances had stood in front of Dr. Ficklen's house, the people of Washington were calling upon her; first among them, General Toombs with cordial offers of aid and hospitality, though there had been sharp differences between him and Mr. Davis. Here, it may be said, she held her last reception as the First Lady of the Confederacy. She had expected to meet her husband, and went away no doubt heavy of heart— herself, her baby, Winnie, and her other little children, and her sister, Maggie Howell, again to be wanderers of woods and waysides. With them went a devoted little band of Confederate soldiers, their volunteer escort, Burton Harrison, the President's secretary, and one or two negro servants whose devotion never faltered.

On a lovely May morning, people sat on the Bank piazza asking anxiously: "Where can Mr. Davis be?" "Is he already captured and killed?" Dr. Robertson, an officer of the bank, and his family lived in the building. With them was General Elzey, on parole, his wife and son. Kate Joyner Robertson and her brother, Willie, sixteen years old and a Confederate Veteran, were on the piazza; also David Faver, seventeen, and a

Confederate Veteran; these boys were members of the Georgia Military Institute Battalion. A description of this battalion was recently given me by Mr. Faver:

"There were as many negroes—body-servants—in our ranks as boys when we started out, spick and span. We saw actual service; guarded the powder magazines at Augusta and Savannah, fought the Yankees at Chattanooga, stood in front of Sherman in South Carolina. Young Scott Todd lost his arm—Dr. Todd, of Atlanta, carries around that empty sleeve today. I bore handsome Tom Hamilton off the field when he was shot. I was just fifteen when I went in; some were younger. Henry Cabaniss and Julius Brown were the smallest boys in the army. We were youngsters who ought to have been in knee pants, but the G. M. I. never quailed before guns or duty! I remember (laughing) when we met the Cits in Charleston. They were all spick and span—'Citadel Cadets' blazoned all over them and their belongings. We were all tattered and torn, nothing of the G. M. I. left about us! Rags was the stamp of the regular, and we 'guyed' the Cits. We had seen fighting and they had not." Sixteen-year-old Lint Stephens, Vice-President Stephens' nephew, was of this juvenile warrior band. On the occasion of his sudden appearance at home to prepare for war, Mr. Stephens asked what he had quit school for. "To fight for the fair sex," he replied. And to this day some people think we fought to keep negroes in slavery!

A "Georgia Cracker" rode in from the Abbeville road, drew rein before the bank, and saluting, drawled: "Is you'uns seen any soldiers roun' here?" There were Confederate uniforms on the piazza. "What kind of soldiers?" he was asked, and General Elzey said: "My friend, you have betrayed yourself by that military salute. You are no ignorant countryman, but a soldier yourself." The horseman spurred close to the piazza. "Are there any Yankees in town?" "None. Tell us, do you know anything about President Davis?" After a little more questioning, the horseman said: "President Davis is not an hour's ride from here."

The piazza was all excitement. "Where should the President be entertained?" Ordinarily, General Toombs was municipal host. Everybody is familiar with the reply he made to a committee consulting him about erecting a hotel in Washington: "We have no need of one. When respectable people come here, they can stop at my house. If they are not respectable, we do not want them at all." Everybody knew that all he had was at the President's command. But—there had been the unpleasantness. "Bring the President here," Mrs. Robertson said promptly. Dr. Robertson added: "As a government building, this is the proper place." Willie Robertson, commissioned to convey the invitation, rode off with the courier, the envy of every other G. M. I. in town. The little "Bats" were ready to go to war again.

Soon, the President dismounted in front of the bank. Mrs. Faver (Kate Joyner Robertson that was) says: "He wore a full suit of Confederate gray. He looked worn, sad, and troubled; said he was tired and went at once to his room. My mother sent a cup of tea to him. That afternoon, or next morning, all the people came to see him. He stood in the parlor door, they filed in, shook hands, and passed out." So, in Washington, he held his last Presidential reception.

"To hear Mr. Davis," Mr. Faver reports, "you would have no idea that he considered the cause lost. He spoke hopefully of our yet unsurrendered forces. Secretary Reagan, General St. John and Major Raphael J. Moses were General Toombs' guests. That night after supper, they walked to the bank; my father's house was opposite General Toombs.' I walked behind them. I think they held what has been called the Last Cabinet Meeting that night."

Mr. Trenholm, too ill to travel, had stopped at Charlotte; Secretary of State Benjamin had left Mr. Davis that morning; at Washington, Secretary of the Navy Mallory went; Secretary of War Breckinridge, whom he was expecting, did not come on time. News reached him of Johnston's surrender. General Upton had passed almost through Washington on his way to receive the surrender of Augusta. The President perceived his escort's peril. To their commander, Captain Campbell, he said: "Your company is too large to pass without observation, and not strong enough to fight. See if there are ten men in it who will volunteer to go with me without question wherever I choose?" Captain Campbell reported: "All volunteer to go with Your Excellency."

He was deeply touched, but would not suffer them to take the risk. With ten men selected by Captain Campbell, and his personal staff, he rode out of Washington, the people weeping as they watched him go. When he was mounting, Rev. Dr. Tupper, the Baptist minister, approached him, uttering words of comfort and encouragement. "'Though He slay me, yet will I trust in Him,'" the President responded gently. He had made disposition of most of his personal belongings, giving the china in his mess-chest to Colonel Weems, the chest to General McLaws; to Mrs. Robertson his ink-stand, table, dressing-case, some tea, coffee, and brandy, portions of which she still retained when last I heard; the dressing-case and ink-stand she had sent to the Confederate Museum at Richmond.

His last official order was written at the old bank; it

appointed Captain H. M. Clarke Acting Treasurer of the Confederacy. The last Treasury Department was an old appletree at General Basil Duke's camp a short distance from Washington, under whose shade Captain Clarke sat while he paid out small amounts in coin to the soldiers. General Duke's Kentuckians, Mr. Davis' faithful last guard, were the remnant of John H. Morgan's famous command.

Soon after his departure, the treasure-train, or a section of it, reached Washington. Boxes of bullion were stored in the bank; Mrs. Faver remembers that officers laughingly told her and her sisters if they would lift one of the boxes, they might have all the gold in it; and they tried, but O, how heavy it was! She recalls some movement on the part of her parents to convey the treasure to Abbeville, but this was not practicable.

"It was a fitting conclusion of the young Government . . . that it marked its last act of authority by a thoughtful loyalty to the comfort of its penniless and starved defenders," says Avery's "History of Georgia," commenting on the fact that under that act Major Raphael J. Moses conveyed to Augusta bullion exceeding $35,000, delivering it to General Molineux on the promise that it would be used to purchase food and other necessaries for needy Confederate soldiers and our sick in hospitals.

Soon after the treasure-train left Washington, some one galloped back and flung into General Toombs' yard a bag containing $5,000 in gold. The General was in straits for money with which to flee the country, but swore with a great round oath he would use no penny of this mysterious gift, and turned it over to Major Moses, who committed it to Captain Abrahams, Federal Commissary, for use in relieving needy Confederates home-returning. At Greensboro, General Joseph E.

Johnston had taken $39,000 for his soldiers. There
have been many stories about this treasure-train.* It
carried no great fortune, and Mr. Davis was no bene-
ficiary. He meant to use it in carrying on the war.

The point has been made that Mr. Davis should have
remained in Richmond and made terms. Since governments were governments, no ruler has followed the
course that would have been. He thought it traitorous
to surrender the whole Confederacy because the Capital
was lost. Even after Lee's surrender the Confederacy
had armies in the field, and a vast domain farther south
where commanders believed positions could be held. He
believed it would be cowardly to fail them, and that it
was his duty to move the seat of government from place
to place through the Confederacy as long as there was
an army to sustain the government. To find precedent,
one has but to turn to European history. In England,
the rightful prince has been chased all over the country
and even across the channel. Mr. Davis believed in
the righteousness of his cause; and that it was his duty
to stand for it to the death.

His determination, on leaving Washington, was to
reach the armies of Maury, Forrest, and Taylor in Alabama and Mississippi; if necessary, withdraw these
across the Mississippi, uniting with Kirby-Smith and
Magruder in Texas, a section "rich in supplies and
lacking in railroads and waterways." There the con-
centrated forces might hold their own until the enemy
"should, in accordance with his repeated declaration,
have agreed, on the basis of a return to the Union, to
acknowledge the Constitutional rights of the States, and
by a convention, or quasi-treaty, to guarantee security of

---

* For full statement, see Captain H. M. Clarke's paper in Southern
Hist. Society Paper, Vol. 9, pp. 542-556, and Paymaster John F.
Whieless' report, Vol. 10, 137.

GENERAL AND MRS. JOHN H. MORGAN

person and property." What Judge Campbell thought could be secured by submission, Mr. Davis was confident could only be attained by keeping in the field a military force whose demands the North, weary of war, might respect. What he sought to do for his people in one way, Judge Campbell sought to do in another. Both failed.

While Mr. Davis was riding out of Washington, Generals Taylor and Maury, near Meridian, Mississippi, were arranging with General Canby, U. S. A., for the surrender of all the Confederate forces in Alabama and Mississippi. These generals were dining together and the bands were playing "Hail Columbia" and "Dixie."

THE COUNSEL OF LEE

CHAPTER VI

THE COUNSEL OF LEE

"A FEW days after the occupation, some drunken soldiers were heard talking in the back yard to our negroes, and it was gathered from what they said that the Federals were afraid General Lee had formed an ambuscade somewhere in the neighbourhood of the city, and that he might fall upon them at any time and deliver Richmond out of their hands. How our people wished it might be so!" Matoaca relates. "Do not buoy yourself up with that hope, my dear," said her monitor. "There's no hope save in the mercy of our conquerors. General Lee is a great soldier, an extraordinary tactician, but he cannot do the impossible. Our army cannot go on fighting forever without money and without food."

When our beloved general came home, the doctrine he taught by precept and example was that of peace. "The stainless sword of Lee" had been laid down in good faith. We had fought a good fight, we had failed, we must accept the inevitable, we must not lose heart, we must work for our country's welfare in peace. The very first heard of him in his modest, unheralded home-returning, he was teaching this.

Young William McCaw, his courier for four years, rode in with him; and General Lee, before going to his own home, delivered William, safe and sound, to his father. Dr. McCaw came out when they stopped in front of his door, and General Lee said:

"Here, Doctor, is your boy. I've brought him home to you."

William was standing beside Traveller, his arm clasped around General Lee's leg, and crying as if his heart would break. The General put his hand on William's head and said:

"No more fighting—that's all over. You've been a good fighter, Will—now I want to see you work for your country's welfare in peace. Be a good boy. I expect a fine Christian manhood of you. Goodbye," and he rode away to his own home, where his invalid wife awaited him.

It was good to have them home again, our men in gray; good though they came gaunt and footsore, ragged and empty-handed. And glad was the man in gray to cross his own threshold, though the wolf was at the door. Our men were ready enough for peace when peace—or what they mistook for peace—came; that is, the mass of them were. They had fought and starved their fill. The cries of destitute women and children called them home. They had no time to pause and cavil over lost issues, or to forge new occasions for quarrel. All they asked now was a chance to make meat and bread and raiment for themselves and those dependent on them.

Yet some young spirits were restive, would have preferred death to surrender. The lesson of utter submission came hard. The freeborn American, fearless of shot and shell, and regarding free speech as his birthright, found the task of keeping close watch over his tongue difficult. General Lee knew the mettle of the fiery young courier to whom he uttered the parting words that have been recorded. To many another youth just out of armor, he gave the same pacific counsel:

"We have laid down the sword. Work for a united country."

RESIDENCE OF ROBERT E. LEE, 1861–65,
Richmond, Va.
Now the home of the Virginia Historical Society.

One high-strung lad seeing a Federal soldier treat a lady rudely on the street (a rare happening in Richmond), knocked him down, and was arrested. The situation was serious. The young man's father went to General Ord and said: "See here, General, that boy's hot from the battle-field. He doesn't know anything but to fight." General Ord's response was: "I'll arrange this matter for you. And you get this boy out of the city tonight."

There happened to be staying in the same house with some of our friends, a young Confederate, Captain Wharton, who had come on sick leave to Richmond before the evacuation, and who, after that event, was very imprudent in expressing his mind freely on the streets, a perilous thing to do in those days. His friends were concerned for his safety. Suddenly he disappeared. Nobody knew what had become of him. Natural conclusion was that free speech had gotten him into trouble. At last a message came: "Please send me something to eat. I am in prison."

Ladies came to know if Matoaca would be one of a committee to wait on the Provost-Marshal General in his behalf. She agreed, and the committee set out for the old Custom House where the Federals held court. They were admitted at once to General Patrick's presence. He was an elderly gentleman, polite, courteous. "I was surprised," says Matoaca, "because I had expected to see something with hoof and horns."

"General," she said, "we have come to see you about a young gentleman, our friend, Captain Wharton. He is in prison, and we suppose the cause of his arrest was imprudent speech. He has been ill for some time, and is too feeble to bear with safety the hardships and confinement of prison life. If we can secure his re-

lease, we will make ourselves responsible for his conduct." She finished her little speech breathless. She
saw the glimmer of a smile way down in his eyes. "I
know nothing about the case," he said kindly. "Of
course, I can not know personally of all that transpires.
But I will inquire into this matter, and see what can
be done for this young gentleman." Soon after, Captain Wharton called on Matoaca. She could hardly
have left General Patrick's presence before an orderly
was dispatched for his release.

Friction resulted from efforts to ram the oath down
everybody's throat at once. I recite this instance because of the part General Lee took and duplicated in
multitudes of cases. Captain George Wise was called
before the Provost to take the oath. "Why must I
take it?" asked he. "My parole covers the ground.
I will not." ",You fought under General Lee, did you
not?" "Yes. And surrendered with him, and gave
my parole. To require this oath of me is to put an
indignity upon me and my general." "I will make a
bargain with you, Captain. Consult General Lee and
abide by his decision."

The captain went to the Lee residence, where he was
received by Mrs. Lee, who informed him that her husband was ill, but would see him. The general was
lying on a lounge, pale, weary-looking, but fully
dressed, in his gray uniform, the three stars on his collar; the three stars—to which any Confederate colonel
was entitled—was the only insignia of rank he ever
wore. "They want me to take this thing, General,"
said the captain, extending a copy of the oath. "My
parole covers it, and I do not think it should be required
of me. What would you advise?"

"I would advise you to take it," he said quietly. "It
is absurd that it should be required of my soldiers, for,

as you say, the parole practically covers it. Nevertheless, take it, I should say." "General, I feel that this is submission to an indignity. If I must continue to swear the same thing over at every street corner, I will seek another country where I can at least preserve my self-respect."

General Lee was silent for a few minutes. Then he said, quietly as before, a deep touch of sadness in his voice: "Do not leave Virginia. Our country needs her young men now."

When the captain told Henry A. Wise that he had taken the oath, the ex-governor said: "You have disgraced the family!" "General Lee advised me to do it." "Oh, that alters the case. Whatever General Lee says is all right, I don't care what it is."

The North regarded General Lee with greater respect and kindness than was extended to our other leaders. A friendly reporter interviewed him, and bold but temperate utterances in behalf of the South appeared in the "New York Herald" as coming from General Lee. Some of the remarks were very characteristic, proving this newspaper man a faithful scribe. When questioned about the political situation, General Lee had said: "I am no politician. I am a soldier—a paroled prisoner." Urged to give his opinion and advised that it might have good effect, he responded:

"The South has for a long time been anxious for peace. In my earnest belief, peace was practicable two years ago, and has been since that time whenever the general government should see fit to give any reasonable chance for the country to escape the consequences which the exasperated North seemed ready to visit upon it. They have been looking for some word or expression of compromise and conciliation from the North upon which they might base a return to the Union, their own views being considered. The question of slavery did not lie in the way at all. The best men of the South have long desired to do away with the institution and were quite willing to see it abolished. But with them in relation to this subject, the question has ever been: 'What will you do with the freed people?' That is the serious question today. Unless some humane course based upon wisdom and Christian principles is adopted, you do them a great injustice in setting them free." He plead for moderation towards the South as the part of wisdom as well as mercy. Oppression would keep the spirit of resistance alive. He did not think men of the South would engage in guerilla warfare as some professed to fear, but it was best not to drive men to desperation. "If a people see that they are to be crushed, they sell their lives as dearly as possible." He spoke of the tendency towards expatriation, deploring it as a misfortune to our common country at a time when one section needed building up so badly, and had, at the best, a terribly depleted force of young, strong men. Throughout, he spoke of the North and South as "we," and expressed his own great willingness to contribute in every way in his power to the establishment of the communal peace and prosperity.

A brave thing for a "rebel" officer to do, he spoke out for Mr. Davis. "What has Mr. Davis done more than any other Southerner that he should be singled out for persecution? He did not originate secession, is not responsible for its beginning; he opposed it strenuously in speech and writing."

Wherever he appeared in Richmond, Federal soldiers treated him with respect. As for our own people, to the day of his death Richmond stood uncovered when General Lee came there and walked the streets. If, as

MRS. ROBERT E. LEE
(Mary Randolph Custis)
Great-granddaughter of Martha Washington

he passed along, he laid his hand on a child's head, the child never forgot it. His words with our young men were words of might, and the cause of peace owes to him a debt that the Peace Angel of the Union will not forget.

"THE SADDEST GOOD FRIDAY"

CHAPTER VII

"The Saddest Good Friday"

In Matoaca's little devotional note-book, I read: "Good Friday, 1865. This is the saddest Good Friday I ever knew. I have spent the whole day praying for our stricken people, our crushed Southland." "The saddest Good Friday I ever knew"; nearly every man and woman in the South might have said that with equal truth.

Her "Journal" of secular events contains a long entry for April 14; it is as if she had poured out all her woes on paper. For the most part it is a tale of feminine trivialities, of patching and mending. "Unless I can get work and make some money," she writes, "we must stay indoors for decency's sake." Her shoes have holes in them: "They are but shoes I cobbled out of bits of stout cloth." The soles are worn so thin her feet are almost on the ground. The family is suffering for food and for all necessaries. "O God, what can I do!" she cries, "I who have never been taught any work that seems to be needed now! Who is there to pay me for the few things I know how to do? I envy our negroes who have been trained to occupations that bring money; they can hire out to the Yankees, and I can't. Our negroes are leaving us. We had to advise them to go. Cato will not. 'Me lef' Mars Ran?' he cried, 'I couldn' think uv it, Miss Mato'ca!'"

Woes of friends and neighbours press upon her heart. Almost every home has, like her own, its empty chair, its hungry mouths, its bare larder, though some are

77

accepting relief from the Christian Commission or from
Federal officers. Of loved ones in prison, they hear no
tidings; from kindred in other parts of the South,
receive no sign. There are no railroads, no mail service. In the presence of the conquerors, they walk
softly and speak with bated breath. The evening
paper publishes threats of arrest for legislators who
may come to town obedient to the call Judge Campbell
issued with Mr. Lincoln's approval.

Good Friday was a day of joy and gladness North.
From newspapers opened eagerly in radiant family
circles men read out such headlines as these: "War
Costs Over. Government Orders Curtailing Further
Purchase of Arms, Ammunition and Commissary
Stores." "Drafting and Recruiting Stopped." "Mili-
tary Restrictions on Trade and Commerce Modified."
Selma, Alabama, with its rich stores of Confederate
cotton, was captured. Mr. Lincoln's conciliatory policy
was commented on as "a wise and sagacious move."
Thursday's stock market had been bullish.

Rachel weeping for her children was comforted because they had not died in vain. Larders were not
bare, clothes were not lacking. The fastings and prayers of the devout were full of praise and thanksgiving.
For the undevout, Good Friday was a feast day and a
day of jollification.

In Charleston, South Carolina, gaping with scars of
shot and shell of her long, long, siege, the roses and
oleanders and palmettoes strove to cover with beauty
the wounds of war, and in their fragrance to breathe
nature's sympathy and faithfulness. Her own desolate people kept within doors. The streets were
thronged with a cheerful, well-clad crowd; the city
was overflowing with Northern men and women
of distinction. In the bay lay Dahlgren's fleet, gay

flags all a-flying. On land and water bands played merrily.

Fort Sumter's anniversary was to be celebrated. The Union flag was to be raised over the ruined pile by General Robert Anderson, who had lost the fort in 1861. In the company duly assembled were Henry Ward Beecher, Theodore Tilton, William Lloyd Garrison, Rev. Dr. Storrs. Mr. Beecher uttered words of kindly sentiment towards the South. He gave God thanks for preserving Lincoln's life, accepting this as a token of divine favor to the Nation. Dr. Storrs read: "'When the Lord turned again the captivity of Zion, we were like them that dream.'" The people: "'Then was our mouth filled with laughter and our tongue with singing.'" And so on through the 126th Psalm. Then: "'Some trust in chariots and some in horses, but we will remember the name of the Lord our God.'" And: "'They are brought low and fallen, but we are risen and stand upright.'"

"The Star-Spangled Banner" was sung, and the guns of Dahlgren's fleet thundered honours to the Stars and Stripes, which, rising slowly and gracefully, fluttered out in triumph against the Southern sky. At sunset, guns boomed again, proud signal to the ending of the perfect day. The city, silent and sad as far as its own people were concerned, rang with the strangers' joy-aunce. Social festivities ruled the hour. General Gillmore entertained at a great banquet. The bay was ablaze with fireworks; all forts were alight; the beautiful Sea Islands, whose owners roamed in destitute exile, gleamed in shining circle, the jewels of the sea.

The 14th was a red-letter day in the National Capital. Everything spoke of victory and gladness. Washington held the two idols of the North—Lincoln and Grant. It was Mr. Lincoln's perfect hour. He went about with a quiet smile on his face. The family breakfast at the White House was very happy; Captain Robert Lincoln was visiting his parents. General Grant was present at the Cabinet meeting during the forenoon, Mr. Lincoln's last. These are some of the President's words:

"I think it providential that this great rebellion is crushed just as Congress has adjourned and there are none of the disturbing elements of that body to hinder and embarrass us. If we are wise and discreet we shall reanimate the States and get their governments in successful operation with order prevailing, and the Union reëstablished before Congress comes together in December. I hope there will be no persecution, no bloody work, after the war is over. No one need expect me to take any part in hanging or killing these men. Enough lives have been sacrificed. We must extinguish resentment if we expect harmony and Union. There is too great a disposition on the part of some of our very good friends to be masters, to interfere with and dictate to these States, to treat the people not as fellow-citizens; there is too little respect for their rights." He made it plain that he meant the words of his second inaugural address, hardly six weeks before, when he promised that his mission should be "to bind up the wounds of the Nation."

"Very cheerful and very hopeful," Mr. Stanton reported, "spoke very kindly of General Lee and others of the Confederacy, and of the establishment of the Government of Virginia." Also, he spoke of the state government in Louisiana, and that which he had mapped out for North Carolina. General Grant was uneasy about Sherman and Johnston. The President said: "I have no doubt that favourable news will come. I had a dream last night, my usual dream which has pre-

MRS. JOSEPH E. JOHNSTON
(Lydia McLane, daughter of Senator McLane, of Delaware.)

ceded every important event of the war. I seemed to be on a singular and indescribable vessel, always the same, moving with great rapidity toward a dark and indefinite shore."

He did not know that on that day Sherman was writing Johnston, "I am empowered to make terms of peace." But he knew he had so empowered Sherman. I can imagine that through his heart the refrain was beating: "There will be no more bloodshed, no more devastation. There shall be no more humiliations for this Southern people, and God will give it into my hands to reunite my country."

He went for a long, quiet drive with his wife. "Mary," he said, "we have had a hard time of it since we came to Washington; but the war is over, and with God's blessing we may hope for four years of peace and happiness. Then we will go back to Illinois and pass the rest of our days in quiet." He longed for quiet. The Sabbath before, while driving along the banks of the James, he said: "Mary, when I die, I would like to lie in a quiet place like this," and related a dream which he felt to be presage of death.

Sailing on the James, he read aloud twice, and in a manner that impressed Charles Sumner, who was present, this passage from Macbeth:

> "'Duncan is in his grave;
> After life's fitful fever he sleeps well;
> Treason has done his worst: nor steel, nor poison,
> Malice domestic, foreign levy, nothing,
> Can touch him further.'"

He was going, safe and whole, from the land of "rebels" to Washington. "We have had a hard time in Washington, Mary." Read Sherman's "Memoirs," and see what little liking great Federal generals had for journeys to Washington; how for peace and safety, they preferred their battle-fields to the place where politicians were wire-pulling and spreading nets.

The conclusion to his perfect day was a box in Ford's Theatre, his wife and a pair of betrothed lovers for company; on the stage Laura Keene in " Our American Cousin." The tragic sequel is indelibly impressed on the brain of every American—the people leaning forward, absorbed in the play, the handsome, slender figure of young Wilkes Booth moving with easy, assured grace towards the President's box, the report of the pistol, the leap of Booth to the stage, falling as the flag caught his foot, rising, brandishing his weapon and crying: "*Sic Semper Tyrannis!*", his escape with a broken ankle through the confused crowds; the dying President borne out to the boarding-house on Tenth Street.

Seward's life was attempted the same evening by Booth's confederate, Lewis Payne, who penetrated to the Secretary's sick-room and wounded him and his son; Payne escaped. General Grant's death was a part of the plot; he and Mrs. Grant had declined invitation to share the President's box, and started west; Mr. Stanton's murder was also intended; but he escaped, scathless of body but bitterer of soul than ever, bitterer than Mr. Seward, who was wounded.

In a letter which Matoaca wrote years afterward, she said: "I well remember the horror that thrilled our little circle when the news came. 'Now, may God have mercy on us!' Uncle exclaimed. He sat silent for a while and then asked: 'Can it be possible that any of our own people could do this thing? Some misguided fanatic?' And then, after a silence: 'Can some enemy of the South have done it? Some enemy of the South who had a grudge against Lincoln, too?' 'What sort of secret service could they have had in Washington that this thing could happen? How was it that the crippled assassin was able to make his escape?' he said when full accounts appeared. The explanations given never explained to him.

"I heard some speak who thought it no more than just retribution upon Mr. Lincoln for the havoc he had wrought in our country. But even the few who spoke thus were horrified when details came. We could not be expected to grieve, from any sense of personal affection, for Mr. Lincoln, whom we had seen only in the position of an implacable foe at the head of a power invading and devastating our land; but our reprobation of the crime of his taking off was none the less. Besides, we did not know what would be done to us. Already there had been talk of trying our officers for treason, of executing them, of exiling them, and in this talk Andrew Johnson had been loudest.

"I remember how one poor woman took the news. She was half-crazed by her losses and troubles; one son had been killed in battle, another had died in prison, of another she could not hear if he were living or dead; her house had been burned; her young daughter, turned out with her in the night, had died of fright and exposure. She ran in, crying: 'Lincoln has been killed! thank God!' Next day she came, still and pale: 'I have prayed it all out of my heart,' she said, 'that is, I'm not glad. But, somehow, I *can't* be sorry. I believe it was the vengeance of the Lord.'"

Jefferson Davis heard of Lincoln's death in Charlotte. A tablet in that beautiful and historic city marks the spot where he stood. He had just arrived from Greensboro, was dismounting, citizens were welcoming him when the dispatch signed by Secretary of War Breckinridge was handed him by Major John Courtney. Mrs. Courtney, the Major's widow, told me that her husband heard the President say: "Oh, the pity of it!" He passed it to a gentleman with the remark, "Here are sad tidings." The Northern press reported that Jefferson Davis cheered when he heard of Lincoln's death.

Mrs. Davis, at the Armistead Burt House, Abbeville, received a message from her husband announcing his arrival in Charlotte and telling of the assassination. Mrs. Davis "burst into tears, which flowed from sorrow and a thorough realization of the inevitable results to the Confederates,"—her own words.

General Johnston and General Sherman were in Mr. Bennett's house near Raleigh. Just before starting to this meeting, General Sherman received a dispatch announcing Mr. Lincoln's assassination. He placed it in his pocket, and, as soon as they were alone, handed it to General Johnston, watching him narrowly. "He did not attempt to conceal his distress," General Sherman relates. "The perspiration came out in large drops on his forehead." His horror and detestation of the deed broke forth; he earnestly hoped General Sherman would not charge this crime to the Confederacy. "I explained," states General Sherman, "that I had not yet revealed the news to my own personal staff or to the army, and that I dreaded the effect when it was made known." He feared that "a worse fate than that of Columbia would befall" Raleigh, particularly if some "foolish man or woman should say or do something that would madden his men." He took pains when making the calamity known to assure his army that he did not consider the South responsible.

Mr. Davis, under arrest, and on the way to Macon, heard that Andrew Johnson had offered a reward of $100,000 for his arrest, charging him, Clement C. Clay and other prominent Southerners with "inciting, concerting, procuring" the "atrocious murder" of President Lincoln. Between threatening soldiery, displaying the proclamation and shouting over his capture, Mr. Davis and his family rode and walked.

At Macon, General Wilson received him with courtesy; when the proclamation was mentioned, Mr. Davis said one person at least in the United States knew the charge to be false, and that was the man who signed it, for Andrew Johnson knew that he preferred Lincoln to himself.

In Augusta, Colonel Randall (author of "Maryland, My Maryland"), meeting Clement C. Clay on the street, informed him of the proclamation. The old ex-Senator at once surrendered, asking trial.*

In Southern cities citizens held meetings condemning the murder and expressing sorrow and regret at the President's death. Ex-Governor Aiken, known as the largest slave-owner in South Carolina, led the movement in Charleston, heading a petition to General Gillmore for use of the Hibernian Hall that the people might have a gathering-place in which to declare their sentiments.

Even the Confederates in prison were heard from. The officers confined at Fort Warren signed with General Ewell a letter to General Grant, expressing to "a soldier who will understand" their detestation of Booth's horrible crime. The commandant of the Fort, Major William Appleton, added a note testifying to their deep sincerity.

---

* The account which I had from Colonel Randall at the home of Mr. John M. Graham, Atlanta, Ga., in the spring of 1905, does not quite coincide with that given by Mrs. Clay in "A Belle of the Fifties." In years elapsing since the war, some confusion of facts in memory is to be expected.

THE WRATH OF THE NORTH

CHAPTER VIII

The Wrath of the North

THE mad act of crazy Wilkes Booth set the whole country crazy. The South was aghast, natural recoil intensified by apprehension. The North, convulsed with anguish, was newly inflamed, and even when the cooler moment came and we were acquitted of any responsibility for Booth's crazy act, the angry humour of a still sore heart was against us. We, of both sections, who suffered so lately as one people in the death of President McKinley, can comprehend the woe and unreason of the moment.

Indignation and memorial meetings simply flayed the South alive. At one in the New York Custom House, when the grieving, exasperated people did not know whether to weep or to curse the more, or to end it by simply hanging us all, Mr. Chittenden rose and said: " Peace, be still! " And declared the death of Lincoln providential, God removing the man of mercy that due punishment might be meted out to rebels. Before the pacific orator finished, people were yelling: " Hang Lee! " and " The rebels deserve damnation! " Pulpits fulminated. Easter sermons demanded the halter, exile, confiscation of property, for " rebels and traitors "; yet some voices rose benignly, as Edward Everett Hale's, Dr. Huntington's, and Rufus Ellis', in words fitting the day. Beecher urged moderation.

The new President, Andrew Johnson, was breathing out threatenings and slaughter before Lincoln's death. Thousands had heard him shout from the southern

89

portico of the Patent Office, "Jeff Davis ought to be hung twenty times as high as Haman!"

In Nicolay and Hay's Life of Lincoln, the following paragraph follows comment upon unanimity in Southern and Northern sentiment: "There was one exception to the general grief too remarkable to be passed over in silence. Among the extreme Radicals in Congress, Mr. Lincoln's determined clemency and liberality towards the Southern people had made an impression so unfavourable that, though they were shocked at his murder, they did not, among themselves, conceal their gratification that he was no longer in the way. In a political caucus held a few hours after the President's death, 'the thought was nearly universal,' to quote the language of one of their most representative members, 'that the accession of Johnson to the Presidency would prove a godsend to the country.'"

The only people who could profit by Lincoln's death were in the Radical wing of the Republican party. These extremists thought Johnson their man. Senator Wade, heading a committee that waited on him, cried: "Johnson, we have faith in you! By the gods, it will be no trouble now running the Government!"

"Treason," said the new President, "is the highest crime in the calendar, and the full penalty for its commission should be visited upon the leaders of the Rebellion. Treason should be made odious." It is told as true "inside history" that the arrest and execution of General Lee had been determined upon; General Grant heard of it and went in the night to see President Johnson and Secretary Stanton and said to them: "If General Lee or any of the officers paroled by me are arrested while keeping the terms of their parole, I will resign my commission in the United States Army."

But on April 15, even General Grant was of a divided mind, for he wired General Ord: "Arrest J. A. Campbell, Mayor Mayo, and members of the old Council who have not yet taken the oath of allegiance, and confine them in Libby Prison . . . arrest all paroled officers and surgeons until they can be sent beyond our lines unless they have taken the oath of allegiance. Extreme rigour will have to be observed whilst assassination is the order of the day with rebels."

General Ord replied: "The two citizens we have seen. They are old, nearly helpless, and, I think, incapable of harm. Lee and staff are in town among the paroled prisoners. Should I arrest them under the circumstances, I think the rebellion here would be reopened. I will risk my life that present paroles will be kept, if you will allow me to so trust the people here, who are ignorant of the assassination, done, I think, by some insane Brutus with but few accomplices. Judge Campbell and Mr. Hunter pressed me earnestly yesterday to send them to Washington to see the President. Would they have done so if guilty?"

General Grant answered: "I leave my dispatch of this date in the light of a suggestion to be executed only as far as you may judge the good of the service demands." But the venerable peace-maker and his associates were not to escape vengeance.

General Halleck, from Richmond, to General Grant, May 5: "Hunter is staying quietly at home, advises all who visit him to support the Union cause. His hostility to Davis did much to make Davis unpopular in Virginia. Considering this, and the fact that President Lincoln advise'? against arresting Hunter, I would much prefer not to arrest him unless specially ordered to do so. All classes are taking the Amnesty Oath; it would be unfortunate to shake by unnecessary arrests this desire for general amnesty. Lee's officers are taking the oath; even Lee himself is considering the propriety of doing so and petitioning President Johnson for pardon."

May 11, Halleck to Stanton: "R. M. T. Hunter has, in accordance with General Grant's orders, been arrested, and is now on a gunboat in the James. Judge Campbell is still at his house. If necessary, he can be confined with Mr. Hunter. He voluntarily submits himself to such punishment as the Government may see fit to impose. He is very destitute and much broken down, and his case excites much sympathy."

Fortress Monroe, May 22, General Halleck wires General Ord, Richmond: "The Secretary of War directs that John A. Campbell be placed in the Libby or some other secure prison. Do this at once." Announcements of arrivals at Fort Pulaski in June would have made a fine page for any hotel desiring a brilliant register, thus: "Ex-Senator R. M. T. Hunter, Virginia; ex-Assistant Secretary of War Judge J. A. Campbell, Alabama; ex-Senator D. L. Yulee, Florida; ex-Governor Clark, Mississippi; ex-Secretary of the Treasury G. A. Trenholm, South Carolina; and so on. Pulaski had rivals in other Federal prisons.

A reward of $25,000 for "Extra Billy" did not bring him in, but he delivered himself up to General Patrick, was paroled, and went to his home in Warrenton, Fauquier, and set to work with a will, though he was, to quote General Halleck, "seventy years old and quite feeble." The rightful Governor of Virginia, he advised her people to cheerful acceptance of Pierpont.

As soon as the aged Governor of Mississippi learned that General Dick Taylor would surrender, he convened the Legislature; his message, recommending the

LIBBY PRISON, RICHMOND, VA.

Before 1861 this building was used as a warehouse, and in 1888–9 was transported by a syndicate to Chicago, and is now known as Libby Prison War Museum.

repeal of the secession ordinance and deploring Lincoln's murder, was not more than read, when General Osband, under orders from Washington, dissolved the Legislature with threats of arrest. Governor Clark was arrested: "The old soldier straightened his mangled limbs as best he could, with great difficulty mounted his crutches, and with a look of defiance, said: 'General Osband, I denounce before high Heaven this unparalleled act of tyranny and usurpation. I am the duly and constitut'onally elected Governor of Mississippi, and would ' ∋sist, if in my power, to the last extremity the enforc' .nent of your order."

Goverr ɔrs, generals and statesmen were arrested in all direc .ons. No exception was made for Alexander H. Ste˙ ∩ens, the invalid, the peace-maker, the gentlest Roma . of them all. At Liberty Hall, Mr. Stephens and , young friend, Robert W. Hull, were playing casi o, when Tim, a negro, ran in, exclaiming: "ℙ ιarster, de town is full uh Yankees! Whole heaps u˙ 'em, gallopin' all about, carryin' guns." Mr. ∫ tephens rose and said to his guest: "I have been expecting this. They have come for me. Excuse me, please, while I pack." He went into his bedroom and began this task, when an officer called. Mr. Stephens met him in the parlor. The officer said, "Are you Alex Stephens?" "That is my name." "I have an order for your arrest." "I would like to have your name and see your order." "I am Captain Saint, of the 4th Iowa, acting under General Upton's orders. Here is the order." Mr. Stephens saw that himself and General Toombs were to be brought before General Upton in Atlanta. "I have been anticipating arrest," he said quietly, "and have been careful not to be out of the way, remaining here at home. General Upton need not have sent an armed force for me. A simple inti-

mation from him that my presence was desired would
have taken me to Atlanta." His negroes were weeping
when he was carried away; one, by special permission,
accompanied him.

He was left under guard in a shanty on the road;
the troops went on to Washington, "to be back in a
little while with Bob Toombs." "Where is General
Toombs?" asked Mr. Stephens, when they returned.
"We don't know," was the rejoinder. "He flanked
us." Thus:

General Toombs, going to the basement doorway of
his house in Washington, exclaimed suddenly: "My
God! the blue-coats!" turned and went rapidly through
his house and out at the back door, saying to his wife:
"Detain them at the front as long as you can." Their
daughter, Mrs. Du Bose, helped her. "Bob Toombs"
was asked for. Mrs. Du Bose went to bring "Bob
Toombs"; she reappeared leading a lovely boy. "Here
is Bob Toombs," she said, "Bob Toombs Du Bose,
named for my father, General Toombs."

Mrs. Toombs took them through the house, showing them into every room—keys of which were lost and
had to be looked for. They would burn the building,
they insisted, if General Toombs was not produced.
"Burn," she said, "and burn me in it. If I knew my
husband's hiding-place, I would not betray him." They
told her to move her furniture out. She obeyed. They
changed their minds about the burning and went off.
General Toombs escaped to the woods, where he
remained hidden until nightfall. His friend, Captain
Charles E. Irvin, got some gold from Mrs. Toombs,
and carried the money to him, together with his mare,
Gray Alice. From Nassau Island he crossed to England, where the doughty "rebel" was mightily liked.

Mr. Davis, Mr. Stephens, Mr. Clay, General

Wheeler, and General Ralls met aboard the steamer at Augusta, all prisoners. The President's arrest occurred the day before Mr. Stephens', near Irwinsville. Picture it. Gray dawn in the Georgia woods. A small encampment of tents, horses, and wagons. Horses saddled and bridled, with pistols in holsters, picketed on the edge of the encampment. A negro watching and listening. Suddenly, he hurries to one of the tents: "Mars Jeff!" His call wakes a man lying fully dressed on one of the cots. "What's the matter, Jim?" "Firin' 'cross de branch, suh. Jes behin' our camp. Marauders, I reckon."

After leaving Washington, Mr. Davis had heard that marauders were in pursuit of his wife's cortege, and turning out of his course, he rode hard across country, found his family, conveyed them beyond the present danger, as he thought, and was about to renew his journey south. Horses for himself and staff were ready, when he heard that marauders were again near; he concluded to wait, and so lay down to rest. At Jim's call, he went to the tent-door, then turned to where his wife bent over her sleeping baby, Winnie. "They are not marauders," he said, "but regular troopers of the United States Army."

She begged him to leave her quickly. His horses and weapons were near the road down which the cavalry was coming. In the darkness of the tent, he caught up what he took to be his raglan, a sleeveless, waterproof garment. It was hers. She, poor soul, threw a shawl over his head. He went out of the tent, she keeping near. "Halt!" cried a trooper, levelling a carbine at him. He dropped his wraps and hurried forward. The trooper, in the dark, might miss aim; a hand under his foot would unhorse him; when Mr. Davis would mount and away. Mrs. Davis saw the carbine, cast her arms about her husband, and lost him his one chance of escape.

In one of her trunks, broken open by pilferers of the attacking party, a hoop-skirt was found. I shall refer to this historic hoop-skirt again.

I left Generals Johnston and Sherman discussing Mr. Lincoln's death and arranging terms of peace, based upon what Sherman recognized as the object of the war—salvation of the Union; and upon instructions received from Mr. Lincoln's own lips in their last interview when the President authorized him to "assure Governor Vance and the people of North Carolina that, as soon as the rebel armies will lay down their arms, they will at once be guaranteed all their rights as citizens of a common country; and that, to avoid anarchy, the State Governments now in existence will be recognized."

"When peace does come, you may call upon me for anything. Then, I will share with you the last crust and watch with you to shield your homes and families against danger from every quarter." Thus Sherman closed his reply to Calhoun's protest against the depopulation of Atlanta. Now that war was over, he was for living up to this.

In soldierly simplicity, he thought he had done an excellent thing in securing Johnston's guarantee of disbandment of all Confederate forces, and settling all fear of guerilla warfare by putting out of arms not only regular Confederates, but any who might claim to be such.

Stanton disposed of the whole matter by ordering Grant to "proceed to the headquarters of Major-General Sherman and direct operations against the enemy." This was, of course, the end to any terms for us. As is known, General Johnston surrendered on the same conditions with Lee.   Grant so ordered his course as not to do Sherman injustice.

General Sherman wrote a spicy letter for Mr. Stanton's benefit: the settlement he had arranged for would be discussed, he said, in a different spirit "two or three years hence, after the Government has experimented a little more in the machinery by which power reaches the scattered people of this vast country known as the South." He had made war "hell"; now, the people of "this unhappy country," as he pityingly designated the land he had devastated, were for peace; and he, than whom none had done more to bring them to that state of mind, was for giving them some of its fruits. "We should not drive a people to anarchy"; for protection to life and property, the South's civil courts and governments should be allowed to remain in operation.

"The assassination has stampeded the civil authorities," "unnerved them," was the conclusion he drew when he went to Washington when, just after the crime, the long roll had been beaten and the city put under martial law; public men were still in dread of assassination. At the grand review in Washington, Sherman, hero of the hour, shook hands with the President and other dignitaries on the stand, but pointedly failed to accept Mr. Stanton's.

After Mr. Lincoln's death, leniency to "rebels" was accounted worse than a weakness. The heavy hand was applauded. It was the fashion to say hard things of us. It was accounted piety and patriotism to condemn "traitors and rebels." Cartoonists, poets, and orators, were in clover; here was a subject on which they could "let themselves out."

THE CHAINING OF JEFFERSON DAVIS

CHAPTER IX

The Chaining of Jefferson Davis

STRANGE and unreal seem those days. One President a fugitive, journeying slowly southward; the other dead, journeying slowly north and west. Aye, the hand of God was heavy on both our peoples. The cup of defeat could not be made more bitter than it was; and into the cup of triumph were gall and wormwood poured.

Hunters pursuing one chieftain with hoarse cries of "rebel!" and "traitor!" For the other, bells tolling, guns booming requiem, great cities hung with black, streets lined with weeping thousands, the catafalque a victor's chariot before which children and maidens scattered flowers. Nearly a month that funeral march lasted—from Washington through Baltimore, Philadelphia, New York, Albany, Cleveland, Columbus, Indianapolis, Chicago—it wound its stately way to Springfield. Wherever it passed, the public pulse beat hotter against the Southern chieftain and his people.

Yet the dead and the hunted were men of one country, born in the same State. Sharp contrasts in many ways, they were yet enough alike in personal appearance to have been brothers. Both were pure men, brave, patriotic; both kindly and true. The dead had said of the living: "Let Jeff escape."

Johnson's proclamation threw the entire South into a white rage and an anguish unutterable, when it charged the assassination to Mr. Davis and other representative men of the South. Swift on it came news that our President was captured, report being spread to cast ridicule upon him that, when caught, he was disguised in his wife's garments. Caricatures, claiming to be truthful portraiture, displayed him in hoops and petticoats and a big poke bonnet, of such flaming contrasts as certainly could not have been found in Mrs. Davis' wardrobe.

In 1904, I saw at a *vaudeville* entertainment in a New York department store, a stereopticon representation of the War of Secession. The climax was Mr. Davis in a pink skirt, red bonnet, yellow bodice, and parti-coloured shawl, struggling with several Federals, while other Federals were rushing to the attack, all armed to the teeth and pointing warlike weapons at this one fantastic figure of a feeble old man. The theatre was full of children. The attraction had been running some time and thousands of young Americans had doubtless accepted its travesties as history. The Northern friend with me was as indignant as myself.

When Mr. Davis' capture was announced in theatres and other places of amusement in the North, people went crazy with joy, clapping their hands and cheering, while bands played "Yankee Doodle" and "Star-Spangled Banner." Many were for having him hung at once. Wendell Phillips wanted him "left to the sting of his own conscience."

Presently, we heard that the "Clyde" was bringing Mr. Davis, his family, General Wheeler, Governor Vance, and others, to Fortress Monroe. And then— will I ever forget how the South felt about that?— that Mr. Davis was a prisoner in a damp, casemated cell, that lights were kept burning in his face all night until he was in danger of blindness; that human eyes were fixed on him night and day, following his every movement; that his jailer would come and look at him

contemptuously and call him "Jeff"; that sightseers
would be brought to peer at him as if he were some
strange wild beast; that his feeble limbs had been
loaded with chains; that he was like to lose his life
through hardships visited upon him! To us who knew
the man personally, his sensitiveness, dignity, and refine-
ment, the tale is harrowing as it could not be to those
who knew him not thus. Yet to all Americans it must
be a regrettable chapter in our history when it is remembered that this man was no common felon, but a prisoner
of State, a distinguished Indian-fighter, a Mexican
veteran, a man who had held a seat in Congress, who
had been Secretary of War of the United States, and
who for four years had stood at the head of the Confederate States.

When they came to put chains upon him, he protested,
said it was an indignity to which as a soldier he would
not submit, that the intention was to dishonour the
South in him; stood with his back to the wall, bade
them kill him at once, fought them off as long as he
could—fought them until they held him down and the
blacksmiths riveted the manacles upon his wasted limbs.
Captain Titlow, who had the work in charge, did not
like his cruel task, but he had no choice but to obey
orders.*

And this was in Fortress Monroe, where of old the
gates fell wide to welcome him when he came as Secretary of War, where guns thundered greeting, soldiers
presented arms, and the highest officer was proud to do
him honour! With bated breath we speak of Russian
prisons. But how is this: "Davis is in prison; he is

* Fac-simile of the order under which Mr. Davis was chained
appears in Charles H. Dana's "Recollections of the Civil War,"
p. 286. The hand that wrote it, when Mr. Davis died, paid generous
tribute to him in the "Sun," saying: "A majestic soul has passed."

not allowed to say a word to any one nor is any one allowed to say a word to him. He is literally in a living tomb. His position is not much better than that of the Turkish Sultan, Bajazet, exposed by his captor, Tamerlane, in a portable iron cage." ("New York Herald," May 26, 1865.) The dispatch seemed positively to gloat over that poor man's misery.

A new fad in feminine attire came into vogue; women wore long, large, and heavy black chains as decorations.

The military murder of Mrs. Surratt stirred us profoundly. Too lowly, simple, and obscure in herself to rank with heroic figures, her execution lifts her to the plane where stand all who fell victims to the troubled times. Suspicion of complicity in Mr. Lincoln's murder, because of her son's intimacy with Wilkes Booth, led to her death. They had her before a military tribunal in Washington, her feet linked with chains.

Several men were executed. Their prison-life and hers was another tale to give one the creeps. They were not allowed to speak to any one, nor was any one allowed to speak to them; they were compelled to wear masks of padded cloth over face and head, an opening at the mouth permitting space for breathing; pictures said to be drawn from life showed them in their cells where the only resting-places were not beds, but bare, rough benches; marched before judges with these same horrible hoods on, marched to the gallows with them on, hanging with them on.

One of the executed, Payne, had been guilty of the attack on Mr. Seward and his son; the others had been dominated and bribed by Booth, but had failed to play the parts assigned them in the awful drama his morbid brain wrought out.

OUR FRIENDS, THE ENEMY

CHAPTER X

Our Friends, the Enemy

THERE was small interchange of civilities between Northern and Southern ladies. The new-comers were in much evidence; Southerners saw them riding and driving in rich attire and handsome equipages, and at the theatre in all the glory of fine toilettes.

There was not so much trouble opening theatres as churches. A good many stage celebrities came to the Richmond Theatre, which was well patronised. Decorated with United States flags, it was opened during the first week of the occupation with "Don Cæsar de Bazan." The "Whig" reported a brilliant audience. Mrs. Lincoln and Mrs. Grant, who had been driving over the city, were formally invited by General Weitzel to attend the play, but did not appear.

The band played every evening in the Square, and our people, ladies especially, were invited to come out. The Square and the Capitol were at one time overrun with negroes. This was stopped. Still, our ladies did not go. Federal officers and their ladies had their music to themselves. "There was no intentional slight or rudness on our part. We did not draw back our skirts in passing Federal soldiers, as was charged in Northern papers; if a few thoughtless girls or women did this, they were not representative. We tried not to give offense; we were heart-broken; we stayed to ourselves; and we were not hypocrites; that was all." So our women aver. In most Southern cities efforts were made to induce the ladies to come out and hear the band play.

The day Governor Pierpont arrived, windows of the Spotswood and Monumental were crowded with Northern ladies waving handkerchiefs. "I only knew from the papers," Matoaca tells, "that the Mansion was decorated with flowers for his reception. Our own windows, which had been as windows of a house of mourning, did not change their aspect for his coming. Our rightful governor was a fugitive; Governor Pierpont was an alien. We were submissive, but we could not rejoice." This was the feminine and social side. On the political and masculine side, he was welcomed. Delegations of prominent Virginians from all counties brought him assurances of coöperation. The new Governor tried to give a clean, patriotic administration.

Northerners held socials in each others' houses and in halls; there were receptions, unattended by Southerners, at the Governor's Mansion and Military Headquarters. It might have been more politic had we gone out of our way to be socially agreeable, but it would not have been sincere. Federal officers and their wives attended our churches. A Northern Methodist Society was formed with a group of adherents, Governor and Mrs. Pierpont, and, later, General and Mrs. Canby among them. "We of the Northern colony were very dependent upon ourselves for social pleasures," an ex-member who now considers herself a Southerner said to me recently. "There were some inter-marriages. I remember an elopement; a Petersburg girl ran away with a Federal officer, and the pair sought asylum at my father's, in Richmond's Northern colony. Miss Van Lew entertained us liberally. She gave a notable reception to Chief Justice Salmon P. Chase and his beautiful daughter, Kate." Miss Van Lew, a resident, was suspected of being a spy during the war.

Our ladies went veiled on the street, the motive that caused them to close their windows impelling them to cover their faces with sorrow's shield. There was not much opportunity for young blue-coats to so much as behold our pretty girls, much less make eyes at them, had they been so minded. That veil as an accompaniment of a lissome figure and graceful carriage must have sometimes acted as a tantalising disguise.

I heard of one very cute happening in which the wind and a veil played part. Mary Triplett, our famous blonde beauty, then in the rosy freshness of early youth, was walking along when the wind took off her veil and carried it to the feet of a young Federal officer. He bent, uplifted the vagrant mask, and, with his cap held before his eyes, restored it. That was a very honest, self-denying Yankee. Perhaps he peeped around the corner of his cap. There was at that time in Richmond a bevy of marvellously lovely buds, Mattie Ould, Miss Triplett's antithesis, among the number.

The entire South seems to have been very rich then in buds of beauty and women of distinction. Or, was it that the fires of adversity brought their charms and virtues into high relief? Names flitting through my mind are legion. Richmond's roll has been given often. Junior members of the Petersburg set were Tabb Bolling, General Rooney Lee's sweetheart (now his widow) ; Molly Bannister, General Lee's pet, who was allowed to ride Traveller; Anne Bannister, Alice Gregory, Betty and Jeannie Osborne, Betty Cabaniss, Betty and Lucy Page, Sally Hardy, Nannie Cocke, Patty Cowles, Julia, Mary and Marion Meade, and others who queened it over General Lee's army and wrought their pretty fingers to the bone for our lads in the trenches. To go farther afield, Georgia had her youthful "Maid of Athens," Jule King, afterwards Mrs. Henry Grady;

in Atlanta were the Clayton sisters, and Maggie Poole,
Augusta Hill, Ella Ezzard, Eugenia Goode, besides a
brilliant married circle.   In South Carolina were Mrs.
James Chesnut, her sister, Mrs. David R. Williams,
and all the fair troop that figure in her "Diary From
Dixie."   Louisiana's endless roster might begin with
the Slocomb family, to which General Butler paid
official tribute, recording that "Mrs. Slocomb equipped
the crack military company of New Orleans, the Washington Artillery, in which her son-in-law, Captain David
Urquhart, is an officer."   Mrs. Urquhart's daughter,
Cora (afterwards Mrs. James Brown Potter), was, I
think, a tiny maiden then.   Beloved for her social
charm and her charities, Mrs. Ida B. Richardson, Mrs.
Urquhart's sister, still lives in the Crescent City.   There
were the Leacock sisters, Mrs. Andrew Gray and Mrs.
Will Howell, the "madonna of New Orleans."   There
was the King family, which produced Grace King,
author and historian.   A Louisiana beauty was Addie
Prescott, whose face and presence gave warrant of the
royal blood of Spain flowing in her veins.   In Mississippi was "Pearl Rivers," afterwards Mrs. Nicholson,
good genius of the "Picayune"; and Mary E. Bryan,
later the genius of the "Sunny South."   Georgia and
Alabama claim Mme. Le Vert, to whose intellect Lamar-
tine paid tribute, and Augusta Evans, whose "Macaria"
ran the blockade in manuscript and came out up North
during the war; that delightful "Belle of the Fifties,"
Mrs. Clement C. Clay, is Alabama's own.   Besides the
"Rose of Texas" (Louise Wigfall), the Lone Star
State has many a winsome "Southern Girl" and woman
to her credit.   Mrs. Roger A. Pryor is Virginia's own.
Among Florida's fair was the "Madonna of the Wickliffe sisters," Mrs. Yulee, Senator Yulee's wife and,
presently, Florida's Vice-Regent for the Ladies' Asso-

MRS. DAVID L. YULEE
(Daughter of Governor Wickliffe, of Kentucky)

She was the wife of Senator Yulee, of Florida, Vice Regent of the
Mount Vernon Association of Florida, and was known as
the " Madonna of the Wickliffe Sisters."

ciation of Mt. Vernon.   Mrs. Sallie Ward Hunt and
Mrs. Sallie Ewing Pope lead a long list in Kentucky,
where Mary Anderson, the actress, was in her tender
teens, and Bertha Honoré (afterwards Mrs. Potter
Palmer) was in pinafores.   To Mississippi and Missouri belongs Theodosia Worthington Valliant; and
to Tennessee Betty Vance, whose beauty's fame was
world-wide, and Mary Wright, later Mrs. Treadwell.
At a ball given Prince Arthur when in this country,
a wealthy belle was selected to lead with him.   The
prince thinking he was to choose his partner, fixed on
Mary Wright, exquisite in poverty's simple white gown,
and asked: "May I lead with her?"   In North
Carolina were Sophia Portridge, women of the houses
of Devereaux, Vance, Mordecai—but I am not writing
the South's "Book of Fair and Noble Women."   I
leave out of my list names brilliant as any in it.
    Of all the fair women I have ever seen, Mary Meade
was fairest.   No portrait can do justice to the picture
memory holds of her as "Bride" to D'Arcy Paul's
"Bridegroom" in the "Mistletoe Bough," which Mrs.
Edwin Morrison staged so handsomely that her ama-
teurs were besought to "star" in the interest of good
causes.   Our fair maids were no idle "lilies of loveliness."   The Meade sisters and others turned talents to
account in mending fallen family fortunes.   Maids and
matrons labored diligently to gather our soldier dead
into safe resting-places.   The "Lyrical Memorial,"
Mrs. Platt's enterprise, like the "Mistletoe Bough"
(later produced), was called for far and wide.   The
day after presentation in Louisville, the Federal Commandant sent Mary Meade, who had impersonated the
South pleading sepulture for her sons, a basket of
flowers with a live white dove in the center.
    Slowly in Richmond interchange of little human kind-

nesses between neighbors established links. General Bartlett, occupying the Haxall house, who had lost a leg in the war, was "the Yankee who conquered my wife," a Southerner bears witness. "I came home one day and found him sitting with her on my steps. He suffered greatly from his old wound, bore it patiently, and by his whole conduct appealed to her sweet womanliness. His staff was quiet and orderly."

The beautiful daughter of one family and her feeble grandmother were the only occupants of the mansion into which General Ord and his wife moved. The pair had no money and were unable to communicate with absent members of the household who had been cut off from home by the accidents of war while visiting in another city. The younger lady was ill with typhoid fever. The general and his wife were very thoughtful and generous in supplying ice, brandy, and other essentials and luxuries.

"Under Heaven," the invalid bore grateful witness when recovering, "I owe my life to General and Mrs. Ord." Her loveliness and helplessness were in themselves an argument to move a heart of stone to mercy; nevertheless, it was virtue and grace that mercy was shown.

We made small appeal for sympathy or aid; were too much inclined to the reverse course, carrying poverty and other troubles with a stiff neck, scantily-clad backs, long-suffering stomachs, and pride and conscience resolved. But—though some form of what we considered oppression was continually before our eyes—our conquerors, when in our midst, were more and more won to pity and then to sympathy. Our commandants might be stern enough when first they came, but when they had lived among us a little while, they softened and saw things in a new light; and the negroes and the carpet-baggers complained of them every one, and the authorities at Washington could not change them fast enough.

Southerners here and in other cities who had Federal boarders were considered fortunate because of the money and protection secured. In such cases, there was usually mutual kindness and consideration, politeness keeping in the background topics on which differences were cruel and sharp; but the sectional dividing lines prevented free social intermingling.

In places garrisoned by soldiers of coarser types and commanded by men less gentlemanly, women sometimes displayed more pronounced disapprobation. Not always with just occasion, but, again, often with cause only too grave. At the best, it was not pleasant to have strange men sauntering, uninvited, into one's yard and through one's house, invading one's kitchen and entertaining housemaids and cooks. That these men wore blue uniforms was unfortunate for us and for the uniform. At that time, the very sight of " army blue " brought terror, anguish and resentment.

Our famous physicians, Maguire and McCaw, were often called to the Northern sick. Dr. McCaw came once direct to Uncle Randolph from the Dents, where he had been summoned to Mrs. Ulysses S. Grant, and Matoaca listened curiously to his and her uncle's cordial discussion of General Grant, who had made friends at the South by his course at Appomattox and his insistence on the cartel.

A conversation occurring between another of our physicians and a feminine patient is not without significance. The lady and the doctor's wife had been friends before the war. " Why has your wife not called upon me, Doctor? " she asked. " Has she forgotten me? " " No, ma'am," he answered gently, and then in a low, kindly voice: "But she cannot—yet—forget all that has happened since you were girls together." "But she should not treasure it against me individually." "She does not, ma'am. But she cannot forget—yet. You would understand if you had been in the beleagured land. If the good women of the North could only imagine themselves in the place of the women of the South during the last four years and in their place now!"

She sighed. "I can see only too plainly that they have suffered unutterably many things that we have been spared. And that they suffer now. It's natural, too, that they should hate to have us here lording it over them."

Very different was the spirit of the wife of a Federal officer stationed at Augusta, Georgia, whose declaration that she hoped to see the day when "black heels should stand on white necks" startled the State of Georgia. Many good ladies came South firm in the belief that all Southerners were negro-beaters, slave-traders, and cut-throats; a folk sadly benighted and needing tutelage in the humanities; and they were not always politic in expressing these opinions.

After war, the war spirit always lingers longest in non-combatants—in women and in men who stayed at home and cheered others on. "The soldiers," said General Grant, "were in favor of a speedy reconstruction on terms least humiliating to the Southern people." He wrote Mrs. Grant from Raleigh, North Carolina, in 1865: "The suffering that must exist in the South . . . will be beyond conception; people who speak of further retaliation and punishment do not conceive of the suffering endured already, or they are heartless and unfeeling."

General Halleck to General Meade, April 30, 1865:

"The Army of the Potomac have shown the people of Virginia how they would be treated as enemies. Let them now prove that they know equally well how to treat the same people as friends."

"The terrible sufferings of the South," our press commented, "have softened the hearts of the stern warriors of the Armies of the Potomac and the Cumberland, and while they are calling for pity and justice for us, politicians and fanatics call for vengeance." General Sherman said: "I do think some political power might be given to the young men who served in the rebel army, for they are a better class than the adventurers who have gone South purely for office."

During an exciting epoch in reconstruction, I was sitting beside a wounded ex-Confederate in an opera-box, listening to a Southern statesman haranguing us on our wrongs, real and heavy enough, heaven knows, heavier than ever those of war had been. "Rather than submit to continued and intensified humiliations," cried the orator, a magnetic man of the sort who was carrying Northern audiences to opposite extremes, "we will buckle on our swords and go to war again!" "It might be observed," remarked my veteran drily, while I clapped my hands, "that if he should buckle on his sword and go to war, it would be what he did not do before." I held my hands quite still during the rest of that speech.

"Our women never were whipped!" I have heard grizzled Confederates say that proudly. "There is a difference," remarked one hoary-headed hero, who, after wearing stars on his collar in Confederate service represented his State in the Federal Congress, "between the political and the feminine war-spirit. The former is too often for personal gain. Woman's is the aftermath of anguish. It has taken a long time to reconstruct

Southern women. Some are not reconstructed yet. Suffering was stamped too deep for effacement. The Northern woman suffered with her Southern sister the agony of anxiety and bereavement. But the Southern had other woes, of which the Northern could have no conception. The armies were upon us. There was devastation. The Southern woman and her loved ones lacked food and raiment, the enemy appropriating what we had and blocking ways by which fresh supplies might come; her home was burned over her head. Sometimes she suffered worse things than starvation, worse things than the destruction of her home.

"And women could only sit still and endure, while we could fight back. Women do not understand that war is a matter of business. I had many friends among the men I fought—splendid, brave fellows. Personally, we were friends, and professionally, enemies. Women never get that point of view."

Woman's war spirit is faithfulness and it is absolutely reckless of personal advantages, as the following incident may illustrate. General Hunton and General Turner knew each other pretty well, although in their own persons they had never met. They had commanded opposing forces and entertained a considerable respect for each other. General Turner was the first Federal officer that came to Lynchburg, when General Hunton's wife and youthful son were refugees; he sent Dr. Murray, a Confederate surgeon, to call upon Mrs. Hunton with the message that she was to suffer for nothing he could supply. General Hunton was in prison, she knew not where; was not sure if he were alive or dead.

She had not the feelings her lord entertained for his distinguished antagonist, and her response was: "Tell

General Turner I would not accept anything from him to save my life!"

Yet she must have been very hungry. She and her youthful son had been reduced to goober-peas. First, her supplies got down to one piece of beef-bone. She thought she would have a soup. For a moment, she left her son to watch the pot, but not to stir the soup. But he thought he would do well to stir it. So he stirred it, and turned the pot over. That day, she had nothing for dinner but goober-peas.

"When I came home," said General Hunton, when asked for this story's sequel, "and she told me about her message to General Turner, I wrote him the nicest letter I knew how to write, thanking him for his kindness to the wife of a man whose only claim on him was that he had fought him the best he knew how.

"I don't think we would ever have had the trouble we had down here," he continued, "if Northern people had known how things really were. In fact, I know we would not. Why, I never had any trouble with Northern men in all my life except that I just fought them all I knew how. And I never had better friends than among my Republican colleagues in Congress after the war. They thought all the more of me because I stood up so stoutly for the old Confederate Cause."

Bonds coming about in the natural, inevitable order through interchange of the humanities were respected. But where they seemed the outcome of vanity, frivolity, or coquetry, that was another matter, a very serious one for the Southern participant. The spirit of the times was morbid, yet a noble loyalty was behind it.

Anywhere in the land, a Southern girl showing partiality for Federal beaux came under the ban. If there were nothing else against it, such a course appeared neither true nor dignified; if it were not treason to our lost Confederacy, it were treason to our own poor boys in gray to flutter over to prosperous conquerors.

Nothing could be more sharply defined in lights and shadows than the life of one beautiful and talented Southern woman who matronised the entertainments of a famous Federal general at a post in one of the Cotton States, and thereby brought upon herself such condemnation as made her wines and roses cost her dear. Yet perhaps such affiliations lessened the rigors of military government for her State.

One of the loveliest of Atlanta's gray-haired dames tells me: "I am unreconstructed yet—Southern to the backbone." Yet she speaks of Sherman's godless cohorts as gently as if she were mother of them all. Her close neighbour was a Yankee encampment. The open ground around her was dotted with tents.

There were "all sorts" among the soldiers. None gave insolence or violence. Pilfering was the great trouble; the rank and file were "awfully thievish." Her kitchen, as usual with Southern kitchens of those days, was a separate building. If for a moment she left her pots and ovens to answer some not-to-be-ignored demand from the house, she found them empty on her return, her dinner gone—a most serious thing when it was as by the skin of her teeth that she got anything at all to cook and any fuel to cook with; and when, moreover, cooking was new and tremendously hard work. "We could not always identify the thief; when we could, we were afraid to incur the enmity of the men. Better have our things stolen than worse happen us, as might if officers punished those men on our report. I kept a still tongue in my head."

Though a wife and mother, she was yet in girlhood's years, very soft and fair; had been "lapped in luxury," with a maid for herself, a nurse for her boy, a servant to do this, that, or the other thing, for her. She thus describes her first essay at the family wash. There was a fine well in her yard, and men came to get water. A big-hearted Irishman caught the little lady struggling over soap-suds. It looked as if she would never get those clothes clean. For one thing, when she tried to wring them, they were streaked with blood from her arms and hands; she had peculiarly fine and tender skin.

"Faith an' be jabbers!" said Pat, "an' what is it that you're thryin' to do?" "Go away, and let me alone!" "Faith, an' if ye don't lave off clanin' thim garmints, they'll be that doirty—" "Go 'way!" "Sure, me choild, an' if ye'll jis' step to the other soide of the tub without puttin' me to the inconvaniance—" He was about to pick her up in his mighty hands. She moved and dropped down, swallowing a sob.

"Sure, an' it's as good a washerwoman as ivver wore breeches I am," said Pat. "An' that's what I've larned in the army." In short order, he had all the clothes hanging snow-white on the line; before he left, he cut enough wood for her ironing. "I'm your Bridget ivery wash-day that comes 'roun'," he said as he swung himself off. He was good as his word. This brother-man did her wash every week. "Sure, an' it's a shame it is," he would say, "the Government fadin' the lazy nagurs an' God an' the divvil can't make 'em wur-r-k."

Through Tony, her son, another link was formed 'twixt late enemies. It was hard for mothers busy at housework to keep track of young children; without fences for definement of yard-limits, and with all old landmarks wiped out, it was easy for children to wander beyond bearings. A lost child was no rarity. One day General and Mrs. Saxton drove up in their carriage, bringing Tony. Tony had lost himself; fright, confusion, lack of food, had made him ill; he had been brought to the attention of the general and his wife, who, instead of sending the child home by a subordinate, came with him themselves, the lady holding the pale little fellow in her arms, comforting and soothing him. Thus began friendship between Mrs. S. and Mrs. Saxton; not only small Tony was now pressed to take airings with Yankees, but his mother. The general did all he could to make life easier for her; had wood hauled and cut for her. The Southern woman's reduction to poverty and menial tasks mortified him, as they mortified many another manly blue-coat, witness of the reduction. "It is pitiable and it is all wrong," said one officer to Mrs. S. "Our people up North simply don't know how things are down here." A lady friend of Mrs. S.'s tells me that she knew a Northern officer— (giving his name)—who resigned his commission because he found himself unable to witness the sufferings of Southern women and children, and have a hand in imposing them.

Rulers who came under just condemnation as "military satraps" governing in a democracy in time of peace by the bayonet, when divorced from the exercise of their office, won praise as men. Thus, General Meade's rule in Georgia is open to severest criticism, yet Ellen Meade Clarke, who saw him as the man and not as the oppressor, says: "I had just married and gone to Atlanta when Sherman ordered the citizens out, which order I hastily obeyed, leaving everything in my Peachtree cottage home. Was among the first to return. Knew all the generals in command; they were all neighbors; General Meade, who was sent to see me by some one bearing our name, proved a good and faithful friend and, on his death-bed, left me his prayer-book."

MISS MARY MEADE, OF PETERSBURG, VA.

She was known far and wide for her loveliness of person and character, her intellectual gifts and social graces.

LOVERS AND PRAYERS

CHAPTER XI

Some military orders were very irritating.
The "Button Order" prohibited our men from wearing Confederate buttons. Many possessed no others
and had not money wherewith to buy. Buttons were
scarce as hens' teeth. The Confederacy had been
reduced to all sorts of makeshifts for buttons. Thorns
from thornbushes had furnished country folks with such
fastenings as pins usually supply, and served convenience
on milady's toilette-table when she went to do up her
hair.

One clause in that monstrous order delighted feminine hearts! It provided as thoughtful concession to
all too glaring poverty that: "When plain buttons
cannot be procured, those formerly used can be covered
with cloth." Richmond ladies looked up all the bits
of crape and bombazine they had, and next morning
their men appeared on the streets with buttons in mourning! "I would never have gotten Uncle out of the
front door if he had realized what I was up to,"
Matoaca relates. "Not that he was not mournful
enough, but he did not want to mourn that way."

Somehow, nobody thought about Sam's button; he
was a boy, only fifteen. He happened to go out near
Camp Grant in his old gray jacket, the only coat he
had; one of his brothers had given it to him months
before. It was held together over his breast by a
single button, his only button. A Yankee sergeant cut

it off with his sword. The jacket fell apart, exposing bepatched and thread-bare underwear. His mother and sisters could not help crying when the boy came in, holding his jacket together with his hand, his face suffused, his eyes full of tears of rage and mortification.

The "Button Trouble" pervaded the entire South. The Tennessee Legislature, Brownlow's machine, discussed a bill imposing a fine of $5 to $25 upon privates, and $25 to $50 upon officers for wearing the "rebel uniform." The gaunt, destitute creatures who were trudging, stumping, limping, through that State on their way from distant battlefields and Northern prisons to their homes, had rarely so much as fifty cents in their pockets. Had that bill become a law enforced, Tennessee prisons must have overflowed with recaptured Confederates, or roads and woods with men in undress.

Many a distinguished soldier, home-returning, ignorant that such an order existed, has been held up at the entrance to his native town by a saucy negro sergeant who would shear him of buttons with a sabre, or march him through the streets to the Provost's office to answer for the crime of having buttons on his clothes.

The provision about covering buttons has always struck me as the unkindest cut of all. How was a man who had no feminine relatives to obey the law? Granted that as a soldier, he had acquired the art of being his own seamstress, how, when he was in the woods or the roads, could he get scraps of cloth and cover buttons?

But of all commands ever issued, the "Marriage Order" was the most extraordinary! That order said people should not get married unless they took the Oath of Allegiance. If they did, they would be arrested. I have forgotten the exact wording, but if you will look

up General Order No. 4,* April 29, and signed by
General Halleck, you can satisfy any curiosity you may
feel. It was a long ukase, saying what-all people
should not do unless they took the oath (some felt like
taking a good many daily!). Naturally, young people
were greatly upset. Many had been engaged a weary
while, to be married soon as the war should be over.

Among those affected was Captain Sloan, whose marriage to Miss Wortham was due the Tuesday following.
The paper containing the order, heavily ringed with
black, darkened the roseate world upon which the bride-
elect opened her lovely eyes Saturday morning. The
same hand that had put the order in mourning had
scribbled on the margin: "If Captain Sloan is not
ready to take that oath, I am."

Her maid informed her that Mr. Carrington, an
elderly friend, fond of a joke, was awaiting her.
Descending to the drawing-room, she found it full of
sympathising neighbours, her betrothed in the midst,
all debating a way out of the difficulty. Not even
sharp-witted lawyers could see one. In times so out of
joint law did not count.

The situation was saved by the fact that General
Halleck had a namesake in Captain Sloan's family.
The Captain's "Uncle Jerry" (otherwise General
Jerry Gilmer, of South Carolina) had called a son

---

* General Halleck to General Stanton (Richmond, April 28, 1865):
"I forward General Orders No. 4. . . . You will perceive from
paragraph V, that measures have been taken to prevent, as far as
possible, the propagation of legitimate rebels." Paragraph V: "No
marriage license will be issued until the parties desiring to be married take the oath of allegiance to the United States; and no clergyman, magistrate, or other party authorized by State laws to perform
the marriage ceremony will officiate in such capacity until himself
and the parties contracting matrimony shall have taken the prescribed
oath of allegiance," all under pains of imprisonment, etc.

"Henry Halleck" in honour of his one-time class-mate at West Point. When the idea of the namesake as basis of appeal dawned on Captain Sloan, day was passing. Miss Wortham's father, who, before the Federal Government had interfered with his dominion as a parent, had been anxious that his very youthful daughter and her betrothed should defer their union, was now quite determined that the rights of the lovers should not be abrogated by Uncle Sam. As member of the Confederate Ambulance Committee, he had been in close touch with Colonel Mulford, Federal Commissioner of Exchange; Judge Ould, Confederate Commissioner, was his personal friend; in combination with these gentlemen, he arranged a meeting twixt lover and war lord.

General Halleck received Hymen's ambassador with courtesy. The story of the namesake won his sympathetic ear. When told what consternation his order was causing—Captain Sloan plead other cases besides his own—the war lord laughed, scribbled something on a slip of official paper and handed it to Captain Sloan, saying: "Let this be known and I suppose there will be a good many weddings before Monday." The slip read like this: "Order No. 4 will not go into effect until Monday morning. H. W. Halleck, General Commanding."

Alas! there were no Sunday papers. The news was disseminated as widely as possible; and three weddings, at least, in high society, happened Sunday in consequence. Mrs. Sloan, a prominent member of Baltimore society, gave her own account of the whole matter in Mrs. Daniel's "Confederate Scrap-Book," which any one may see at the Confederate Museum.

"The gown I wore the day after my marriage," she relates, "was a buff calico with tiny dots in it, and as it was prettily and becomingly made, I looked as well, and I know I was as happy, as if it had been one of Worth's or Redfern's most bewildering conceits—and I am sure it was as expensive, as it cost $30 a yard."

General Halleck's order was not unique. Restrictions on marriage had been incorporated in the State Constitution of Missouri, 1864, a section prescribing that "No person shall practice law, be competent as bishop, priest, deacon, minister, elder, or other clergyman of any religious persuasion, sect, or denomination, teach, preach, or solemnise marriage until such person shall have first taken the oath required as to voters." "Under these provisions," commented Senator Vest, from whom I borrow, "the parent who had given a piece of bread or a cup of water to a son in the Confederate service, or who had in any way expressed sympathy for such son, was prohibited from registering as voter, serving as juror, or holding any office or acting as trustee, or practicing law, or teaching in any school, or preaching the Gospel, or solemnising the marriage rite." *

Strictly construed, the test-oath imposed by Congress in 1867, like that of Missouri, excluded from franchise and office, the parent who had given a piece of bread or a cup of water or his sympathy to a son in the Confederate service; and the negrò who had made wheat and corn for his master's family, as the applicant must swear that he had not "given aid or comfort to" Confederates.

The Missouri test-oath was one that prominent Union men, among them General Francis P. Blair, leader of the Union Party in his State, a man who had taken

---

* "Why Solid South," Hilary Herbert. To this book I owe a large debt for information, as does every other present-day writer on reconstruction.

part in the siege of Vicksburg and marched with Sherman to the sea, were unable to take. Americans beholding his statue in Statuary Hall, Washington, as that of one of the two sons Missouri most delights to honour, will find food for curious reflection in the fact that General Blair, going in full Federal uniform to register as a voter, was not allowed to do so. Visitors to Blair Hall at the St. Louis Exposition may have been reminded of this little incident of reconstruction. In 1867, Father John A. Cummings was arrested and tried for performing parochial duties without taking the oath. A bill forbidding women to marry until they took the oath was passed by Tennessee's Senate, but the House rejected it. This bill, like Missouri's law, discriminated against ministers of the Gospel; those who had sympathised with "rebels" or in any way aided them, were condemned to work on the public roads and other degrading forms of expiation.

There was no appreciable reluctance on the part of the people to take the oath of allegiance. They could honestly swear for the future to sustain the Government of the United States, but few, or no decent people, even Unionists, living among Confederates, could vow they had given no "aid or comfort" to one. The test-oath cultivated hypocrisy in natives and invited carpet-baggers. A native who would take it was eligible to office, while the honest man who would not lie, was denied a right to vote.

In readiness to take the oath of allegiance, people rushed so promptly to tribunals of administration that the sincerity of the South was questioned at the North, where it could not be understood how sharp was our need to have formalities of submission over and done with, that we might get to work. One striking cartoon pictured Columbia upon a throne gloomily regarding

From a portrait by de Franca, photographed by Doerr, Louisville, Ky.

MRS. HENRY L. POPE
(Sarah Moore Ewing)

First Kentucky State Regent D. A. R.

a procession that came bending, bowing, kneeling, creeping, crawling, to her feet, General Lee leader and most abject, with Howell Cobb, Wade Hampton, and other distinguished Southerners around him. Beneath was this: "Can I trust these men?" On the opposite page, a one-legged negro soldier held out his hand; beneath was: "Franchise? And not this man?"

A few people had serious scruples of conscience against taking the oath. I know of two or three whose attitude, considering their personalities, was amusing and pathetic. There was one good lady, Mrs. Wellington, who walked all the way from Petersburg to Richmond, a distance of twenty miles, for fear the oath might be required if she boarded a car!

I turn to Matoaca's journal:

"I have been visiting Cousin Mary in Powhatan. Of course they have military government there, too. Soldiers ride up, enter without invitation, walk through the house, seat themselves at the piano and play; promenade to the rear, go into the kitchen, sit down and talk with the darkeys.

"At church, I saw officers wearing side-arms. They come regularly to watch if we pray for the President of the United States. I hope they were edified; a number stood straight up during that prayer. Among the most erect were the M. girls, who have very *retroussé* noses. The Yankees reported: 'Not only do they stand up when the President is prayed for, but they turn up their noses.' They sent word back: 'A mightier power than the Yankee Army turned up our noses.'

"I hear they have dealt severely with Rev. Mr. Wingfield because he would not read that prayer for the President. When brought up for it, he told the examining officer he could not—it was a matter of conscience. They put a ball and chain on him and made him sweep the streets. And these people are the exponents of 'freedom,' and 'liberty of conscience.' They come from a land whose slogan is these words! They have no right to force us to pray according to their views. For myself, I kneel during the prayer, I try to pray it; I seek to feel it, since to pray without feeling is mockery. But I don't feel it.

"Uncle advised: 'My daughter, no man needs your prayers more than the President of the United States. He has great and grave responsibilities. We must desire that a higher power shall direct him. The President is surrounded by advisers bent on revenge, so bent on it that they seem to care nothing whatever for the Union—the real union of the North and South.' So I bow my head, and I try—God knows I try! But thoughts of all the blood that has been shed, of the homes that have been burned, the suffering and starvation endured, will rush into my mind as I kneel. Dear Christ! did you know how hard a command you laid upon us when you said, 'Pray for your enemies?'"

An entry after Mr. Lincoln's death says: "How can I pray that prayer in the face of this?" Below is pasted Johnson's proclamation charging the assassination to Mr. Davis and other Southern leaders. This follows: "How *can* I pray for the President of the United States? That proclamation is an insult flung in the face of the whole South! And we have to take it."

They had as much trouble at Washington over our prayers as over our few buttons and clothes.

The Sunday after the evacuation—one week from the day on which the messenger came from General Lee to Mr. Davis—the Federals were represented in St. Paul's by distinguished and respectful worshippers.

Nearly all women present were in black. When the moment came for the petition for "the President of the Confederate States and all others in authority," you could have heard a pin fall. The congregation had kinsmen in armies still under the authority of the President of the Confederacy; they were full of anxiety; their hearts were torn and troubled. Were they here before God to abjure their own? Were they to utter prayer that was mockery? To require them to pray for the President of the United States was like calling upon the martyrs of old to burn incense to strange gods. Dr. Minnegerode read the prayer, omitting the words "for the President of the Confederate States," simply saying "for all in authority." Generals Weitzel, Shepley and Ripley had consented that it was to be thus.

Assistant Secretary of War Dana writes to Secretary of War Stanton: "On Friday, I asked Weitzel about what he was going to do in regard to opening the churches on Sunday. He said ministers would be warned against treasonable utterances and be told they must put up loyal prayers."

It seems that after this conversation the determination of the Commandant and his Staff to wrest piety and patriotism out of the rebels at one fell swoop, underwent modification, partly, perhaps, as a concession to the Almighty, of whom it was fair to presume that He might not be altogether pleased with prayers offered on the point of a sword.

Scandalised at official laxity in getting just dues from Heaven for the United States, Dana continues: "It shakes my faith a good deal in Weitzel." In subsequent letters he says it was Shepley's or Ripley's fault; Weitzel really thought the people ought to be made to pray right; the crime was somehow fastened finally

on Judge Campbell's back, and Weitzel was informed
that he must have no further oral communications with
this dangerous and seditious person. Thus Mr.
Stanton rounded up Weitzel: "If you have consented
that services should be performed in the Episcopal
Churches of Richmond without the usual prayer said in
loyal churches for the President, your action is strongly
condemned by this Department. I am not willing to
believe that an officer of the United States commanding in Richmond would consent to such an omission
of respect for the President of the United States."
Weitzel: "Do you desire that I should order this
form of prayer in Episcopal, Hebrew, Roman Catholic,
and other churches where they have a liturgy?"
Stanton: "No mark of respect must be omitted to
President Lincoln which was rendered to the rebel, Jeff
Davis." Weitzel: "Dispatch received. Order will
be issued in accordance therewith."

Is it any wonder that Grant and Sherman between
them finally said to President Johnson: "Mr. President, you should make some order that we of the army
are not bound to obey the orders of Mr. Stanton as
Secretary of War."

The Episcopal clergy presented the case clearly to
General Weitzel and his Staff, who, as reasonable men,
appreciated the situation. "The Church and State are
not one in this country; we, as men, in all good faith
take the oath of allegiance required of us. As priests,
we are under ecclesiastical jurisdiction; we cannot add
to the liturgy. A convention of the Church must be
called. Meanwhile, we, of course, omit words held
treasonable, reciting, 'for all in authority,' which surely
includes the President. Forcing public feeling will be
unwise; members will absent themselves, or go to a
church which, not using any ritual, is not under com-

pulsion; the order is, in effect, discrimination against the Episcopal Church."

Our people, they said, "desire by quiet and inoffensive conduct to respond to the liberal policy of those in command; they deeply appreciate the conciliatory measures adopted, and all the more regret to appear as dissenters." They wrote to President Johnson, asking opportunity for action by heads of the diocese; they said that when the South seceded, standing forms had obtained for months till change was so wrought. That letter went the rounds of the War, State, and Executive Departments, and was returned "disapproved," and the Episcopal Churches of Richmond were actually closed by military order until they would say that prayer.

Even President Lincoln was moved to write General Weitzel, asking what it meant that he hadn't made people pray as they ought! "You told me not to insist upon little things," said Weitzel.

Had we been let alone in the matter of praying for the President, we would all very soon have come to see the subject in the light in which Uncle Randolph presented it. As it was, conscientious prelates were in straitened positions, not wishing to lead their people in petitions which the latter would resent or regard at the best as empty formula. Omission of the prayer altogether was recommended by Bishop Wilmer, of Alabama, as the wisest course for the moment; General Woods suspended the Bishop and all clergy of his diocese; they were not to preach or to lead in church service; and, I believe, were not to marry the living, baptise the new-born, or bury the dead. President Johnson set such orders aside as soon as he came to his senses after the shock of Mr. Lincoln's death.

General McPherson commanded pastors of Vicksburg (1864) to read the prescribed prayer for the

President at each and every service; pastors of churches without such prescribed form were instructed to invent one. The Bishop of Natchez, William Henry Elder, was banished because he would not read the prayer. Some young ladies, of Vicksburg, were banished because they rose and left the church, on Christmas morning, when a minister read it. An order signed by General McPherson, served on each, said she was "hereby banished and must leave the Federal lines within forty-eight hours under penalty of imprisonment." No extension of time for getting "their things ready" was allowed. Permission was given for the mother of one delinquent to chaperon the bevy, which, with due ceremony, was deported under flag of truce, hundreds of Federal soldiers watching.

One Sunday in New Orleans under Butler's rule, Major Strong was at Dr. Goodrich's church; time came for prayer for the Confederacy; there was silence. Major Strong rose and thundered: "Stop, sir! I close this church in ten minutes!" Rev. Dr. Leacock * wrote Butler a tender letter begging him not to force people to perjury in taking the oath through fear, prefacing: "No man more desires restoration of the Union than I." Helen Gray, Dr. Leacock's granddaughter, tells me: "My grandfather was arrested in church and marched through the city in ecclesiastical robes to answer for not praying as Butler bade; Rev. Dr. Goodrich and Rev. Mr. Fulton (now Editor of the 'Church Standard') were also arrested. Butler sent them North to be imprisoned in Fort Lafayette. The levee was thronged with people, many weeping to see them go. They were met at New York by influential

---

* An Englishman of Queen's College; the Bishop of London had sent him as Chaplain to Lord Sligo, Governor of Jamaica, but at this time he was Rector of Christ Church, New Orleans.

MRS. WILLIAM HOWELL
(Mary Leacock)

MRS. ANDREW GRAY
(Lina Leacock)

Daughters of the Rev. Dr. Leacock, of Christ Church, New Orleans.

citizens, among these Samuel Morse, the inventor, who offered them his purse, carriage and horses. They were paroled and entertained at the Astor House. Some people were bitter and small towards them; many were kind, among these, I think, was Bishop Potter. Hon. Reverdy Johnson took up their case. Grandfather served St. Mark's, Niagara, Canada, in the rector's absence; the people presented him, through Mrs. Dr. Marston, with a purse; he served at Chamblee, where the people also presented him with a purse. Mrs. Greenleaf, Henry W. Longfellow's sister, sent him a purse of $500; she had attended his church during ante-bellum visits to New Orleans, and she loved him dearly. Rev. F. E. Chubbuck, the Yankee Chaplain appointed to succeed my grandfather, called on my grandmother, expressed regrets and sympathies, and offered to do anything he could for her. I tell the tale as it has come to me." Government reports confirm this in essentials.

Of course, denominations not using a liturgy, had an advantage, but they were not exempt. Major B. K. Davis, Lexington, Mo., April 25, 1865, to Major-General Dodge: "On the 7th of April, from the well-known disloyalty of the churches of this place, I issued an order that pastors of all churches return thanks for our late victories. The pastor of the M. E. Church declined to do so, and I took the keys of his church."

In Huntsville, Alabama, 1862, Rev. F. A. Ross, Presbyterian minister, was arrested and sent north by General Rousseau because, when commanded to pray for the Yankees, he prayed: "We beseech thee, O Lord, to bless our enemies and remove them from our midst as soon as seemeth good in Thy sight!" *

---

* "Civil War & Reconstruction in Alabama," W. L. Fleming.

"The Confederate Veteran" tells this of General Lee. At Communion in St. Paul's soon after the occupation, the first person to walk up to the altar and kneel was a negro man. Manner and moment made the act sinister, a challenge, not an expression of piety. The congregation sat, stunned and still, not knowing what to do. General Lee rose, walked quietly up the aisle and knelt near the negro. The people followed and service proceeded as if no innovation had been attempted. The custom by which whites preceded negroes to the altar originated, not in contempt for negroes, but in ideas of what was right, orderly and proper. So far were whites from despising negroes in religious fellowship that it was not strange for both races to assemble in plantation chapels and join in worship conducted by the black preacher in the white preacher's absence. I sometimes think those old Southerners knew the negro better than we ever can. But just after the war, they were not supposed to know anything of value on any subject.

Wherever there was a press, it was muzzled by policy if not by such direct commands as General Sherman's in Savannah, when he ordained that there should be no more than two newspapers, and forbade "any libelous publication, mischievous matter, premature acts, exaggerated statements, *or any comments whatever upon the acts of the constituted authorities,*" on pain of heavy penalties to editors and proprietors. Some people say we ought, even now, for the family honour, to hush up everything unpleasant and discreditable. Not so! It is not well for men in power to think that their acts are not to be inquired into some day.

CLUBBED TO HIS KNEES

CHAPTER XII

CLUBBED TO HIS KNEES

As illustrations of embarrassments we had to face, I have chiefly chosen incidents showing a kindly and forbearing spirit on the part of Federal commanders, because I desire to pay tribute wherever I may to men in blue, remembering that Southern boys are now wearing the blue and that all men wearing the blue are ours. I have chiefly chosen incidents in which the Federal officers, being gentlemen and brave men—being decent and human—revolted against exercise of cruelty to a fallen foe.

Truth compels the shield's reverse.

In Richmond, one officer in position went to a prominent citizen and demanded $600 of him, threatening to confiscate and sell his home if he did not give it. This citizen, a lawyer and man of business, knew the threat could not be executed, and refused to meet the demand. Others not so wise paid such claims. In all parts of the South, many people, among them widows and orphans, were thus impoverished beyond the pinched condition in which war left them. Some sold their remnants of furniture, the very beds they slept on, a part of their scanty raiment, and in one case on official record, "the coverlid off the baby's bed," to satisfy the spurious claims of men misusing authority.

An instance illustrating our helplessness is that of Captain Bayard, who came out of the war with some make-shift crutches, a brave heart, and a love affair as the sum total of his capital in life. He made his first money by clerical work for sympathetic Federal officials. This he invested in a new suit of clothes; "They are right nice-looking," he said with modest pride when conveying the pleasing intelligence to one interested; and he bought a pair of artificial feet.

Then he set out to see his sweetheart, feeling very proud. It was the first time he had tried his feet on the street, and he was not walking with any sense of security, but had safely traversed a square or two and was crossing a street, when a Federal officer came galloping along and very nearly ran over him; he threw up his cane. The horse shied, the cavalryman jumped off and knocked him down. As fast as he struggled up, the cavalryman knocked him down again. A burly man ran to his assistance; the cavalryman struck this man such a blow that it made tears spring in his eyes; then mounted and galloped off. "He was obliged to see," said the captain, "that I was a cripple, and that I could not get out of his way or withstand his blows."

The worst Virginia had to bear was as nothing to what the Carolinas suffered. There was that poor boy, who was hung in Raleigh on Lovejoy's tree—where the Governor's Mansion now stands. He had fired off a pistol; had hurt nobody—had not attempted to hurt anybody; it was just a boy's thoughtless, crazy deed.

Entering Rosemont Cemetery, Newberry, S. C., one perceives on a tall marble shaft "The Lone Star of Texas" and this: "Calvin S. Crozier, Born at Brandon, Mississippi, August 1840, Murdered at Newberry, S. C., September 8, 1865."

At the close of the war, there were some 99,000 Confederates in Federal prisons, whose release, beginning in May, continued throughout the summer.

Among these was Crozier, slender, boyish in appearance, brave, thin to emaciation, pitifully weak and homesick. It was a far cry to his home in sunny Galveston, but he had traversed three States when he fell ill in North Carolina. A Good Samaritan nursed him, and set him on his way again. At Orangeburg, S. C., a gentleman placed two young ladies, journeying in the same direction, under his care. To Crozier, the trust was sacred. At Newberry, the train was derailed by obstructions placed on the track by negro soldiers of the 33d U. S. Regiment, which, under command of Colonel Trowbridge, white, was on its way from Anderson to Columbia. Crozier got out with others to see what was the matter. Returning, he found the coach invaded by two half-drunk negro soldiers, cursing and using indecent language. He called upon them to desist, directing their attention to the presence of ladies. They replied that they "didn't care a d—!" One attempted gross familiarities with one of the ladies. Crozier ejected him; the second negro interfered; there was a struggle in the dark; one negro fled unhurt; the other, with a slight cut, ran towards camp, yelling: "I'm cut by a d—d rebel!" Black soldiers came in a mob.

The narrative, as told on the monument, concludes: "The infuriated soldiers seized a citizen of Newberry, upon whom they were about to execute savage revenge, when Crozier came promptly forward and avowed his own responsibility. He was hurried in the night-time to the bivouac of the regiment to which the soldiers belonged, was kept under guard all night, was not allowed communication with any citizen, was condemned to die without even the form of a trial, and was shot to death about daylight the following morning, and his body mutilated."

He had been ordered to dig his own grave, but refused. A hole had been dug, he was made to kneel on its brink, the column fired upon him, he tumbled into it, and then the black troops jumped on it, laughing, dancing, stamping. The only mercy shown him was by one humane negro, who, eager to save his life, besought him to deny his identity as the striker of the blow. White citizens watched their moment, removed his remains, and gave them Christian burial.

There was the burning of Brenham, Texas, September 7, 1866. Federal soldiers from the post attended a negro ball, and so outraged the decencies that negro men closed the festivities. The soldiers pursued the negro managers, one of whom fled for safety to a mansion, where a party of young white people were assembled. The pursuers abused him in profane and obscene terms. The gentlemen reminded them that ladies were in hearing; they said they "didn't care a d—!" and drew pistols on the whites. A difficulty ensued, two soldiers were wounded, their comrades carried them to camp, returned and fired the town. The incendiaries were never punished, their commander spiriting them away when investigation was begun.*

"Numbers of our citizens were murdered by the soldiers of the United States, and in some instances deliberately shot down by them, in the presence of their wives and children," writes Hon. Charles Stewart, of reconstruction times, early and late, in Texas, and cites the diabolical midnight murder of W. A. Burns and Dallas, his son, giving the testimony of Sarah, daughter of one, sister of the other, and witness of the horrible deed, from the performance of which the assassins walked away "laughing." "Let no one suppose that

* See Stewart on "Texas" in "Why Solid South," by Hilary Herbert and others.

the instances given were isolated cases of oppression that might occur under any Government, however good," says Mr. Stewart. "They were of such frequent occurrence as to excite the alarm of good people."

Federal posts were a protection to the people, affording a sense of peace and security, or the reverse, according to the character of the commanders. To show how differently different men would determine the same issue, it may be cited that General Wilde confiscated the home of Mrs. Robert Toombs to the uses of the Freedmen's Bureau, ordering her to give possession and limiting the supplies she might remove to two weeks' provisions. General Steedman humanely revoked this order, restoring her home to Mrs. Toombs. There was no rule by which to forecast the course a military potentate, ignorant of civil law, might pursue. The mood he was in, the dinner he had eaten, the course of a flirtation on hand, motives of personal spite, gain or favoritism, might determine a decision affecting seriously a whole community, who would be powerless to appeal against it, his caprice being law.

In a previous chapter I have told a story showing General Saxton in a most attractive light. In his "Provisional Governorship of South Carolina," Governor Perry says: "The poor refugees (of the Sea Islands) were without fortune, money or the means of living! Many had nothing to eat except bread and water, and were thankful if they could get bread. I appointed W. H. Trescott to go to Washington and represent them in trying to recover their lands. He procured an order for the restoration, but General Saxton or some of his sub-agents thwarted in some way the design and purport of this order, and I believe the negroes are still in possession."

So, in some places you will hear Southerners say that,

save for domestic and industrial upheavals resulting from emancipation and for the privations of acute poverty, they suffered no extreme trials while under the strictly martial regime—were victims of no act of tyranny from local Federal authorities; in other places, you will hear words reflecting praise on such authorities; in others, evidence is plain that inhabitants endured worse things of military satraps than Israel suffered of Pharaoh.

As the days went by, there were fresh occasions for the conclusion: "The officers who gave Captain Bayard work and the officer who knocked him down are types of two classes of our conquerors and rulers. One is ready to help the cripple to his feet, the other to knock him down again and again. Congress will club the cripple with the negro ballot." "If that be true," said some, "the cripple will rise no more. Let me go hence ere my eyes behold it. Spilled blood and ruin wrought I can forgive, but not this thing!"

NEW FASHIONS

CHAPTER XIII

NEW FASHIONS: A LITTLE BONNET AND AN ALPACA SKIRT

THE confessions of Matoaca:

" I will never forget how queer we thought the dress of the Northern ladies. A great many came to Richmond, and Military Headquarters was very gay. Band answered band in the neighbourhood of Clay and Twelfth Streets, and the sound of music and dancing feet reached us through our closed shutters.

" Some ladies wore on the streets white petticoats, braided with black, under their dresses, which were looped up over these. Their gowns were short walking length, and their feet could be seen quite plainly. That style would be becoming to us, we said to ourselves, thinking of our small feet—at least I said so to myself. Up to that time we had considered it immodest to show our feet, our long dresses and hoop-skirts concealing them. We had been wearing coal-scuttle bonnets of plaited straw, trimmed with corn-shuck rosettes. I made fifteen one spring, acquired a fine name as a milliner, and was paid for my work.

" I recall one that was quite stunning. I got hold of a bit of much-worn white ribbon and dyed it an exquisite shade of green, with a tea made of coffee-berries. Coffee-berries dye a lovely green; you might remember that if you are ever in a war and blockaded. Our straw-and-shuck bonnets were pretty. How I wish I had kept mine as a souvenir—and other specimens of my home-made things! But we threw all our home-

147

made things away—we were so tired of make-shifts!—
and got new ones as soon as we could. How eager we
were to see the fashions! We had had no fashions for
a long time.

"When the Northern ladies appeared on the streets,
they did not seem to have on any bonnets at all. They
wore tiny, three-cornered affairs tied on with narrow
strings, and all their hair showing in the back. We
thought them the most absurd and trifling things! But
we made haste to get some. How did we see the fashions when we kept our blinds closed? Why, we could
peep through the shutters, of course. Remember, we
had seen no fashions for a long time. Then, too, after
the earlier days, we did not keep our windows shut.

"I began braiding me a skirt at once. The Yankees
couldn't teach me anything about braid! To the
longest day I live, I will remember the reign of skirt-
braid during the Confederacy! There was quite a
while when we had no other trimming, yet had that in
abundance, a large lot having been run through the
blockade; it came to the Department. The Department
got to be a sort of Woman's Exchange. Prices were
absurd. I paid $75 for a paper of pins and thought it
high, but before the war was over, I was thankful to
get a paper for $100. I bought, once, a cashmere
dress for the price of a calico, $25 a yard, because it
was a little damaged in running the blockade. At the
same time, Mrs. Jefferson Davis bought a calico dress
pattern for $500 and a lawn for $1,000; one of my
friends paid $1,400 for a silk, another, $1,100 for a
black merino. Mine was the best bargain. It lasted
excellently. I made it over in the new fashion after
the evacuation. One of the styles brought by the
Northern ladies was black alpaca skirts fringed. I got
one as soon as I could.

"The Yankees introduced some new fashions in other things besides clothes that I remember vividly, one being canned fruit. I had never seen any canned fruit before the Yankees came. Perhaps we had had canned fruit, but I do not remember it. Pleasant innovations in food were like to leave lasting impressions on one who had been living on next to nothing for an indefinite period."

The mystery of her purchase of the alpaca skirt and the little bonnet is solved by her journal:

"I am prospering with my needlework. I sew early and late. My friends who are better off give me work, paying me as generously as they can. Mammy Jane has sold some of my embroideries to Northern ladies. Many ladies, widows and orphans, are seeking employment as teachers. The great trouble is that so few people are able to engage them or to pay for help of any kind. Still, we all manage to help each other somehow.

"Nannie, our young bride, is raising lettuce, radish, nasturtiums, in her back yard for sale. She is painting her house herself (with her husband's help). She is going to give the lettuce towards paying the church debt. She has nothing else to give. I think I will raise something to buy window-panes for this house. Window-panes patched with paper are all the fashion in this town.

"The weather is very hot now. After supper, we go up on Gamble's Hill, our fashionable cooling-off resort, to get a breath of fresh air; then come back and work till late in the night. O, for a glimpse of the mountains! a breath of mountain air! But I can only dream of the Greenbrier White and the Old Sweet Springs!

"Last night, on Gamble's Hill, we observed near us

a party whom we recognized by accent and good clothes as Northerners. One of the ladies, looking down on our city, said: 'Behold the fruits of secession!' Below us in the moonlight lay Richmond on her noble river, beautiful in spite of her wounds. A gentleman spoke: 'Massachusetts thought of seceding once. I am sorry for these people.' How I wanted to shout: 'Behold the fruits of invasion!' But, of course, I did not. I thanked our advocate with my eyes."

A few had a little store laid up previous to the evacuation. A short time before that, the Confederate Government was selling some silver coin at $1 for $60 in notes; at Danville, it was sold for $70; and thrifty ones who could, bought.

Women who had been social queens, who had had everything heart could wish, and a retinue of servants happy to obey their behests and needing nothing, now found themselves reduced to harder case than their negroes had ever known, and gratefully and gracefully availed themselves of the lowliest tasks by which they might earn enough to buy a dress for the baby, a pair of shoes for little bare feet, coffee or tea or other luxury for an invalid dear one, or a bit of any sort of food to replenish a nearly empty larder.

The first greenbacks were brought to one family by a former dining-room servant. His mistress, unable to pay him wages, had advised him to seek employment elsewhere. At the end of a week, he returned, saying: "Mistiss, here is five dollahs. I'm makin' twenty dollahs a month, an' rations, waitin' on one uh de Yankee officers. I'll bring you my wages evvy week." "John," she said, "I don't know how to take it, for I don't see how I can ever pay it back." He knew she was in dire straits. "You took care uh me all my life, Mistiss, an' learnt me how to work. I orter do whut

I kin fuh you." Seeing her still hesitate: "You got property, you kin raise money on presen'y. Den you kin pay me back, but I'd be proud ef you wouldn' bother yo'se'f." Could her son have done more? The Old South had many negroes as good and true. Was the system altogether wrong that developed such characters?

Some of our people had Northern friends and relatives who contrived money to them. Mrs. Gracebridge was one of the fortunate; and everybody was glad. No one deserved better of fate or friends. She had entertained many refugees, was the most hospitable soul in the world. Had her table been large enough to seat the world, the world would have been welcome. From her nephew, living in New York, an officer of the United States Navy came with a message and money.

She had a way of addressing everybody as "my dear friend." Her household teasingly warned her that she was going to call this messenger "my dear friend." "Never!" she exclaimed. "Never in the world will I call a Yankee, 'my dear friend!' Never! How can you say such a thing to me! I am surprised, astonished, at the suggestion!" They listened, and before she and her guest had exchanged three sentences, heard her calling him "my dear friend," in spite of the insistent evidence of his gorgeous blue uniform, gold lace and brass buttons, that he was decidedly a Yankee.

It was a custom, rooted and grounded in her being, to offer refreshments to guests; when nothing else was left with which to show good feeling, she would bring in some lumps of white sugar, a rarity and a luxury, and pass this around. Never will spying intimates forget the expression of that naval officer's countenance when, at her call, a little black hand-maid presented on an old-fashioned silver salver, in an exquisite saucer, a few lumps of white sugar! He looked hard at it; then grasped the situation and a lump, glancing first at her, then at the sugar, as if he did not know whether to laugh or to cry.

She was a delightful woman. She and her two little darkeys afforded her friends no end of diversion. She had never managed her negroes in slavery-time. After the war, everybody's darkeys did as they pleased; hers did a little more so. At this pair, she constantly exclaimed, in great surprise: "They don't mind a word I say!" "My dear lady!" she was reminded, "you must expect that. They are free. They don't belong to you now."

And she would ask: "If they don't belong to me, whose are they?" That was to her a hopeless enigma. They had to belong to somebody. It was out of decency and humanity that they should have nobody to belong to! They would stand behind her chair, giggling and bubbling over with merriment.

THE GENERAL IN THE CORNFIELD

CHAPTER XIV

THE GENERAL IN THE CORNFIELD

WE did anything and everything we could to make a living. Prominent citizens became pie-sellers. Colonel Cary, of General Magruder's Staff, came home to find his family desperately poor, as were all respectable folks. He was a brave soldier, an able officer; before the war, principal of a male academy at Hampton. Now, he did not know to what he could turn his hand for the support of himself and family. He walked around his place, came in and said to his wife: "My dear, I have taken stock of our assets. You pride yourself on your apple-pies. We have an apple-tree, and a cow. I will gather the apples and milk the cow, and you will make the pies, and I will go around and sell them."

Armed with pies, he met his aforetime antagonists at Camp Grant and conquered them quite. The pies were delicious; the seller was a soldier, an officer of distinction, in hard luck; and the men at Camp Grant were soldiers, too. There was sharp demand and good price; only the élite—officers of rank—could afford to indulge in these confections. Well it was that Yankee mothers had cultivated in their sons an appetite for pies. One Savannah lady made thirty dollars selling pies to Sherman's soldiers; in Georgia's aristocratic "City by the Sea," high-bred dames stood at basement windows selling cakes and pies to whoever would buy.

Colonel Cary had thrifty rivals throughout Dixie. A once rich planter near Columbia made a living by selling flowers; a Charleston aristocrat peddled tea by the pound and molasses by the quart to his former slaves. General Stephen Elliott, Sumter's gallant defender, sold fish and oysters which he caught with his own hands. His friend, Captain Stoney, did likewise. Gentlemen of position and formerly of wealth did not pause to consider whether they would be discredited by pursuing occupations quite as humble. Men of high attainments, without capital, without any basis upon which to make a new start in life except "grit," did whatever they could find to do and made merry over it.

Yet reporters going over our battle-swept, war-scarred land from whose fields our laboring class had been by one fell stroke diverted, judged us by evidences of inertia seen from windows of creepy little cars—(where we had any cars at all)—that stopped every few hours to take on wood or water or to repair something or other. For a long time, there was good reason why our creepy railroads should be a doubly sore subject. Under the reconstruction governments every State paid thousands of dollars for railroads that were never built.

All that Southern white men did, according to some ready scribes, was to sit around cross-roads stores, expectorate tobacco-juice, swap jokes, and abuse Yankees and niggers. In honesty, it must be confessed there was too much of this done, any being too much. Every section has its corps of idlers, its crew of yarn-spinners and drinkers, even in ordinary times when war has not left upon men the inevitable demoralisation that follows in its train. Had railway travellers gone into cotton and cornfields and tobacco lots, they would have found there much of the flower and chivalry of the Old South "leading the row." Sons of fathers who had been the wealthiest and most influential men in Dixie came home from the war to swing the hoe and drive the plow as resolutely as ever they had manned a battery or charged the breastworks.

But the young men of the South were not born tillers of the soil; not fitted by inheritance or education for manual toil. They were descendants of generations who had not labored with their hands but had occupied themselves as lawyers, doctors, politicians, gentlemen of leisure, and agriculturists commanding large working forces. Our nation might have been gainer had the Government devised measures by which talented men could have been at once bound to its interests and their gifts utilised for the common advantage. Instead of which, they were threatened with trial for treason, with execution or exile, were disfranchised, disqualified, put under the ban. Many who would have made brilliant and useful servants of the Republic were driven abroad and found honourable service in Mexico, Brazil, Egypt and Europe.

It is difficult for us at this day to realise what little promise life held for the young American of the South; difficult even for the South of the present to appreciate the irritations and humiliations that vexed and chafed him. Many felt that they had no longer a country.

Mischief was inevitable as the result of repressed or distorted energies, thwarted or stifled ambition. Some whose record for courage and steadiness on the field of battle reflects glory on our common country, failed utterly at adaptation. But as the patient effort of the great body politic changed the times and opened opportunity, middle-age and youth were ready to rush in with a will, occupying and improving fields of industry.

But the old people of the South never reacted. Many simply sat down and died, succumbing to bereavement, hardships and heartbreak. They felt that their country was dead. Men of their own blood, their brothers, had set an alien race, an ignorant race, half-human, half-savage, above them; were insisting that they should send their children to school with children of this race, while their consciences cried out against the mere discussion of this thing as an evil to themselves and the negro, and against the thing itself as crime. Intermarriage was discussed in legislative halls; bills sanctioning it were introduced; and the horrible black, social evil due to passions of the white man and the half-human, half-savage woman—the incubus, the nightmare, under which the whole section had groaned with groanings that cannot be uttered—was flung in their faces as more than fair reason.

With reconstruction there was strengthening of the tendency towards expatriation. Despair and disgust drove many away; and more would have gone had means been at hand. Whole families left the South and made homes in Europe; among these, a goodly proportion were proud old Huguenots from South Carolina. In some of the Cotton States it looked as if more white men were to be lost thus than had been lost in battle. In December, 1867, Mr. Charles Nathan, of New Orleans, announced through the press that he had contracted with the Emperor of Brazil to transport 1,000 yearly to that empire.

Many went into the enemy's country—went North. Their reports to old neighbours were that they liked the enemy immensely at home; the enemy was serenely unconscious of the mischief his fad was working in other people's homes. He set down everything ill that happened South to the Southern whites' "race prejudice"; and sipped his own soup and ate his own pie in peace. The immigrant learned that it was wise to hold his tongue when discussion of the negro came up. He was considered not to know anything worth hearing upon the subject. His most careful and rational utterances would be met with a pitying look which said as plainly as words lips polite withheld: " Race prejudice hallucination!"

General Lee raised no uncertain voice against expatriation; from his prison cell, Jefferson Davis deplored it in the first letters he was allowed to write. Lee set prompt example in doing what his hand found to do, and in choosing a task rather for public service than for private gain. I quote a letter written by Mrs. Lee to Miss Mason, dated Derwent, Virginia, December, 1865:

"The papers will have told you that General Lee has decided to accept the position at Lexington. I do not think he is very fond of teaching, but he is willing to do anything that will give him an honourable support. He starts tomorrow *en cheval* for Lexington. He prefers that way, and, besides, does not like to part even for a time from his beloved steed, the companion of many a hard-fought battle. . . . The kindness of the people of Virginia to us has been truly great, and they seem never to tire. The settlement of Palmore's surrounding us does not suffer us to want for anything their gardens or farms can furnish. . . . My heart sinks when I hear of the destitution and misery which abound further South—gentle and refined women reduced to abject poverty, and no hope of relief."

Far more lucrative positions had been offered him; salaries without work, for the mere use of his name. Solicitations came from abroad, and brilliant opportunities invited across the ocean. He took the helm at Washington College with this avowal: " I have a self-imposed task which I must accomplish. I have led the young men of the South in battle. I have seen many of them fall under my standard. I shall devote my life

now to training young men to do their duty in life."
Urged in 1867 to run for office, he declined, believing
that his candidacy might not contribute to sectional
unification.   As nearly perfect was this man as men
are made.   Our National Capitol is the poorer because
his statue is not there.   If it ever is, I should like to
see on its pedestal Grant's tribute: "There was no use
to urge him to do anything against his ideas of what
was right."

When the crippled and impoverished General Hood
refused to receive money raised by subscription, the
"Albany Evening Journal" commented: "It is the
first instance we have ever seen recorded of a 'Southern
gentleman' too proud or self-reliant to accept filthy
lucre, come from what source it may."   The "Petersburg Index-Appeal" responded:

"Hood has only done what Lee did a dozen times, what Beaure-
gard did, what Magruder did, and what President Davis did. The
noble response of Magruder to the people of Texas, who contributed
a handsome purse to procure him a fine plantation, was the impulse
and utterance of the universal spirit of the Southern soldier: 'No,
gentlemen, when I espoused the cause of the South, I embraced
poverty and willingly accepted it.'"

Near Columbia, on the ruins of his handsome home
which Sherman burned, General Wade Hampton, clever
at wood-work, built with his own hands and with the
help of his faithful negroes, a lowly cottage to shelter
himself and family.   A section was added at a time,
and, without any preconceived design on his part, the
structure stood, when completed, a perfect cross.   Miss
Isabella Martin, looking upon it one day, exclaimed:
"General, you have here the Southern Cross!"   So
"Southern Cross" the place was called.   Here, Mrs.
Wade Hampton, who, as Miss McDuffie, had been the
richest heiress in South Carolina, and as such and as

Hampton's wife, the guardian angel of many black folk, wrought and ruled with wisdom and with sweetness unsoured by reverses.   South Carolina offered Hampton a home, as Virginia and then Washington College offered Lee, but Hampton, almost in want, refused.

This is the plight in which General M. C. Butler, Hampton's aide, came out of the war: "Twenty-nine years old, with one leg gone, a wife and three children to support, seventy slaves emancipated, a debt of $15,000, and, in his pocket, $1.75 in cash." That was the situation of thousands.   It took manhood to make something of it.

For months after the surrender, Confederates were passing through the country to their homes, and hospitality was free to every ragged and footsore soldier; the poor best the larder of every mansion afforded was at the command of the gray-jacket.   How diffidently proud men would ask for bread, their empty pockets shaming them!   When any man turned them off with cold words, it was not well for his neighbours to know, for so, he was like to have no more respectable guests. The soldiers were good company, bringing news from far and wide.   Most were cheerful, glad they were going home, undaunted by long tramps ahead.   The soldier was used to hard marches.   Now that his course was set towards where loved ones watched for his coming, life had its rosy outlook that turned to gray for some who reached the spot where home had stood to find only a bank of ashes.   Reports of country through which they came were often summed up: "White folks in the fields, negroes flocking to towns.   Freedmen's Bureau offices everywhere thronged with blacks."

A man who belonged to the "Crippled Squad," not one of whom had a full complement of arms and legs, told this story: As four of them were limping along near Lexington, they noticed a gray-headed white man in rough, mud-stained clothes turning furrows with a plow, and behind him a white girl dropping corn. Taking him for a hired man, they hallooed: "Hello, there!" The man raised his head. "Say," they called, "can you tell us where we can get something to eat?" He waved them towards a house, where a lady who was on the porch, asked them to have a seat and wait while she had food cooked.

They had an idea that she prepared with her own hands the dinner to which they presently sat down, of hot hoe-cakes, buttermilk, and a little meat so smothered in lettuce leaves that it looked a great deal. When they had cleared up the table, she said: "I am having more bread cooked if you can wait a few minutes. I am sorry we have not more meat and milk. I know this has been a very light repast for hungry men, but we have entertained others this morning, and we have not much left. We hate to send our soldiers hungry from the door; they ought to have the best of everything when they have fought so long and bravely and suffered so much." The way she spoke made them proud of the arms and legs they didn't have.

Now that hunger was somewhat appeased, they began to note surroundings. The dwelling was that of a military man and a man of piety and culture. A lad running in addressed the lady as "Mrs. Pendleton," and said something about "where General Pendleton is plowing."

They stumbled to their crutches! and in blushing confusion, made humble apologies, all the instincts of the soldier shocked at the liberties they had taken with an officer of such high grade, and at the ease of manner with which they had sat at his table to be served by his wife. They knew their host for William Nelson Pendleton, late Brigadier-General, C. S. A., Chief of Artillery of the Army of Northern Virginia, a fighting preacher. She smiled when they blundered out the excuse that they had mistaken him for a day-labourer.

"The mistake has been made before," she said. "Indeed, the General is a day-labourer in his own field, and it does not mortify him in the least now that all our people have to work. He is thankful his strength is sufficient, and for the help that the schoolboys and his daughters give him." She put bread into their haversacks and sent them on their way rejoicing. The day-labourer and his plow were close to the roadside, and as they passed, they drew themselves up in line and brought all the hands they had to their ragged caps in salute.

Dr. Robert G. Stephens, of Atlanta, tells me of a Confederate soldier who, returning armless to his Georgia home, made his wife hitch him to a plow which she drove; and they made a crop. A Northern missionary said in 1867, to a Philadelphia audience, that he had seen in North Carolina, a white mother hitch herself to a plow which her eleven-year-old son drove, while another child dropped into the furrows seeds Northern charity had given. I saw in Virginia's Black Belt a white woman driving a plow to which her young daughters, one a nursing mother, were hitched; and near the same time and place an old negro driving a milch-cow to his cart. "Uncle Eph, aren't you ashamed," I asked, "to work your milch-cow?" "Law, Miss, milch-white-'oman wuk. Huccom cow can't wuk?"

TOURNAMENTS AND PARTIES

CHAPTER XV

TOURNAMENTS AND STARVATION PARTIES

IT would seem that times were too hard and life too bitter for merry-making. Not so. With less than half a chance to be glad, the Southerner will laugh and dance and sing—and make love. At least, he used to. The Southerner is no longer minstrel, lover, and cavalier. He is becoming a money-maker. With cannons at our gates and shells driving us into cellars, guitars were tinkling, pianos were not dumb, tripping feet were not stayed by fear and sorrow. When boys in gray came from camp, women felt it the part of love and patriotism to give them good cheer, wearing smiles while they were by, keeping tears for them when absent.

With the war over and our boys coming home for good, ah, it was not hard to laugh, sing and dance, poor as we were! "Soldiers coming up the road," "Some soldiers here for tonight," the master of the house would say, and doors would fling wide. "Nice fellows, I know," or "I knew this one's father, and that one's uncle is Governor—and this one went to school with our Frank; and these fought side by side with friends of ours," or "Their names are so-and-so," or just, "They are gentlemen." Maidens would make themselves fair; wardrobes held few or no changes, but one could dress one's hair another way, put a rose in one's tresses, draw forth the many-times-washed-over or thrice-dyed ribbon for adornment. After supper, there would be music in the parlor, and perhaps dancing. But not always! too often, the guest's feet were not shod for dancing. It might be that he was clothed from shirt to shoe in garments from the host's own store. Many a soldier would decline entering the great house and beg off from presentations, feeling the barn a more fitting shelter for his rags, and the company of ladies a gift the gods must withhold.

Joy reigned in every household when its owner came home from the war, joy that defeat at arms could not kill. The war was over! it had not ended as we had prayed, but there was to be no crying over spilt milk if young people had their way.

Departure of old servants and installation of new and untried ones was attended with untold vexation, but none of this was allowed to interfere with the pleasure and happiness of young people when it was possible to prevent it. Southern mistresses kept domestic difficulties in the background or made merry over them. On the surface, domestic machinery might seem to move without a hitch, when in reality it was in so severe a state of dislocation that the semblance of smooth operation was little short of a miracle.

Reserves of cotton and tobacco that had escaped the attention of the Yankee Army sold high. Fortunate possessors were soon flush with greenbacks which were put in quick circulation. It was a case of a little new bonnet and an alpaca skirt with girls everywhere; women had done without clothes so long, they felt they just must have some now; our boys had gone in rags so long, they must have new clothes, too; everybody had lived so hard and been so sad, there must be joy now, love-making and dancing. The "Starvation Party" did not go out of fashion with war. Festal boards were often thinly spread, but one danced not the less lightly for that. Enough it was to wing the feet to know that the bronzed young soldier with his

MISS ADDIE PRESCOTT
(A Louisiana Belle)
Afterwards Mrs. R. G. H. Kean, of Lynchburg, Va.

arm about your waist must leave you no more for the battle.

To show how little one could be festive on, we will take a peep at a starvation party given on a plantation near Lexington, North Carolina, by Mrs. Page, soon after General Kilpatrick's troops vacated the mansion. "We had all been so miserable," Mrs. Page tells, "that I was just bound to have some fun. So I gave a dining."

She invited ten ladies, who all came wondering what on earth she could set before them. They walked; there was not a carriage in the neighbourhood. They were all cultured, refined women, wives and daughters of men of prominence, and accustomed to elegant entertainment. A few days before, one of them had sent to Mrs. Page for something to eat, saying she had not a mouthful in the house, and Mrs. Page had shared with her a small supply of Western pork and hardtack which her faithful coloured man, Frank, had gotten from the Yankees. Mrs. Page had now no pork left. Her garden had been destroyed. She had not a chair in the house, and but one cooking utensil, a large iron pot. And not a fork, spoon, cup, plate or other table appointment.

With pomp and merriment, Mrs. Drane, a clergyman's widow, the company's dean and a great favourite with everybody, was installed at the head of the bare, mutilated table, where rude benches served as seats. Mrs. Marmaduke Johnston, of Petersburg, was accorded second place of honour. The *menu* consisted of a pudding of corn-meal and dried whortle-berries sweetened with sorghum; and beer made of persimmons and honeyshucks, also sweetened with sorghum. The many-sided Frank was butler. The pudding, filling the half of a large gourd, was placed in front of Mrs.

Drane, and she, using hardtack as spoon, dipped it up, depositing it daintily on other hardtack which answered for plates and saucers.

The beer was served from another gourd into cups made of newspapers folded into shape; the ladies drank quickly that the liquid might not soak through and be lost. They enjoyed the beverage and the pudding greatly and assured their hostess that they had rarely attended a more delightful feast. The pudding had been boiled in the large iron pot, and Frank had transferred it to the gourd. In his kitchen and pantry, gourds of various sorts and sizes seemed to ask: "Why were vessels of iron, pewter, and copper ever invented, and what need has the world of china-ware so long as we grow on the backyard fence?"

How Frank's mistress, a frail-looking, hospitable, resourceful little woman, provided for herself and family and helped her friends out of next to nothing; how her cheerfulness, industry, and enterprise never failed her or others; and how Frank aided her, would in itself fill a book.

But then it is a story of Southern verve and inventiveness that could be duplicated over and over again.

Did not Sir George Campbell write in an English magazine of how much he enjoyed a dinner in a Southern mansion, when all the feast was a dish of roasted apples and a plate of corn-bread? Not a word of apology was uttered by his host or hostess; converse was so cultured and pleasing, welcome so sincere, that the poverty of the board was not to be weighed in the balance. This host who had so much and so little to give his guest was Colonel Washington Ball, nearest living kinsman to General George Washington.

The fall of 1865 was, in Virginia at least, a bountiful one. Planters' sons had come home, gone into the fields, worked till the crop was all laid by; and then, there was no lack of gaiety.   A favourite form of diversion was the tournament, which furnished fine sport for cavalry riders trained under Stuart and Fitz Lee.

One of the most brilliant took place in 1866, at a famous plantation on the North Anna River.   The race-track had been beaten down smooth and hard beforehand by the daily training of knights.   It was in a fair stretch of meadow-land beyond the lawns and orchards.   The time was October, the weather ideal, the golden haze of Indian Summer mellowing every line of landscape.   On the day appointed the grounds were crowded with carriages, wagonettes, buggies and vehicles of every sort, some very shabby, but borrowing brightness from the fair young faces within.

The knights were about twenty-five.   Their steeds were not so richly caparisoned as Scott's in "Ivanhoe," but the riders bestrode them with perhaps greater ease and grace than heavy armor permitted mediæval predecessors.   Some wore plumed hats that had covered their heads in real cavalry charges, and more than one warrior's waist was girt with the red silk sash that had belted him when he rode at the head of his men as Fitz Lee's captain.   A number were in full Confederate uniform, carrying their gray jackets as jauntily as if no battle had ever been lost to them.   One of these attracted peculiar attention.   He was of very distinguished appearance; and from his arm floated a long streamer of crape.   Every one was guessing his name till the herald cried: "Knight of Liberty Lost!"   The mourning knight swept before the crowd, bearing off on the point of his spear the three rings which marked his victory for at least that run.

For this sport, three gibbet-like structures stand equal distances apart on a straight race-track.   From the arm of each, a hook depends and on each hook a ring is hung. Each knight, with lance poised and aimed, rides full tilt down this track and takes off all the rings he can in a given number of rides. He who captures most rings is victor. It is his right to choose the Queen of Love and Beauty, riding up to her on the field and offering a ring upon his spear. The knight winning the second highest number chooses the First Maid of Honour; and so on, until there is a royal quartette of queen and maids.

The tournament was to the South what baseball is to the nation; it was intensely exciting and picturesque, and, by reason of the guerdon won, poetic, investing an ordinary mortal with such power as Paris exercised when he gave the golden apple to Venus. It had spice of peril to make it attractive, if "danger's self is lure alone." Fine horsemanship, a steady hand, and sure eye were essentials.

"Liberty Lost" won, and the mourning knight laid his laurels at the feet of a beautiful girl who has since reigned as a social queen in a Northern home. The coronation took place in the mansion that evening. After a flowery address, each knight knelt and offered a crown to his fair one. The symbols of royalty were wreaths of artificial flowers, the queen's shaped like a coronet, with sprays forming points. Her majesty wore a gown that had belonged to her great-grandmother; very rich silk in a bayadere pattern, that served as becoming sheath for her slim blonde loveliness. After the coronation, the knights led their fair ones out in the "Royal Set" which opened the ball.

Perhaps it is better to say that George Walker, the negro fiddler, opened the ball. He was the most famous man of his craft in the Piedmont region. There he was that night in all his glory at the head of his band

of banjoists, violinists and violincellist; he was grandeur
and gloss personified when he made preliminary bow and
flourish, held his bow aloft, and set the ball in motion!
"Honour yo' pardners!"
"And didn't we do as George told us to do!"
Matoaca says. "Such dance-provoking melodies fol-
lowed as almost bewitched one's feet. 'Life on the
Ocean Wave,' 'Down-town Girls Won't You Come
Out Tonight and Dance by the Light of the Moon!'
'Fisher's Horn-Pipe' and 'Ole Zip Coon' were some
of them. Not high-sounding to folks of today, but
didn't they make feet twinkle! People did what was
called 'taking steps' in those days. I can almost hear
George's fiddle now, and hear him calling: 'Ladies
to the right! Gents to the right! Ladies to the center!
Gents to the center! Hands all 'roun' an' promenade
all!' Who could yell 'Do se do!' and 'Sashay all!'
with such a swing?"

About one o'clock all marched in to supper, the queen
and her knights and maidens leading. It was hard
times in Virginia, but the table groaned under such
things as folks then thought ought to adorn a festal
board. There was not lacking the mighty saddle-o'-
mutton, roast pig with apple in his mouth, Smithfield
ham, roast turkey, and due accompaniments. The company marched back to the ball-room, and presently
marched again to a second supper embracing sweets of
all descriptions.

Commencements at schools and colleges, which the
South began to restore and refill as quickly as she was
able, brought the young people together and were strong
features in our social life. So were Sunday schools;
and, in the country, protracted meetings or religious
revivals. And barbecues. Who that has gone out to a
frolic in the Southern woods and feasted on shote or

mutton roasted over a pit and basted with vinegar and red pepper gravy, can forget what a barbecue is!

Summer resorts became again meeting-grounds for old friends, and new. Social gatherings at the Greenbrier White Sulphur were notable. General Lee was there with his daughter, and the first to lead in extending courtesies to Northern guests attracted to the White by the reputation of that famous watering-place. Again, our women were at their ancient haunts, wearing silks and laces as they were prospering under the new order or as their great-grandmothers' trunks, like that of Love and Beauty's Queen, held reserves not yet exhausted. And under the silks and laces, hearts cried out for loved ones who would gather on the green lawns and dance in the great halls no more. But heroism presented a smiling face and took up life's measure again.

In cities changes were not so acute as in the country, where people, without horses and vehicles, were unable to visit each other. The larger the planter, the more extreme his family's isolation was like to be, his land and his neighbours' lands stretching for miles between houses. I heard a planter's wife say, "Yours is the first white woman's face I have seen for six months." Her little daughter murmured mournfully: "And I haven't seen a little white girl to play with for longer than that." Multitudes who had kept open house could no longer. To a people in whom the social instinct was so strong and hospitality second nature, abrupt ending of neighbourly intercourse was a hard blow.

Stay and bankrupt laws for the benefit of the debtor class and bearing much hardship on creditors, often orphan minors, were passed, and under these planters were sold out and moved to new places, their overseers often succeeding them and reigning in their stead. It

MRS. DAVID URQUHART, OF NEW ORLEANS
A famous hostess, distinguished for her social graces
and her good deeds.

was not an unknown thing for men to manage to get themselves sold out under these laws, thus evading payment of obligations and at the same time securing a certain quota for themselves, which the law allowed. It seemed to me that many who took it were better off than before. There were unfortunates who had to pay security debts for bankrupts. Much hard feeling was engendered.

Some measure for relief of the debtor class was necessary. A man who had contracted debts on the basis of thousands of acres at fifteen to fifty dollars an acre, and owning a hundred or more negroes, worth a thousand dollars each, could not meet in full such engagements when his land would not bring two dollars an acre, when his negroes were set free, and hired labour, if he had wherewithal to hire, could not be relied on. Some men took the Bankrupt Law for protection, then set themselves to work and paid obligations which could not be exacted by law.

THE BONDAGE OF THE FREE

CHAPTER XVI

THE BONDAGE OF THE FREE

"HAD slavery lasted a few years longer," I have heard my mother say, "it would have killed Julia, my head-woman, and me. Our burden of work and responsibility was simply staggering."

In the ante-bellum life of the mistress of a Southern plantation there was no menial occupation, but administrative work was large and exacting. The giving out of rations, clothes, medicines, nursing of the sick, cutting out of garments, sewing, spinning, knitting, had to be directed. The everlasting teaching and training, the watch-care of sometimes several hundred semi-civilized, semi-savage people of all ages, dispositions and tempers, were on the white woman's hands.

The kitchen was but one department of that big school of domestic science, the home on a Southern plantation, where cooks, nurses, maids, butlers, seamstresses and laundresses had understudies or pupils; and the white mistress, to whom every student's progress was a matter of keen personal interest and usually of affectionate concern, was principal and director. The typical Southern plantation was, in effect, a great social settlement for the uplift of Africans.

For a complete picture of plantation life, I beg my readers to turn to that chapter in the "Life of Leonidas Polk" written by his son, Dr. W. M. Polk, which describes "Leighton" in the sugar-lands on Bayou La Fourche. Read of the industrial work and then of the Sabbath, when the negroes assembled in the bishop's

179

house where the chaplain conducted the service while the bishop sat at the head of his servants.   Worship over, women withdrew into another room, where Mrs. Polk or the family governess gave them instruction; the children into still another, where Bishop Polk's daughter taught them; the men remained with the chaplain for examination and admonition.   The bishop made great efforts to preserve the sanctity of family life among his servants.   He christened their babies; their weddings were celebrated in his own home, decorated and illuminated for them.   The honour coveted by his children was to hold aloft the silver candlesticks while their father read the marriage service.   If a couple misbehaved, they were compelled to marry, but without a wedding-feast.

Andrew P. Calhoun, eldest son of John C. Calhoun, was President of the South Carolina Agricultural College and owner of large lands in Alabama and South Carolina.   He took pride in raising everything consumed on his plantations.   In the New York home of his son, Mr. Patrick Calhoun, three of his old servants live; his wife's maid says proudly: "I have counted thirty things on my Miss' dinner-table that were grown on the place."   Cotton and wool were grown on the place and carded, spun, dyed, woven into cloth by negro women; in great rooms, well lighted, well aired, well equipped, negro cutters, fitters and seamstresses fashioned neat and comfortable garments for a contented, well-cared-for laboring force.   Mrs. Calhoun devoted as much time to this department of plantation work, which included the industrial and moral education of negro women, as Mr. Calhoun devoted to the general management of his lands and the industrial and moral uplift of negro men.   The Polk and Calhoun plantations were types of thousands; and their owners types

FRANCES DEVEREUX POLK
(Wife of General Leonidas Polk, the Warrior Bishop.)
She was the spiritual and industrial educator of many negroes, and
the mistress of a large sugar plantation.

of thousands of planters who applied the same principles, if sometimes on lesser scale, to farming operations.
No institutional work can take the place of work of
this kind. It is like play to the real thing. Without
decrying Hampton, Petersburg and Tuskegee, it can
be said with truth that these institutions and many more
in combination would be unable to do for a savage race
what the old planters and the old plantation system of
the South did for Africa's barbarians. Employers of
white labor might sit at the feet of those old planters
and learn wisdom. Professor Morrison, of the Chair
of History and Sociology at Clemson College, tells me
that the instruction of students in their duty to their
servants constituted a recognised department in some
Southern colleges.

Mammy Julia was my mother's assistant superintendent, so to speak. "I could trust almost anything to
her," her mistress bore testimony, "for she appreciated
responsibility and was faithfulness itself. I don't know
a negro of the new order who can hold a candle to her."
Mammy Julia and my mother had no rest night or day.
Black folks were coming with troubles, wants, quarrels,
ailments, births, marriages and deaths, from morning
till night and night till morning again. "I was glad
and thankful—on my own account—when slavery ended
and I ceased to belong, body and soul, to my negroes."
As my mother, so said other Southern mistresses.

Perhaps the Southern matron's point of view may be
somewhat surprising to those who have thought that
under ante-bellum conditions, slavery was all on the
negro's side and that all Southern people were fiercely
bent on keeping him in bonds. Many did not believe
in slavery and were trying to end it.

Mrs. Robert E. Lee's father and uncle freed some
five hundred slaves, with General Lee's approval, thus

alienating from her over $500,000 worth of property. The Hampton family, of South Carolina, sent to Liberia a great colony of freed slaves, who presently plead to be brought home. General Preston, Confederate, of Kentucky, freed his negroes; he would not sell, and could not afford to keep, them; they were " over-running and ruining his plantation, and clearing up forests for firewood; slavery is the curse of the South."

Many families had arranged for a gradual emancipation, a fixed percentage of slaves being freed by each generation. By will and otherwise, they provided against division of families, an evil not peculiar to slavery, as immigrant ships of today, big foundling asylums, and train-loads of home-seeking children bear evidence.

But freedom as it came, was inversion, revolution. Whenever I pass "The House Upside Down" at a World's Fair, I am reminded of the South after freedom. In "South Carolina Women in the Confederacy," * Mrs. Harby tells how Mrs. Postell Geddings was in the kitchen getting Dr. Geddings' supper, while her maid, in her best silk gown, sat in the parlour and entertained Yankee officers. Charleston ladies cooked, swept, scrubbed, split wood, fed horses, milked and watered the cattle; while filling their own places as feminine heads of the house, they were servants-of-all-work and man of the house. Mrs. Crittendon gives an anecdote matching Mrs. Geddings'. A Columbia lady saw in Sherman's motley train an old negress arrayed in her mistress' antiquated, ante-bellum finery, lolling on the cushions of her mistress' carriage, and fanning (in

---

* A collection of records, sketches, etc., edited and published by Mrs. Taylor, Mrs. Smythe, Mrs. Kohn, Miss Poppenheim and Miss Washington, of that State. Owner, August Kohn, Columbia, S. C. For confirmation of first chapter of this book, see same.

winter) with a huge ostrich-feather fan. "Why, Aunt Sallie, where are you going?" she called out impulsively. "Law, honey! I'se gwine right back intuh de Union!" and on rode Aunt Sallie, feathers and flowers on her enormous poke-bonnet all a-flutter.

Mrs. Jewett, of Stony Creek, saw her negro man walking behind the Yankee Army with her husband's suit of clothes done up in a red silk handkerchief and slung on a stick over his shoulder. Her two mulatto nurse-girls laid down their charges, attired themselves in her best apparel and went; her seamstress stopped sewing, jumped on a horse behind a soldier who invited her, and away she rode.

As victorious armies went through the country, they told the negroes, "You are free!" Negroes accepted the tidings in different ways. Old Aunt Hannah was not sure but that the assurance was an insult. "Law, marster!" she said, "I ain' no free nigger! I *is* got a marster an' mistiss! Dee right dar in de great house. Ef you don' b'lieve me, you go dar an' see." "You're a d—d fool!" he cried and rode on. "Sambo, you're free!" Some negroes picked up the master's saddle, flung it on the master's horse, jumped on his back and rode away with the Yankees. After every Yankee army swarmed a great black crowd on foot, men, women, and children. They had to be fed and cared for; they wearied their deliverers.

Yankees told my father's negroes they were free, but they did not accept the statement until "Ole Marster" made it. I remember the night. They were called together in the back yard—a great green space with blossomy altheas and fruit-trees and tall oaks around, and the scent of honeysuckles and Sweet Betseys making the air fragrant. He stood on the porch beside a table with a candle on it. I, at his knee, looked up at him and out on the sea of uplifted black faces. Some carried pine torches. He read from a paper, I do not know what, perhaps the emancipation proclamation. They listened silently. Then he spoke, his voice trembling:

"You do not belong to me any more. You are free. You have been like my own children. I have never felt that you were slaves. I have felt that you were charges put into my hands by God and that I had to render account to Him of how I raised you, how I treated you. I want you all to do well. You will have to work, if not for me, for somebody else. Heretofore, you have worked for me and I have supported you, fed you, clothed you, given you comfortable homes, paid your doctors' bills, bought your medicines, taken care of your babies before they could take care of themselves; when you were sick, your mistress and I have nursed you; we have laid your dead away. I don't think anybody else can have the same feeling for you that she and I have. I have been trying to think out a plan for paying wages or a part of the crop that would suit us all; but I haven't finished thinking it out. I want to know what you think. Now, you can stay just as you have been staying and work just as you have been working, and we will plan together what is best. Or, you can go. My crops must be worked, and I want to know what arrangements to make. Ben! Dick! Moses! Abram! line up, everybody out there. As you pass this porch, tell me if you mean to stay; you needn't promise for longer than this year, you know. If you want to go somewhere else, say so—and no hard thoughts!"

The long line passed. One and all they said: "I gwi stay wid you, Marster." A few put it in different words. Uncle Andrew, the dean of the body, with wool as white as snow, a widower who went sparking every Sunday in my grandfather's coat and my grandfather's silk hat, said: "Law, Marster! I ain' got nowhar tuh go ef I was gwine!" Some wiped their eyes, and my father had tears in his.

Next morning, old Uncle Eph, Andrew's mate, was missing; his aged wife was in great distress. She came to my father reproachfully: "Marster," she said, "I wish you wouldn' put all dat foolishness 'bout freedom in Eph's hade. He so ole I dunno what gwi become uh him 'long de road. When I wake up dis mo'nin', he done tied all his close up in his hankercher and done lit out." In a few days he returned, the butt of the quarters for many a day. "I jes wanter see whut it feel lak tuh be free," he said, "an' I wanter to go back to Ole Marster's plantation whar I was born. It don' look de same dar, an' I done see nuff uh freedom."

Presently my father was making out contracts and explaining them over and over; he would sign his name, the negro would make his mark, the witnesses sign; and the bond for a year's work and wages or part of the crop, was complete. At first, contracts had to be ratified by a Freedmen's Bureau agent, who charged master and servant each fifty cents or more. After one of our neighbours told his negroes they were free, they all promised to stay, as had ours. Next morning all but two were gone. In a few days all returned. The Bureau Agent had made them come back.

Many negroes leaving home fared worse than Uncle Eph. After the fall of Richmond, Mr. Hill, who had been a high official of the Confederacy, went back to his plantation, where he found but three negroes remaining, the rest having departed for Washington, the negro heaven. One of these, a man of seventy, said he must go, too. His ex-master could not dissuade him. He was comfortably quartered and Mr. Hill told him he would be cared for the rest of his life. Nothing would do but he must sell his chickens and his little crop of tobacco to one of the other negroes and go. Mr. Hill gave him provisions for ten days, had the wagon hitched up and sent him to Culpeper, where he was to take the train. On Culpeper's outskirts was the usual collection of negroes, snack-house, bad whiskey, gambling, and kindred evils. Here Uncle John stopped. He had started with $15 cash. In less than a week his money was gone and he was thrown out on the common.

Mr. Hill, summoned before the Provost-Marshal on the charge of having driven Uncle John off, said: "The man sitting out there in my buggy can tell you whether I did that." The testimony of the black witness was conclusive, the Provost dismissed the case. Mr. Hill went to the commons.

Lying in the sun, stone-blind, was Uncle John. He raised his head and listened. "Mistuh, fuh Gawd's sake, please do suppin fuh me!" "Old man, why are you here?" "Lemme hear dat voice again!" "Uncle John!" "Bless de Lawd, Marster! you done come. Marster, a 'oman robbed me uf all I had an' den th'owed me out. Fuh Gawd's sake, take me home!" "I will have you cared for tonight, and tomorrow I will come in the wagon for you." "Lawd, Marster, I sho is glad I gwine home! I kin res' easy in my min', now I *know* I gwine home!"

Mr. Hill returned to the Provost: "I shall come or send for the old man tomorrow," he said. "Meanwhile, he must be cared for." The Provost was indifferent. This was one of many cases. "If you do not provide food and shelter for that negro," he was sharply assured, "I shall report you to the authorities

at Washington." The Provost promised and sent two
orderlies to attend to the matter. Next morning the
master was back. The old man was dead. He had
been put in the scale-house, an open shed. There,
instead of in his old home surrounded by friends who
loved him, Uncle John had breathed his last.

From many other stories, companions in pathos, I
choose Mammy Lisbeth's. Her son went with the
Yankee army. She grieved for him till her mistress'
heart ached. The mistress returned one day from a
visit to find Lisbeth much excited. "Law, Miss, I done
hyerd f'om my chile!" "How, Mammy?" "A
Yankee soldier come by an' I ax 'im is he seed my son
whar he been goin' 'long? An' I tell 'im all 'bout how
my chile look. An' he say he done been seen 'im.
An' I say, 'Law, mister, ain't my chile gwi come home?'
An' he gimme de answer: 'He can't come ef he ain'
got no money.' An' I answer, 'Law, marster, I got
a fi'-dollar gol' piece my ole miss dat's done dade gimme
long time ago. Does you know any safe passin'?'
An' he answer, jes ez kin', how he gwine datter way
hisse'f, an' he'll kyar it. I run in de house an' got dat
fi'-dollar gol' piece an' gi' to 'im. An' now my chile's
comin' home, Miss! my chile's comin' home! He say,
'In 'bout two weeks, you go to de kyars evvy day an'
look fuh im.'" Her mistress had not the heart to tell
her the man had robbed her. Never before had a white
man robbed her; it was second nature to trust the white
face.

"It is heart-breaking," her mistress wrote, "to see
how she watches for him. She is at the depot every
day, scanning the face of every coloured passenger
getting off. I've been to the Bureau making inquiries.
The Agent says if he could catch the rascal, the robber,
he would string him up by the thumbs, but her descrip-

tion fits any strolling private. He says: 'Any woman who would trust a stranger so with her money deserves to be fooled. I wouldn't trouble about it, Madam!' Yankees do not understand our coloured people and us. How can I help being troubled by anything that troubles Mammy Lisbeth?"

Here is another old letter: "Cousin mine: I came home from school a few days ago. Railroads all broken up and it took several days to make the journey in the carriage, stopping over-night along the route. At most houses, there was hardly anything to offer but shelter, but hospitality was perfect. Only cornbread and sassafras tea at one place; no servants to render attention; silver gone; famliy portraits punctured with bayonets; furniture and mirrors broken. Reaching home, found everything strange because of great change in domestic regime. Our cook, who has reigned in our kitchen for thirty years, is in Richmond, coining money out of a restaurant. Most of our servants have gone to the city. Our old butler and Mammy abide. I think it would have killed me had Mammy gone!

"I cannot tell you how it oppressed me to miss the familiar black faces I have loved all my life, and to feel that our negroes cared so little for us, and left at the first invitation. I have something strange to tell you. Mammy has been free since before I was born. I never knew till now. I was utterly wretched, and exclaimed: 'Well, Mammy, I reckon you'll go too!' She took it as a deadly insult; I had to humble myself. While she was mad, the secret burst out: 'Ef I'd wanted to go, I could ha' gone long time ago. No Yankees sot me free! My marster sot me free.' She showed me her manumission papers in grandfather's hand, which she has worn for I don't know how long, in a little oil-silk bag around her neck, never caring to

use them.   Domestic cares are making me gray!   But
I get some fun trying to do things I never did before,
while Mammy scolds me for 'demeaning' myself."
There was honour in the "gritty" way the Southern
housewife adapted herself to the situation, humour in
the way spoiled maidens played the part of milkmaid
or of Bridget.

"Do you know how to make lightbread?" one of
our friends inquired, and proceeded to brag of her
new accomplishments, adding: "I had never gotten
a meal in my life until the morning after the Yankees
passed, when I woke to find not a single servant on the
place.   There was a lone cow left.   I essayed to milk
her, but retired in dire confusion.   I couldn't make
the milk go in the pail to save my life!   It squirted in
my face and eyes and all over my hair.   The cow
switched her tail around and cut my countenance, made
demonstrations with her hind feet, and I retired.   One
of my daughters sat on the milking-stool and milked
away as if she had been born to it."

"The first meal I got," another friend wrote, "my
sons cooked.   They learned how in the army.   I thought
the house was coming down while they were beating the
biscuit!   They drove me from the kitchen.   'We don't
hate the Yankees for thrashing us,' they said, 'but God
knows we hate them for turning our women into hewers
of wood and drawers of water.'   Now, I'm as good a
cook as my boys.   Can do everything domestic except
kill a chicken.   I turn the chicken loose every time."

"I write in a merry vein," was another recital,
"because it is no good to write in any other.   But I
have the heart-break over things.   I see this big plantation, once so beautifully kept up, going to rack and
ruin.   I see the negroes I trained so carefully deterio-
rating every day.   We suffer from theft, are humiliated

by impertinence; and cannot help ourselves. Negroes call upon me daily for services that I, in Christian duty, must render whether I am able or not. And I cannot call upon them for one thing but I must pay twice over—and I have nothing to pay with. This is the first rule in their lesson of freedom—to get all they can out of white folks and give as little as possible in return."

Letters teemed with experiences like this: "We went to sleep one night with a plantation full of negroes, and woke to find not one on the place—every servant gone to Sherman in Atlanta. Negroes are camped out all around that city. We had thought there was a strong bond of affection on their side as well as ours! We have ministered to them in sickness, infancy, and age. But poor creatures! they don't know what freedom is, and they are crazy. They think it the opening of the door of Heaven. Some put me in mind of birds born and raised in a cage and suddenly turned loose and helpless; others, of hawks, minks and weasels, released to do mischief.

"We heard that there was much suffering in the camps; presently our negroes were all back, some ill from exposure. Maum Lucindy sent word for us to send for her, she was sick. Without a vehicle or team on the place, it looked like an impossible proposition, but my little boys patched up the relics of an old cart, borrowed the only steer in the neighbourhood, and got Maum Lucindy back. The raiders swept us clean of everything. We are unable to feed ourselves. How we shall feed and clothe the negroes when we cannot make them work, I do not know."

My cousin, Mrs. Meredith, of Brunswick, Virginia, congratulated herself, when only one of her servants deserted his post to join Sheridan's trail of camp-followers. A week after Simeon's departure, she woke

one morning to discover that six women had decamped,
one leaving her two little children in her cabin from
which came pitiful wails of " Mammy! " " Mammy! "
Simeon had come in the night, and related of Black's
and White's (now Blackstone) where a garrison had
been established, that calico dresses were as plentiful
as leaves on trees and that coloured women were parad-
ing the streets with white soldiers for beaux.   My
cousin, Mrs. White, said a whole wagon-load of negro
women passed her house going to Blackstone, and that
one of them insisted upon presenting her with a four-
year-old child, declaring it too much trouble.   It was
not an unknown thing for negro mothers to leave their
children along the roadsides.

Blackstone drew recruits until there was just one
woman-servant remaining with the Merediths.   Why
she stayed was a mystery, but as she was "the only
pebble on the beach," everything was done to make
home attractive.   One day she asked permission (why,
could not be imagined) to go visiting.   She did not
return.   Shortly, Captain Meredith was haled before
the Freedmen's Bureau at Black's and White's to answer
the charge of thrashing Viny.   Marched into court, he
took a chair.   " Get up," said the Bureau Agent, "and
give the lady a seat."   He rose, and Viny dropped into
it.   She was shamefaced and brazen by turns; finally,
burst into tears and begged " Mars Tawm's " pardon,
saying she had brought the charge because she had
" no 'scuse for leavin' " and had to invent one;
" nevver knowed Mars Tawm was gwi be brung in cote
'bout it."

The early stirrings of the social equality problem
were curious.   Adventurous Aunt Susan tried the experi-
ment of " eatin' wid white folks."   She was bursting
to tell us about it, yet loath to reveal her degradation—

"White folks dat'll eat wid me ain't fitten fuh me to
eat wid," being the negro position. "But dese folks
was rale quality, Miss," Susan said when murder was
out. "I kinder skittish when dee fus' ax me to set
down wid 'em. I couldn' eat na'er mouthful wid white
folks a-lookin' at me an' a rale nice white gal handin'
vittles. An' presen'ly, mum, ef I didn' see dat white
gal settin' in de kitchen eatin' her vittles by herse'f.
Rale nice white gal! I say, 'Huccum you didn' eat
wid tur white folks?' She say, 'I de servant.'"

Mrs. Betts, of Halifax (Va.), was in her kitchen, her
cook, who was in her debt, having failed to put in
an appearance. The cook's husband approached the
verandah and requested a dollar. "Where is Jane?"
he was asked. "Why hasn't she been here to do her
work?" "She are keepin' parlour." "What is that?"
"Settin' up in de house hol'in' her han's. De Civilise
Bill done been fulfill an' niggers an' white folks jes
alike now."

Coloured applicant for menial position would say to
the door-opener: "Tell dat white 'oman in dar a cullud
lady out here want to hire." "De cullud lady" was
capricious. My sister in Atlanta engaged one for every
day in one month, in fact, engaged more than that
average, engaged every one applying, hoping if ten
promised to come in time to get breakfast, one might
appear.

With two hundred black trial justices, South Carolina
had more than her share of funny happenings, as of
tragic. A gentleman who had to appear before some
tribunal, wrote us: "Whom do you suppose I found
in the seat of law? Pete, my erstwhile stable-boy. He
does not know A from Z, had not the faintest idea of
what was to be done. 'Mars Charles,' he said, 'you
jes fix 'tup, please, suh. You jes write down whut you

think orter be wroted, an' I'll put my mark anywhar you tell me.'"

Into a store in Wilmington sauntered a sable alderman whom the merchant had known from boyhood as "Sam." "What's the matter with Sam?" the merchant asked as Sam stalked out. Soon, Sam stalked back. "Suh, you didn' treat me wid proper respecks." "How, Sam?" "You called me 'Sam,' which my name is Mr. Gary." "You're a d—d fool! There's the door!" Gary had the merchant up in the mayor's court. "What's the trouble?" asked the mayor. "Dis man consulted me." "You ought to feel flattered! What did he do to you?" "He called me 'Sam,' suh." "Ain't that your name?" "My name's Mr. Gary." "Ain't it Sam, too?" "Yessuh, but—" "Well, there ain't any law to compel a man to call another 'Mister.' Case dismissed." "Dar gwi be a law 'bout dat," muttered Sam.

Washington was the place of miracles. When Uncle Peter went there, some tricksters told him his wool could be made straight and his colour changed—"Said dee could make it jes lak white folks' ha'r," he informed his mistress mournfully, when he had paid the price— nearly his entire capital—and returned home with flaming red wool. His wife did not know him, or pretended not to, and drove him out of the house. He appealed to his mistress and she made Manda behave herself.

"Ole Miss," asked my mother's little handmaiden, "now, I'se free, is I gwi tu'n white lak white folks?" "You must not be ashamed of the skin God gave you, Patsy," said her mistress kindly. "Your skin is all right." "But I druther be white, Ole Miss." And there was something pathetic in the aspiration.

Some of the older and more intelligent blacks held

their children back from doffing with undignified haste old ways for new. But in most cases, the Simian quality showed itself promptly ascendant. Negroes did things they saw white people do, not because these things were right or seemly, but because white people did them, selecting for imitation trifles in conduct which they thought marked the social dividing line between white and black. As, for instance, they dropped the old sweet "Daddy" and "Mammy" for the dreadful "Pa" and "Ma," or the infantile "Popper" and "Mommer" which white people inflict upon parents. It would be laughable to hear a big buck negro addressing his sire as "Popper."

I have seen in a Southern street-car all blacks sitting and all whites standing; have seen a big black woman enter a car and flounce herself down almost into the lap of a white man; have seen white ladies pushed off sidewalks by black men. The new manners of the blacks were painful, revolting, absurd. The freedman's misbehaviour was to be condoned only by pity that accepted his inferiority as excuse. Southerners had taken great pains and pride in teaching their negroes good manners; they wanted them to be courtly and polished, and it must be said for the negroes, they took polish well. It was with keen regret that their old preceptors saw them throw all their fine schooling in etiquette to the winds.

Interest in and affection for negroes made these new manners the more obnoxious. Here, in one woman's statement, is the point illustrated: "I considered Mammy part of our family; my family pride would have been aggrieved, I would have tingled with mortification, to see her so far forget what was due herself as to push herself into places where she was not wanted. These are things she could not possibly do of herself, her own good taste, perfect breeding, and sturdy self-respect forbidding. But her husband and son quickly succumbed to the demoralisation of freedom and were vulgar and troublesome; we were in fear and trembling lest they should lead her into some situation in church, theatre, or car, where she would find herself conspicuous and from which she would not know how to withdraw until officially escorted out in the midst of trouble created by her men."

Many worthy negroes, the old, infirm and children, lost needed protection. Negroes had not been permitted to get drunk—except around corn-shucking and Christmas. There was no such restraint now. Formerly, a negro, if so disposed, could not beat his child unmercifully. Now, women and children might feel a heavy hand unknown before. White people might not interfere in family disputes as formerly, though they continued, at personal risk, to do what they could. A case in point was that of Mr. R., a respected merchant of Petersburg, who ejected his cook's drunken husband from the kitchen where the brute was cruelly maltreating her. The old gentleman was arrested and marched through the streets, as I have been told, by negro sergeants to trial before a negro magistrate.

A characteristic common to uncultured motherhood is over-indulgence and over-severity by turns. When provoked, the negro mother would descend like a fury upon her offspring, beating it as a former master would never have suffered her to abuse his property. A word or suggestion from a white would bring fresh blows upon the luckless wight, the mother thinking thus to demonstrate independence and ownership.

Under freedom, negroes developed bodily ills from

which they had seemed immune. A consumptive of the race was rarely heard of before freedom. After freedom, they began to die of pulmonary complaints. There were frequent epidemics of typhoid fever, quarters not being well kept. "The race is dying out," said prophets. Negroes began to grow mad. An insane negro was rarely heard of during slavery. Regular hours, regular work, chiefly out of doors, sobriety, freedom from care and responsibility, had kept the negro singularly exempt from insanity and various other afflictions that curse the white. Big lunatic asylums established for negroes soon after the war and their continual enlargement tell their own story.*

Freedom broke up families. Under stress of temptation, the young and strong deserted the aged, the feeble, the children, leaving these to shift for themselves or to remain a burden upon a master or mistress themselves impoverished and, perhaps, old and infirm.

In the face of so much distraction, demoralisation and disorder, the example of those negroes who were not affected by it shines out with greater clearness as witness for the best that is in the race. Thousands stood steadfastly to their posts, superior to temptations which might have shaken white people, performing their duties faithfully, caring for their children, sick and aged, shirking no debt of love and gratitude to past owners. Some negroes still live in families for which their ancestors worked, the bond of centuries never having been broken.

When this is true, the tie between white and black is yet strong, sweet and tender, like the tie of blood. The venerable "uncles" and "aunties" with their courtly

---

* Syphilitic diseases, from which under slavery negroes were nearly exempt, combine with tuberculosis to undermine racial health.

MRS. ANDREW PICKENS CALHOUN

Daughter of General Duff Green, of Georgia, and daughter-in-law of John C. Calhoun, the statesman, of South Carolina.

This picture was taken when Mrs. Calhoun was 71 years of age.

manners, their good warm hearts, their love for the whites, are swiftly passing away, and their like will not be seen again. They were America's black pearl; and America had as good reason to be proud of her faithful and efficient serving-class as of her Anglo-Saxons. They were needed; they filled an honourable and worthy place and filled it well.

This is not to justify slavery. Slavery was forced upon this country over Colonial protests, particularly from Southern sections fearing negroisation of territory; the slave-trade was profitable to the English Crown; our forefathers, coming into independence, faced a problem of awful magnitude in the light of Santo Domingo horrors; New England's slave-ships and Eli Whitney's cotton-gin complicated it; it is curious to read in the proceedings of the Sixth Congress how Mr. John Brown, of Rhode Island, urged that this Nation should not be deprived of a right, enjoyed by every civilised country, of bringing slaves from Africa *—particularly as transference to a Christian land was a benefit to Africans, a belief held by many who believed that the Bible sanctioned slavery. Through kindliness of temperament on both sides and the clan feeling fostered by the old plantation life of the South, the white man and the negro made the best they could of an evil thing. But the world has now well learned that a superior race cannot afford to take an inferior into such close company as slavery implies. For the service of the bond-slave the master ever pays to the uttermost in things precious as service, imparting refinements, ideals, standards, morals, manners, graces; in the end he pays that which he considers more precious than service; he pays his blood, and in more ways than one.

* See Susan Pendleton Lee's "History of Virginia."

BACK TO VOODOOISM

CHAPTER XVII

BACK TO VOODOOISM

THE average master and mistress of the old South were missionaries without the name. Religious instruction was a feature of the negro quarters on the Southern plantation—the social settlements for Africans in America.

Masters and mistresses, if themselves religious, usually held Sabbath services and Sunday schools for blacks. Some delegated this task, employing preachers and teachers. Charles Cotesworth Pinckney was the first rice planter to introduce systematic religious instruction among negroes on the Santee, influenced thereto by Bishop Capers. He subscribed to the Methodist Episcopal Mission for them, and a minister came every week to catechise the children and every Sabbath to preach at the negro church which Mr. Pinckney, with the assistance of his neighbours, established for the blacks on his own and neighbouring plantations. Soon fifty chapels on his model sprang up along the seaboard. In the Methodist churchyard in Columbia, a modest monument marks the grave of Bishop Capers, " Founder of the Mission to the Slaves." Nearby sleeps Rev. William Martin, who was a distinguished preacher to whites and a faithful missionary to blacks. In Zion Presbyterian Church, Charleston, built largely through the efforts of Mr. Robert Adger, no less a preacher than Rev. Dr. Girardeau ministered to negroes. The South entrusted the spiritual care of her negroes to her best and ablest, and what she did for them is inter-

woven with all her history. You will hear to-day how
the great clock on top of the church on Mr. Plowden
Weston's plantation kept time for plantations up and
down the Waccamaw. In that chapel, Rev. Mr.
Glenrie and an English catechist diligently taught the
blacks. After Sherman's visit to Columbia, Trinity
(Episcopal) Church had no Communion service; the
sacred vessels of precious metals belonging to the negro
chapel on the Hampton place were borrowed for
Trinity's white congregation.

The rule where negroes were not so numerous as to
require separate churches was for both races to worship
in one building. Slavery usages were modelled on
manorial customs in England, where a section of church
or chapel is set apart for the peasantry, another for
gentry and nobility. The gallery, or some other section of our churches, was reserved for servants, who
thus had the same religious teaching we had; there
being more of them, they were often in larger evidence
than whites at worship. After whites communed, they
received the Sacrament from the same hands at the same
altar. Their names were on our church rolls. Our
pastors often officiated at their funerals; sometimes an
old "exhorter" of their own colour did this; sometimes
our pastors married them, but this ceremony was not
infrequently performed by their masters.

The Old African Church, of Richmond, was once
that city's largest auditorium. In it great meetings
were held by whites, and famous speakers and artists
(Adelina Patti for one) were heard. One of Mr.
Davis' last addresses as President was made there. The
regular congregation was black and their pastor was
Rev. Robert Ryland, D. D., President of Richmond
College; "Brother Ryland," they called him. He
taught them with utmost conscientiousness; they loved

him and he them.   When called upon for the marriage ceremony, he would go to the home of their owners, and marry them in the "white folks' house" or on the lawn before a company of whites and blacks.   Then, as fee, a large iced cake would be presented to him by a groomsman with great pomp.

After the war, the old church was pulled down, and a new one erected by the negroes with assistance of whites North and South.   Then they wrote Dr. Ryland, who had gone to Kentucky, asking him to return and dedicate it.   He answered affectionately, saying he appreciated greatly this evidence of their regard and that nothing would give him greater pleasure, but he was too poor to come; he would be with them in spirit. They replied that the question of expense was none of his business; it was theirs.   He wrote that they must apply the sum thus set aside to current expenses, to meet which it would be needed.   They answered that they would be hurt if he did not come; they wanted no one else to dedicate their church.   So he came, stopping at Mr. Maury's.

He was greatly touched when he met his old friends, the congregation receiving him standing.   So much feeling was displayed on their part, such deep emotion experienced on his, that he had to retire to the study before he could command himself sufficiently to preach.

In religious life, after the war, the negro's and the white man's path parted quickly.   Negro galleries in white churches soon stood empty.   Negroes were being taught that they ought to sit cheek by jowl in the same pews with whites or stay away from white churches.

With freedom, the negro, *en masse,* relapsed promptly into the voodooism of Africa.   Emotional extravaganzas, which for the sake of his health and sanity, if for nothing else, had been held in check by his owners, were indulged without restraint. It was as if a force long repressed burst forth. "Moans," "shouts" and "trance meetings" could be heard for miles. It was weird. I have sat many a night in the window of our house on the big plantation and listened to shouting, jumping, stamping, dancing, in a cabin over a mile distant; in the gray dawn, negroes would come creeping back, exhausted, and unfit for duty.

In some localities, devil-dancing, as imported from Africa centuries ago, still continues. I have heard of one place in South Carolina where worshippers throw the trance-smitten into a creek, as the only measure sufficiently heroic to bring them out of coma. Devil-worship was rife in Louisiana just after the war.

One of my negro friends tells me: "Soon atter de war, dar wuz a trance-meetin' in dis neighbourhood dat lasted a week. De cook at marster's would git a answer jes befo' dinner dat ef he didn' bring a part uv evvything he cooked to de meetin', 'de Lawd would snatch de breath outen his body.' He brung it. Young gals dee'd be layin' 'roun' in trances. A gal would come to meetin' w'arin' a jacket a white lady gin 'er. One uh de gals in a trance would say: 'De Lawd say if sich an' sich a one don' pull dat jacket off, he gwi snatch de breath out dar body.' One ole man broke dat meetin' up. Two uv his gran'sons was lyin' out in a trance. He come down dar, wid a han'-full uh hickory switches an' laid de licks on dem gran'chillun. Evvybody took out an' run. Dat broke de meetin' up.

"Endurin' slavery, dar marsters wouldn' 'low niggers tuh do all dat foolishness. When freedom come, dee lis'n to bad advice an' lef' de white folks' chu'ches an' go to doin' all sorts uh nawnsense. Now dee done learnt better again. Dee goin' back sorter to de white folks' chu-ches. Heap uh Pristopals lak dar use tuh be. In Furginny, Bishop Randolph come 'roun' an' confirm all our classes. An' de Baptis'es dee talk 'bout takin' de cullud Baptis'es under dar watch-keer. An' all our folks dee done learnt heap better an' all what I been tellin' you. I don' want you tuh put dat in no book lessen you say we-all done improved."

Southern men who stand at the head of educational movements for negroes, state that they have advanced greatly in a religious sense, their own educated ministry contributing to this end. Among those old half-voodoo shouters and dreamers of dreams were negroes of exalted Christian character and true piety, and, industrially, of far more worth to society than the average educated product. I have known sensible negroes who believed that they "travelled" to heaven and to hell.*

It has been urged that darkness would have been quickly turned to light had Southern masters and mistresses performed their full duty in the spiritual instruction of their slaves. To change the fibre of a race is not a thing quickly done even where undivided and intense effort is bent in this direction. The negro, as he came here from Africa, changed much more quickly for the better in every respect than under freedom he could have done. It has been charged that we had laws against teaching negroes to read. I never heard of them until after the war. All of us tried to teach darkeys to read, and nothing was ever done to anybody

---

* Among Southerners assuring me that education is advancing negroes, I may mention ex-Mayor Ellyson, of Richmond, and Judge Watkins, of Farmville, who credit educated negro clergy with such moral improvement in the race. Both gentlemen were deeply interested in the educational work at Petersburg. Said Mayor Ellyson: "We take equal care in selecting teachers for both races."

about it. If there were such laws, we paid no attention to them, and they were framed for the negroes' and our protection against fanatics.*

I have treated this subject to show the swing back to savagery the instant the master-hand was removed; one cause of demoralisation in field and kitchen; the superstitious, volatile, inflammable material upon which political sharpers played without scruple.

---

* Such laws were adopted after 1830 in Alabama, Georgia and South Carolina, when secret agents of the abollitionists were spreading incendiary literature. It is a fact, though not generally understood, that abolition extremists arrested several emancipation movements in the South; whites dared not release to the guidance of fanatics a mass of semi-savages in whose minds doctrines of insurrection had been sown. See recent articles on Slavery in the "Confederate Veteran"; "The Gospel to the Slaves"; "An Inquiry into the Law of Negro Slavery in the United States; with an Historical Sketch of Slavery," by Thomas R. R. Cobb; and Southern histories of the Southern States.

THE FREEDMEN'S BUREAU

CHAPTER XVIII

THE FREEDMEN'S BUREAU

FEDERAL authorities had a terrific problem to deal with in four millions of slaves suddenly let loose. Military commanders found themselves between the devil and the deep sea.

Varied instructions were given to bring order out of chaos. "Freedmen that will use any disrespectful language to their former masters will be severely punished," is part of a ukase issued by Captain Nunan, at Milledgeville, in fervent if distracted effort for the general weal. By action if not by order, some others settled the matter this way: "Former masters that will use any disrespectful language to their former slaves will be severely punished"; as witness the case where a venerable lady, bearing in her own and that of her husband two of the proudest names in her State, was marched through the streets to answer before a military tribunal the charge of having used offensive language to her cook.

With hordes of negroes pilfering and pillaging, new rulers had an elephant on their hands. No vagrant laws enacted by Southern Legislatures in 1865-6 surpassed in severity many of the early military mandates with penalties for infraction. The strongest argument in palliation of the reconstruction acts is found in these laws which were construed into an attempt to re-enslave the negro. The South had no vagrant class before the war and was provided with no laws to meet conditions of vagrancy which followed emancipation with overwhelming force.

Comparing these laws with New England's, we find that in many respects the former were modelled on the latter, from which the words "ball and chain," "master and mistress" and the apprentice system, which Mr. Blaine declared so heinous, might well have been borrowed, though New England never faced so grave a vagrancy problem as that which confronted the South.

Negroes flocked to cities, thick as blackbirds. Federal commanders issued orders: "Keep negroes from the cities." "The Government is feeding too many idlers." "Make them stay on the plantations." "Impress upon them the necessity of making a crop, or famine is imminent throughout the South." "Do not let the young and able-bodied desert their children, sick, and aged." As well call to order the wild things of the woods! In various places something like the old "patter-roller" system of slavery was adopted by the Federals, wandering negroes being required to show passes from employers, saying why they were abroad.

General Schofield's Code for the Government of Freedmen in North Carolina (May, 1865) says: "Former masters are constituted guardians of minors in the absence of parents or other near relatives capable of supporting them." The Radicals made great capital out of a similar provision in Southern vagrancy laws.

Accounts of confusion worse confounded wrung this from the "New York Times" (May 17, 1865) : "The horse-stealing, lemonade and cake-vending phase of freedom is destined to brief existence. The negro misunderstands the motives which made the most laborious, hard-working people on the face of the globe clamour for his emancipation. You are free, Sambo, but you must work. Be virtuous, too, O Dinah! 'Whew! Gor Almighty! bress my soul!'"

The "Chicago Times" (July 7, 1865) gives a Western view: "There is chance in this country for philanthropy, a good opening for abolitionists. It is to relieve twenty-eight millions of whites held in cruel bondage by four million blacks, a bondage which retards our growth, distracts our thoughts, absorbs our efforts, drives us to war, ruptures our government, disturbs our tranquillity, and threatens direfully our future. There never was such a race of slaves as we; there never was another people ground so completely in the dust as this nation. Our negro masters crack their whips over our legislators and our religion."

The Freedmen's Bureau was created March 3, 1865, for the care and supervision of negroes in Federal lines. Branches were rapidly established throughout the South and invested with almost unlimited powers in matters concerning freedmen. An agency's efficiency depended upon the agent's personality. If he were discreet and self-respecting, its influence was wholesome; if he were the reverse, it was a curse. If he were inclined to peculate, the agency gave opportunity; if he were cruel—well, negroes who were hung up by the thumbs, or well annointed with molasses and tied out where flies could find them had opinions.

I recall two stories which show how wide a divergence there might be between the operations of two stations. A planter went to the agent in his vicinity and said: "Captain, I don't know what to do with the darkeys on my place. They will not work, and are committing depredations on myself and neighbours." The agent went out and addressed the negroes: "Men, what makes you think you can live without work? The Government is not going to support any people in idleness on account of their complexions. I shall not issue food to another of you. I have charged this planter to bring before me any case of stealing. If you stay on this plantation, you are to work for the owner."

In a week, the planter reported that they still refused to labour or to leave; property was disappearing, wanton damage was being done; but it was impossible to spot thieves and vandals. The agent, a man of war, went up in a hurry, and his language made the air blue! "If I come again," was his parting salutation, "I'll bring my cannon, and if you don't hoe, plow, or do whatever is required, I'll blow you all to pieces!" They went to work.

A gentleman of Fauquier tells me: "When I got home from prison, July, 1865, I found good feelings existing between whites and their former slaves; everything was going on as before the war except that negroes were free and received wages. After a while there came down a Bureau Agent who declared all contracts null and void and that no negro should work for a white except under contract written and approved by him. This demoralised the negroes and engendered distrust of whites."

"If a large planter was making contracts," I heard Mr. Martin, of the Tennessee Legislature, relate, "the agent would intermeddle. I had to make all mine in the presence of one. These agents had to be bribed to do a white man justice. A negro would not readily get into trouble with a gentleman of means and position when he would make short work of shooting a poor white. Yet the former had owned slaves and the latter had not."

Planters, making contracts, might have to journey from remote points (sometimes a distance of fifty miles over bad roads), wherever a Bureau was located, whites and blacks suffering expense, and loss of time. Both had to fee the agent. A contract binding on the

white was not binding on the negro, who was irrespon-
sible. If the Bureau wrought much mischief, it also
wrought good, for there were some whites ready to take
advantage of the negro's ignorance in driving hard
bargains with him; sorrowfully be it said, if able to
tip the agent, they would usually be able to drive the
hard bargain.

After examination for the Government into Bureau
operations, Generals Fullerton and Steedman reported,
May, 1866: "Negroes regard the Bureau as an indication that people of the North look upon the whites here
as their natural enemies, which is calculated to excite
suspicion and bad feeling. Only the worthless and idle
ask interference, the industrious do not apply. The
effect produced by a certain class of agents, is bitterness
and antagonism between whites and freedmen, a growing prejudice on the part of-planters to the Government
and expectations on the part of freedmen that can never
be realised. Where there has been no such interference or bad advice given, there is a growing feeling of
kindness between races and good order and harmony
prevail." They condemned the "arbitrary, unnecessary and offensive interference by the agents with the
relations of the Southern planters and their freedmen."

General Grant had reported (Dec. 18, 1865) to
President Johnson, after a Southern tour: "The belief
widely spread among freedmen that the lands of former
owners will, at least in part, be divided among them,
has come through agents of this Bureau. This belief
is seriously interfering with the willingness of the freedmen to make contracts."

Whether agents originated or simply winked at the
red, white and blue stick enterprise, I am unable to say.
Into a neighborhood would come strangers from the
North, seeking private interviews with negroes possess-

ing a little cash or having access to somebody else's cash; to these would be shown, with pledges of secrecy, packages of red, white and blue sticks, four to each package. "Get up before light on such a date, plant a stick at the four corners of any piece of land not over a mile square, and the land is yours. Be wary, or the rebels will get ahead of you."

Packages were five dollars each. One gentleman found a set for which he had lent part of the purchase money planted on his land. If a negro had not the whole sum, the seller would "trust" him for the balance till he "should come into possession of the land."

Generals Fullerton and Steedman advised discontinuance of the Bureau in Virginia; and some similar recommendation must have accompanied the report for Florida and the Carolinas which contained such revelations as this about the Trent River Settlement, where 4,000 blacks lived in "deplorable condition" under the superintendency of Rev. Mr. Fitz, formerly U. S. A. Chaplain. "Four intelligent Northern ladies," teaching school in the Settlement, witnessed the harsh treatment of negroes by Mr. Fitz, such as suspension by the thumbs for hours; imprisonment of children for playing on the Sabbath; making negroes pay for huts; taxing them; turning them out on the streets. Interesting statements were given in regard to the "planting officials" who impressed negroes to work lands under such overseers as few Southern masters (outside of "Uncle Tom's Cabin") would have permitted to drive negroes they owned, the officials reaping profits.

The Bureau had ways of making whites know their place. One could gather a book of stories like this, told me recently by an aged lady, whose name I can give to any one entitled to ask: "Captain B., of the Freedmen's Bureau, was a very hard man. He took up farms around and put negroes on them. We had a large place; he held that over a year and everything was destroyed. Saturdays, Captain B. would send many negroes out there—and it was pandemonium! My husband was in prison. My father was eighty; he would not complain, but I would. We went to the Bureau repeatedly about the outrages. Captain B. was obsequious, offered father wine; but he did not stop the outrages. Once he asked: 'Have you not had any remuneration for your place?' 'No,' I said, 'and we are not asking it. We only beg you to make the negroes you send out there behave decently.' He said he would do anything for us, but did nothing; at last, I went direct to General Stoneman, and he helped us."

Not long after Generals Grant's, Fullerton's, and Steedman's reports, Congress enlarged the powers of the Bureau. Coincident with this, the negro became a voter, the Bureau a political machine, the agent a candidate. The Bureau had been active in securing negro enfranchisement. It was natural that ambitious agents should send hair-raising stories North of the Southerner's guile, cruelty and injustice, and touching ones of the negro's heavenly-mindedness in general and of his fitness to be an elector and law-maker in particular; all proving the propriety and necessity of his possession of the ballot for self-protection and defense.

In signal instances, the Bureau became the negro's protector in crime, as when its officials demanded at one time of Governor Throckmorton, of Texas, pardon and release of two hundred and twenty-seven negroes from the penitentiary, some of whom had been confined for burglary, arson, rape, murder.

The Bureau did not in the end escape condemnation from those for whom it was created, and who, on acquisition of the ballot, became its "spoiled darlings."

"De ossifers eat up all de niggers' rations, steal all dey money, w'ar all dey Sunday clo'se," said Hodges, of Princess Anne, in Virginia's Black and Tan Convention. The failure of the Freedmen's Savings Bank was a scandal costing pain and humiliation to all honest Northerners connected with the institution, and many a negro his little hoard and his disposition to accumulate.

It is not fair to overlook benefits conferred by the Bureau because it failed to perform the one great and fine task it might have accomplished, as the freedman's first monitor, in teaching him that freedom enlarges responsibility and brings no exemption from toil. If much harm, great good was also done in distribution of Government rations, in which whites sometimes received share with blacks. In numbers of places, both races found the agent a sturdy friend and wise counsellor.*

No one who knows General O. O. Howard, who was Commissioner, can, I think, doubt the sincerity and purity of purpose which animated him and scores of his subordinates. From the start, the Bureau must have been a difficult organization to handle; once the negro entered into count as a possible or actual political factor, the combined wisdom of Solomon and Moses could not have made its administration a success nor fulfilled the Government's benign intention in creating it.

---

* See University of Iowa Studies, "Freedmen's Bureau," by Paul Skeels Pierce.

PRISONER OF FORTRESS MONROE

CHAPTER XIX

THE PRISONER OF FORTRESS MONROE

AN extract from a letter by Mrs. Robert E. Lee to Miss Mason, from Derwent, September 10, 1865, may interest my readers: "I have just received, dear Miss Em, a long letter from Mrs. Davis in reply to one of mine. She was in Augusta, Ga.; says she is confined to that State. She has sent her children to kindred in Canada. Says she knows nothing whatever of her husband, except what she has seen in the papers. Says any letter sent her under care of Mr. Schley will reach her safely. She writes very sadly, as she well may, for I know of no one so much to be pitied. . . . She represents a most uncomfortable state of affairs in Augusta. No one, white or black, can be out after ten o'clock at night without a pass. . . . We must wait God's time to raise us up again. That will be the best time." In a later letter, Mrs. Lee said: "I cannot help feeling uneasy about Mr. Davis. May God protect him, and grant him deliverance!"

The whole South was anxious about Mr. Davis. Those who had come in close touch with him felt a peculiar sympathy for him inspired by a side of his character not generally recognized, as his manner often conveyed an impression of coldness and sternness. Under his reserve, was an almost feminine tenderness revealed in many stories his close friends tell. Thus: One night, Judge Minor, to see the President on business of state, sat with him in the room of the "White House" where the telegraph wire came in at the window (now, Alabama Room in the Confederate Museum), when in stumbles little Joe, in night-gown, saying: "Papa, I want to say my prayers." The President, caressing his child, despatched a message, answered Judge Minor's immediate question, and saying, "Excuse me a moment," led his little one's devotions. He was of wide reading and wonderful memory, yet was ignorant of "Mother Goose" until he heard his children babbling the jingles. Mrs. Davis brought "Babes in the Wood" to his notice. He suffered from insomnia after visits to the hospitals; his wife would try to read him to sleep. One night she picked up the "Babes" as the one thing at hand, and was astonished to find the poem unknown to him; at the children's desertion he rose, exclaiming: "Was there no one to help those poor tender babies? The thought is agonizing!" A part of his childhood was spent in a Kentucky monastery, where the good monks did not bethink themselves to teach him nursery rhymes.

There was the story of the soldier's widow, to answer whose call the President left his breakfast unfinished. Mrs. Davis found him trying to comfort and to induce her to partake of a tray of delicacies sent in by his order. She was trying to find her husband's body, and feared that as he was a poor private due aid might not be given her; she had been certain that she would receive scant attention from the Chief Magistrate. But he was telling her that the country's strength and protection lay in her private soldier. "My father, Madam, was a private in the Revolution, and I am more proud of what he did for his country than if he had been an officer expecting the world's praise. Tell your sorrows to my wife. She will take you in her carriage wherever you wish to go, and aid you all she can."

Dr. Craven, Mr. Davis' Federal physician at Fortress Monroe, testifies in his book to his patient's unusual depth and quickness of sympathy: "Despite a certain exterior cynicism of manner, no patient ever crossed my path who, suffering so much himself, appeared to feel so warmly and tenderly for others." In Confederate hospitals, he had not limited pity to wearers of the gray. A "White House" guest told me of his robbing his scant table more than once for a sick Federal who had served with him in Mexico. Another laughingly remarked: "I don't see how he managed to rob his table of a delicacy. When I sat down to it, it had none to spare. Yet certainly he might have kept a bountiful board, for Government stores were accessible to Government officials, and the President might have had first choice in purchasing blockade goods. But the simplicity of our White House regime was an object-lesson. I recall seeing Mr. Davis in home-spun, home-made clothes at State receptions. That required very positive patriotism if one could do better! 'Do look at Mr. Davis!' Mrs. Davis whispered, 'He *will* wear those clothes, and they look lop-sided!' Their deficiencies were more noticeable because he was so polished and elegant."

One of the faithful shows me in her scrap-book a dispatch, of May 25, 1865, in the "Philadelphia Inquirer": "Jeff does not pine in solitude. An officer and two soldiers remain continually in the cell with him." And then points to these words from the pen of Hugh McCulloch, Mr. Davis' visitor from Washington: "He had the bearing of a brave and high-born gentleman, who, knowing he would have been highly honoured if the Southern States had achieved their independence, would not and could not demean himself as a criminal because they had not." She tells how men who had served under Mr. Davis in Mexico were among his guards at Fortress Monroe and showed him respect and kindness; and how almost everybody there grew to like him, he was so kind and courteous, and to the common soldier as to the strapped and starred officer.

Our ladies sent articles for his comfort to Mr. Davis, but knew not if he received them. Dr. Minnegerode's efforts to see him were for a weary while without success. It seemed that his pastor, at least, might have had this privilege without question, especially such as Dr. Minnegerode, a man of signal peace and piety who had carried the consolations of religion and such comforts as he could collect in an almost famine-stricken city to Federals in prison. His first endeavour, a letter of request to President Johnson, met no response. Finally, appeal was made through Rev. Dr. Hall, Mr. Stanton's pastor; to the committee of ladies waiting on him, Dr. Hall said he did not wish to read the petition, wished to have nothing to do with the matter; they besought, he read, and secured privilege of intercourse between pastor and prisoner.

For months, Mr. Davis was not allowed to correspond with his wife; was allowed no book but the Bible; June 8, 1865, Stanton reproved General Miles for permitting the prison chaplain to visit him. He was unprepared for his pastor's coming, when Dr. Minnegerode, conducted by General Miles, entered his cell. In a sermon in St. Paul's after Mr. Davis' death, Dr. Minnegerode described this meeting. Mr. Davis had been removed (on medical insistence) from the casemate, and was "in an end room on the second floor of Carroll Hall, with a passage and windows on each side of the room, and an anteroom in front, separated by an open grated door—a sentinel on each passage and before the grated door of the anteroom; six eyes always

Photographed in 1890

A VIEW OF FORTRESS MUNROE

Showing section of casemates overlooking the moat. In a casemate of this fort Mr. Davis was confined.

upon him, day and night." With these eyes looking on, the long-parted friends, the pastor and the prisoner, met.

When the question of Holy Communion was broached, Mr. Davis hesitated. "He was a pure and pious man, and felt the need and value of the means of grace. But could he take the Sacrament in the proper spirit—in a forgiving mind? He was too upright and conscientious to eat and drink unworthily—that is, not at peace with God and man, as far as in him lay." In the afternoon, General Miles took the pastor to the prisoner again. Mr. Davis was ready to pray, "Father, forgive them!" "Then came the Communion. It was night. The fortress was so still that you could hear a pin fall. General Miles, with his back to us, leaned against the fire-place in the anteroom, his head on his hands—not moving; sentinels stood like statues."

Of Mr. Davis' treatment, Dr. Minnegerode said: "The officers were polite and sympathetic; the common soldiers—not one adopted the practice of high dignitaries who spoke sneeringly of him as 'Jeff.' Not one but spoke of him in a subdued and kindly tone as 'Mr. Davis.' I went whenever I could," he adds, "to see my friend, and precious were the hours spent with that lowly, patient, God-fearing soul. It was in these private interviews that I learned to appreciate his noble, Christian character—'pure in heart,' unselfish, without guile, and loyal unto death to his conscience and convictions." The prisoner's health failed fast. Officers thought it would be wise and humane to allow him more liberty; they knew that he not only had no desire to escape, but could not be induced to do so. He was begging for trial. The pastor, encouraged by Dr. Hall, called on Mr. Stanton. He had hoped to find the man of iron softened by sorrow; Mr. Stanton had lost a son; his remaining child was on his knees. His greeting was like ice—a bow and nothing more. The pastor expressed thanks for permit to visit the prisoner, and respectfully broaching the subject of Mr. Davis' health, suggested that, as he neither would nor could escape, he be allowed the liberty of the fort. Mr. Stanton broke his silence: "It makes no difference what the state of Jeff Davis' health is. His trial will come on, no doubt. Time enough till that settles it." "It settled it in my leaving the presence of that man," said the pastor. "I realise," Dr. Craven protested, "the painful responsibilities of my position. If Mr. Davis were to die in prison, without trial, subject to such indignities as have been visited upon his attenuated frame, the world would form unjust conclusions, but conclusions with enough colour to pass them into history." Arguments breathing similar appreciation of the situation began to appear in the Northern press, while men of prominence, advocating the application of the great principles of justice and humanity to his case, called for his release or trial; such lawyers as William B. Reed, of Philadelphia, and Charles O'Conor, of New York, tendered him free services. Strong friends were gathering around his wife. The Northern heart was waking. General Grant was one of those who used his influence to mitigate the severity of Mr. Davis' imprisonment.

Again and again Mrs. Davis had implored permission to go to him. "I will take any parole—do anything, if you will only let me see him! For the love of God and His merciful Son, do not refuse me!" was her cry to the War Department, January, 1866. No reply. Then, this telegram to Andrew Johnson from Montreal, April 25, 1866: "I hear my husband's health is failing rapidly. Can I come to see him?

Can you refuse me? Varina Davis." Stanton acquiesced in Johnson's consent. And the husband and wife were reunited.

Official reports to Washington, changing their tone, referred to him as "State Prisoner Davis" instead of merely "Jeff Davis." The "National Republican," a Government organ, declared: "Something ought in justice to be done about his case. By every principle of justice as guaranteed by the Constitution, he ought to be released or brought to trial." It would have simplified matters had he asked pardon of the National Government. But this he never did, though friends, grieving over his sufferings, urged him. He did not hold that the South had committed treason or that he, in being her Chief Magistrate, was Arch-Traitor. Questions of difference between the States had been tried in the court of arms; the South had lost, had accepted conditions of defeat, would abide by them; that was all there was to it. Northern men were coming to see the question in the same light.

Through indignities visited upon him who had been our Chief Magistrate was the South most deeply aggrieved and humiliated; through the action of Horace Greeley and other Northern men coming to his rescue was the first real balm of healing laid upon the wound that gaped between the sections. That wound would have healed quickly, had not the most profound humiliation of all, the negro ballot and white disfranchisement, been forced upon us.

Among relics in the Confederate Museum is a mask which Mr. Davis wore at Fortress Monroe. His wife sent it to him when she heard that the everlasting light in his eyes and the everlasting eyes of guards upon him were robbing him of sleep and threatening his eyesight and his reason. Over a mantel is Jefferson Davis' bond in a frame; under his name are those of his sureties, Horace Greeley's leading the signatures of Cornelius Vanderbilt, Gerrit Smith, Benjamin Wood, and Augustus Schell, all of New York; A. Welsh and D. K. Jackson, of Philadelphia; and Southern sureties, W. H. McFarland, Richard Barton Haxall, Isaac Davenport, Abraham Warwick, Gustavus A. Myers, W. Crump, James Lyons, John A. Meredith, W. H. Lyons, John Minor Botts, Thomas W. Boswell, James Thomas. Thousands of Southerners would have rejoiced to sign that bond; but it must be pleasing now to visitors of both sections to see Northern and Southern names upon it. The mask and the bond tell the story.

RECONSTRUCTION ORATORY

CHAPTER XX

RECONSTRUCTION ORATORY

NORTHERN visitors, drawn to Richmond in the Spring of 1867, to the Davis trial, came upon the heels of a riot if not squarely into the midst of one. Friday, May 10, began with a mass-meeting at one of the old Chimborazo buildings, where negroes of both sexes, various ages, and in all kinds of rags and raiment, congregated. Nothing could exceed the cheerfulness with which their initiation fees and monthly dues were received by the white Treasurer of the National Political Aid Society, while their names were called by the white Secretary—the one officer a carpet-bagger, the other a scalawag. Initiation fee was a quarter, monthly dues a dime; the Treasurer's table was piled with a hillock of small change. The Secretary added 400 names to a roll of 2,000.

A negro leader, asked by a Northern reporter, "What's this money to be used for?" replied: "We gwi sen' speakers all 'roun' de country, boss; gwi open de eyes er de cullud folks, an' show 'em how dee gotter vote. Some niggers out in de country don' know whe'er dee free er not—hoein' an' plowin' fuh white folks jes lak dee always been doin'. An' dee gwi vote lak white folks tell 'em ef dar ain' suppin' did. De country's gwi go tuh obstruction ef us whar knows don' molighten dem whar don' know. Dat huccum you sees what you does see." When collection had been taken up, a young carpet-bagger led in speech-making:

"Dear friends: I rejoice to find myself in this noble

229

company of patriots. I see before me men and women who are bulwarks of the nation; ready to give their money, to work, to die, if need be, for freedom. Freedom, my friends, is another name for the great Republican Party. ("Hise yo' mouf tellin' dat truf!" "Dat's so!" "Halleluia!" "Glory be tuh Gawd!") The Republican Party gave you freedom and will preserve it inviolate! (Applause; whispers: "What dat he spoken 'bout?" "Sho use big words!" "Dat man got sense. He know what he talkin' 'bout ef we don't!") That party was unknown in this grand old State until a few months ago. It has been rotten-egged!—("Now ain't dat a shame!") although its speakers have only advocated the teachings of the Holy Bible. ("Glory Halleluia!" "Glory to de Lamb!" "Jesus, my Marster!") The Republican Party is your friend that has led you out of the Wilderness into the Promised Land!" Glories and halleluias reached climax in which two sisters were carried out shouting. "Disshere gitten' too much lak er 'ligious meetin' tuh suit me," a sinner observed.

"You do not need for me to tell you never to vote for one of these white traitors and rebels who held you as slaves. ("Dat we ain't!" "We'll see 'em in h— fust!") We have fought for you on the field of battle. Now you must organize and fight for yourselves. ("We gwi do it, too! Dat we is! We gwi fight!") We have given you freedom. We intend to give you property. We, the Republican Party, propose to confiscate the land of these white rebels and traitors and give it to you, to whom it justly belongs—forty acres and a mule and $100 to every one of you! (The Chairman exhausted himself seeking to subdue enthusiasm.) The Republican Party cannot do this unless you give it your support. All that it asks is your vote and your influence. If the white men of the South carry the elections, they will put you back into slavery."

A scalawag delivered the gem of the occasion: "Ladies and gentlemen: I am happy to embrace this privilege of speaking to you. I desire to address first and very especially a few words to these ladies, for they wield an influence of which they are little aware. Whether poor or rich, however humble they may be, women exert a powerful influence over the hearts of men. I have been gratified to see you bringing your mites to the cause of truth. Emulate, my fair friends, the example of your ancestors who came over in the Mayflower, emulate your ancestors, the patriotic women of '76. Give your whole hearts, and all your influence to this noble work. And in benefits that will come to you, you shall be repaid an hundred-fold for every quarter and dime you here deposit!" The meeting closed with race-hatred stirred up to white heat in black breasts.

Later in the day, Richmond firemen were entertaining visiting Delaware firemen with water-throwing. A policeman requested a negro, standing within reserved space, to move; Sambo would not budge; the officer pushed him back; Sambo struck the officer; there was a hubbub. A white bystander was struck, and struck back; a barber on the corner jerked up his pole and ran, waving it and yelling: "Come on, freedmen! Now's de time to save yo' nation!" Negroes of all sizes, sexes and ages, some half-clad, many drunk, poured into the street; brickbats flew; the officer was knocked down, his prisoner liberated. Screams of "Dem p'licemens shan't 'res' nobody, dat dee shan't!" "Time done come fuh us tuh stan' up fuh our rights!" were heard on all sides. The police, under orders not to fire, tried to disperse or hold them at bay, exercising marvellous patience when blacks shook fists in their faces, saying: "I dar you tuh shoot! I jes dar you tuh shoot!"

Mayor Mayo addressed the crowd: "I command you in the name of the Commonwealth to go to your homes, every one, white and black; I give you my word every case shall be looked into and justice done." They moved a square, muttering: "Give us our rights, now— de cullud man's rights!" An ambulance rumbled up. Negroes broke into cheers. In it sat General Schofield, Federal Commandant, and General Brown, of the Freedmen's Bureau. "Speech! speech!" they called. "I want you to go to your homes and remain there," said General Schofield. They made no motion to obey, but called for a speech. "I did not come here to make a speech. I command you to disperse." They did not budge. The war lord was not there to trifle. In double-quick time, Company H of the Twenty-Ninth was on the ground and sent the crowd about its business. That night six companies were marched in from Camp Grant and disposed about the city at Mayor Mayo's discretion.

High carnival in the Old African Church wound up the day. An educated coloured man from Boston presided, and Carpet-Bagger-Philanthropist Hayward (who, having had the cold shoulder turned on him in Massachusetts, had come to Virginia) held forth: "The papers have made conspicuous my remarks that the negro is better than the white man Why, I had no idea anybody was so stupid as to doubt it. When I contemplate such a noble race, and look upon you as you appear to me tonight, I could wish my own face were black!" "Ne'm min', boss!" sang out a sympathetic auditor, "Yo' heart's black! Dat's good enough!" The speaker was nonplussed for a second.

"When I go to Massachusetts, shall I tell the people there that you are determined to ride in the same cars on which white men and women ride?" "Yes! Yes!" "Shall I tell them you intend to go in and take your seats in any church where the Gospel is preached?" "Yes! Yes! Dat we is!" "Shall I tell them you intend to occupy any boxes in the theatre you pay your money for?" "You sho kin, boss!" "Yes, yes!" "Shall I tell them you intend to enjoy, *in whatever manner you see fit,* any rights and privileges which the citizens of Massachusetts enjoy?" "Dat you kin!" "Tell 'em we gwi have our rights!"

"If you cannot get them for yourselves, the young men of the Bay State will come down and help you. We have made you free. We will give you what you want." The coloured gentleman from Boston had to employ all his parliamentary skill before applause could be subdued for the speaker to continue. "You are brave. I am astonished at evidences of your bravery. To any who might be reckless, I give warning. You would not endanger the life of the illustrious Underwood, would you?" (Judge Underwood, boss of the black ring, was in town to try Mr. Davis.) "Dat we wouldn'!" "*Well, then, as soon as he leaves, you may have a high carnival in whatever way you please. It is not for me to advise you what to do, for great masses do generally what they have a mind to.*"

Wrought up to frenzy, the negroes fairly shook the house; the chairman made sincere efforts to bring the meeting to order. The young white Secretary of the National Political Aid Society arose and said: "Mr. Speaker, you may tell the people of Massachusetts that the coloured people of Richmond are determined to go into any bar-room, theatre, hotel, or car they wish to enter." "Yes, you tell 'em dat! We will! We will!"

Next morning, our war lord brought Hayward up in short order. The meeting had come to his notice through Cowardin's report in the "Dispatch." The hearing was rich, a cluster of bright newspaper men being present, among them the "New York Herald" reporter, who endorsed Mr. Cowardin's account, and declared Hayward's speech inflammatory. It developed that negroes had been petitioning to Washington for General Schofield's removal, a compliment paid all his predecessors.

The idle and excitable negroes must not be accepted as fully representative of their race. Those not heard from were the worthy ones, remaining at the houses of their white employers or in their own homes, and performing faithfully their regular duties. They were in the minority, but I believe the race would prefer now that these humble toilers should be considered representative rather than the other class. Lending neither aid nor encouragement to insurrectionary methods, they yet dared not openly oppose the incendiary spirit which, had it been carried far enough, might have swept them, too, off their feet as their kindred became involved. Negroes stick together and conceal each other's defections; this does not proceed altogether from race loyalty; they fear each other; dread covert acts of vengeance and being "conjured." Mysterious afflictions overtake the "conjured" or bewitched.

THE PRISONER FREE

CHAPTER XXI

THE PRISONER FREE

ON a beautiful May afternoon, two years after Mr. Davis' capture, the "John Sylvester" swung to the wharf at Rocketts and the prisoner walked forth, smiling quietly upon the people who, on the other side of the blue cordon of sentinels, watched the gangway, crying, "It is he! it is he!" Always slender, he was shadowy now, worn and thin to emaciation. He did not carry himself like a martyr. Only his attenuation, the sharpness of his features, the care-worn, haggard appearance of the face, the hair nearly all gray, the general indications of having aged ten years in two, made any appeal for sympathy. With him were his wife, Judge Ould, and Mr. James Lyons, Dr. Cooper, Mr. Burton Harrison, and General Burton, General Miles' successor, whose prisoner he yet was, but whose attitude was more that of friend than custodian.

A reserved and dignified city is the Capital on the James, taking joys sedately; but that day she wore her heart on her sleeve; she cheered and wept. The green hills, streets, sidewalks, were alive with people; porches, windows, balconies, roofs, were thronged; Main Street was a lane of uncovered heads as two carriages rolled swiftly towards the Spotswood, one holding Mr. Davis, General Burton, Dr. Cooper and Mr. Harrison; the other, Mrs. Davis and Mrs. Lyons, Mr. Lyons and Judge Ould; an escort of Federal cavalry bringing up the rear with clattering hoofs and clanging sabres. It was more like a victor's home-returning

237

than the bringing of a prisoner to trial. Yet through popular joy there throbbed the tragic note that marks the difference between the huzzas of a conquering people for their leader, and the welcoming "God bless you!" of a people subdued.

This difference was noticeable at the Spotswood, which famous hostelry entertained many Northern guests. A double line of policemen, dividing the crowd, formed an avenue from sidewalk to ladies' entrance. This crowd, it seems, had its hat on. Among our own people may have been some who thought it not wise in their own or the prisoner's interests to show him too much honour. But as the emaciated, careworn man with the lofty bearing, stepped from the carriage, a voice, quiet but distinct, broke the impressive stillness: "Hats off, Virginians!" Instantly every man stood uncovered.

Monday he went to trial. The Court Room in the old Custom House was packed. In the persons of representative men, North and South were there for his vindication of the charge of high treason. Were he guilty, then were we all of the South, and should be sentenced with him.

Reporters for Northern papers were present with their Southern brethren of scratch-pad and pencil. The jury-box was a novelty to Northerners. In it sat a motley crew of negroes and whites. For portrait in part of the presiding judge, I refer to the case of McVeigh vs. Underwood, as reported in Twenty-third Grattan, decided in favour of McVeigh. When the Federal Army occupied Alexandria, John C. Underwood used his position as United States District Judge to acquire the homestead, fully furnished, of Dr. McVeigh, then in Richmond. He confiscated it to the United States, denied McVeigh a hearing, sold it,

AN HISTORICAL PETIT JURY

This is the Petit Jury impaneled to try President Jefferson Davis, being the first mixed Petit Jury ever impaneled in the United States. Judge Underwood, not Chief Justice Chase, presided.

bought it in his wife's name for $2,850 when it was worth not less than $20,000, and had her deed it to himself. The first time thereafter that Dr. McVeigh met the able jurist face to face on a street in Richmond, the good doctor, one of the most amiable of men, before he knew what he was doing, slapped the able jurist over and went about his business; whereupon, the Honourable the United States Circuit Court picked himself up and went about his, which was sitting in judgment on cases in equity. In 1873, Dr. McVeigh's home was restored to him by law, the United States Supreme Court pronouncing Underwood's course "a blot upon our jurisprudence and civilisation." Underwood was in possession when he presided at the trial of Jefferson Davis.

His personal appearance has been described as "repellant; his head drooping; his hair long; his eyes shifty and unpleasing, and like a basilisk's; his clothes ill-fitting;" he "came into court, fawning, creeping, shuffling; ascended the bench in a manner awkward and ungainly; lifted his head like a turtle." "Hear ye! hear ye! Silence is commanded while the Honourable the United States Circuit Court is in session!" calls the crier on this May morning.

General Burton, with soldierly simplicity, transfers the prisoner from the military to the civil power; Underwood embarrasses the officer and shames every lawyer present by a fatuous response abasing the bench before the bayonet. Erect, serene, undefiant, surrounded by mighty men of the Northern and Southern bar—O'Conor, Reed, Shea, Randolph Tucker, Ould— Jefferson Davis faces his judge, his own clear, fearless glance meeting squarely the "basilisk eye."

The like of Underwood's charge to the jury was never heard before in this land. It caused one long blush from Maine to Texas, Massachusetts to California; and resembled the Spanish War that came years after in that it gave Americans a common grievance. This poor, political bigot thought to please his Northern hearers by describing Richmond as "comely and spacious as a goodly apple on a gilded sepulchre where bloody treason flourished its whips of scorpions" and a "place where licentiousness has ruled until a majority of the births are illegitimate," and "the pulpit prostituted by full-fed gay Lotharios." But the thing is too loathsome to quote! Northern reporters said it was not a charge, took no cognisance of the matter before the Court, was a "vulgar, inflammatory stump speech." The "New York Herald" pronounced it "The strangest mixture of drivel and nonsense that ever disgraced a bench," and "without a parallel, with its foulmouthed abuse of Richmond." "A disgrace to the American bench," declared the "New York World." "He has brought shame upon the entire bench of the country, for to the people of other countries he is a representative of American judges."

There was no trial. Motion was made and granted for a continuance of the case to November, and bail given in bond for $100,000, which Horace Greeley signed first, the crowd cheering him as he went up to write his name, which was followed by signatures of other well-known men of both sections. "The Marshal will discharge the prisoner!" a noble sentence in the judge's mouth at last! Applause shakes the Court Room. Men surge forward; Mr. Davis is surrounded; his friends, his lawyers, his sureties, crowd about him; the North and the South are shaking hands; a lovefeast is on. Human nature is at its best. The prisoner is free. When he appears on the portico the crowd grows wild with joy. Somebody wrote North that they heard the old "Rebel yell" once more, and that something or other unpleasant ought to be done to us because we would "holler" like that whenever we got excited.

It looks as if his carriage will never get back to the Spotswood, people press about him so, laughing, crying, congratulating, cheering. Negroes climb upon the carriage steps, shaking his hand, kissing it, shouting: "God bless Mars Davis!" No man was ever more beloved by negroes he owned or knew.

The South was unchained. The South was set free. No! That fall the first election at which negroes voted and whites—the majority disqualified by test-oath provision—did not vote, was held to send delegates to a convention presided over by John C. Underwood. This convention—the Black and Tan—made a new Constitution for the Old Dominion.

"If black men will riot, I will fear that emancipation is a failure." So spoke the great abolitionist, Gerritt Smith, from the pulpit of the Old African Church Tuesday night after the Davis trial. "Riots in Richmond, Charleston, and New Orleans have made me sick at heart." On the platform with him were Horace Greeley, Governor Pierpont, Colonel Lewis and Judge Underwood. His audience consisted of negroes, prominent white citizens of Richmond, Federal officers and their wives. The negroes, as ready to be swayed by good advice as bad, listened attentively to the wisest, most conservative addresses they had heard from civilians of the North, or than they were again to hear for a long time. Gerrit Smith, who was pouring out his money like water for their education, told them:

"I do not consider the white people of the South traitors. The South is not alone responsible for slavery.

Northern as well as Southern ships brought negroes to this shore. When Northern States passed laws abolishing slavery in their borders, Northern people brought their negroes down here and sold them before those laws could take effect. I have been chased in the North by a pro-slavery mob—never in the South." Referring to the South's impoverished condition, he said he wished the Federal Government would give the section six years' exemption from the Federal tax to make rapid rehabilitation possible. He plead for harmony between races; urged whites to encourage blacks by selling lands to them cheap; urged blacks to frugality, industry, sobriety; plead with them not to drink. "Why cannot you love the whites among whom you have been born and raised?" he asked. "We do! we do!" cried the poor darkeys who had yelled, "We will! we will!" when Hayward was inciting them to mischief.

Horace Greeley said: "I have heard in Richmond that coloured people would not buy homes or lands because they are expecting these through confiscation. Believe me, friends, you can much sooner earn a home. Confiscation is a slow, legal process. (Underwood had not found it so.) Thaddeus Stevens, the great man who leads the movement—and perhaps one of the greatest men who ever sat in Congress—is the only advocate of such a course, among all our representatives and senators. If it has not taken place in the two years since the war, we may not hope for it now. Famine, disaster, and deadly feuds would follow confiscation." His voice, too, was raised against calling Southern whites "traitors." "This seems to me," he said, "to brand with the crime of treason—of felony— millions of our fellow-countrymen."

It is to be said in reference to one part of Gerrit Smith's advice, that Southerners were only too ready

to sell their lands at any price or on any terms to whoever would buy. Had the negroes applied the industrial education which they then possessed they might
have become owners of half the territory of the South.
Politicians and theorists who diverted negroid energies
into other channels were unconsciously serving Nature's
purpose, the preservation of the Anglo-Saxon race.
Upon every measure that might thwart that purpose,
Nature seems to smile serenely, turning it to reverse
account.

. . . .

A lively account of the seating of the first negro in
the Congress of the United States was contained in
a letter of February, 1870, from my friend, Miss
Winfield, stopping in Washington. "Revels," she
wrote, "occupies the seat of Jefferson Davis. The
Republicans made as much of the ceremony as possible.
To me it was infinitely sad, and infinitely absurd. We
run everything in the ground in America. Here, away
from the South, where the tragedy of it all is not so
oppressively before me and where I see only the political
clap-trap of the whole African business, I am prone
to lose sight of the graver side and find things simply
funny."

A lively discussion preceded the seating. Senator
Wilson said something very handsome about the "Swan
Song of Slavery" and God's hand in the present state
of affairs; as he was soaring above the impious Democrats, Mr. Casserly, one of the last-named sinners,
bounced up and asked: "I would like to know when
and where the Senator from Massachusetts obtained a
commission to represent the Almighty in the Senate?
I have not heard of such authorisation, and if such
person has been selected for that office, it is only another
illustration of the truism that the ways of Providence

are mysterious and past finding out." Laughter put the "Swan Song" off key; Casserly said something about senators being made now, not by the voice of God and the people, but by the power of the bayonet, when somebody flung back at him, "You use the shelalah in New York!"

"But the ceremony!" Miss Winfield wrote. "Nothing has so impressed me since the ball to Prince Arthur, nor has anything so amused me unless it be the pipe-stem pantaloons our gentlemen wear in imitation of His Royal Highness. Senator Wilson conducted Revels to the Speaker's desk with a fine air that said: 'Massachusetts has done it all!' Vice-President Colfax administered the oath with such unction as you never saw, then shook hands with great warmth with Revels— nobody ever before saw him greet a novitiate so cordially! But then, those others were only white men! With pomp and circumstance the sergeant-at-arms led the hero of the hour to his exalted position. 'Some day,' said my companion, 'history will record this as showing how far the race-madness of a people can go under political spurs.' Republican Senators fell over each other to shake Revels' hand and congratulate him. Poor Mississippi! And Revels is not even a native. General Ames, of Maine, is her other senator. Poor Mississippi!"

A LITTLE PLAIN HISTORY

CHAPTER XXII

A LITTLE PLAIN HISTORY

FOR clearness in what has gone before and what follows, I must write a little plain history.

Many who ought to have known Mr. Lincoln's mind, among these General Sherman, with whom Mr. Lincoln had conversed freely, believed it his purpose to recognise existing State Governments in the South upon their compliance with certain conditions. These governments were given no option; governors calling legislatures for the purpose of expressing submission, were clapped into prison. Thus, these States were without civil State Governments, and under martial law. Some local governments and courts continued in operation subject to military power; military tribunals and Freedmen's Bureaus were established.

Beginning May 29, 1865, with North Carolina, President Johnson reconstructed the South on the plan Mr. Lincoln had approved, appointing for each State a Provisional Governor empowered to call a convention to make a new State Constitution or remodel the old to meet new conditions. His policy was to appoint a citizen known for anti-Secession or Union sentiments, yet holding the faith and respect of his State, as Perry, of South Carolina; Sharkey, of Mississippi; Hamilton, of Texas. The conventions abolished slavery, annulled the secession ordinance, repudiated the Confederate debt, acknowledged the authority of the United States. An election was held for State officers and members of the legislature, voters qualifying as previous to 1861, and by taking the amnesty oath of May 29. Legislatures reënacted the convention's work of annulling secession, abolishing slavery, repudiating debt; and passed civil rights bills giving the negro status as a citizen, but without the franchise, though some leaders advised conferring it in a qualified form; they passed vagrancy laws which the North interpreted as an effort at reënslavement.

Congress met December, 1865; President Johnson announced that all but two of the Southern States had reorganised their governments under the conditions required. Their representatives were in Washington to take their seats. With bitter, angry, contemptuous words, Congress refused to seat them. April 2, 1866, President Johnson proclaimed that in the South "the laws can be sustained by proper civil authority, State and Federal; the people are well and loyally disposed;" military occupation, martial law, military tribunals and the suspension of the writ of *habeas corpus* "are in time of peace, dangerous to public liberty," "incompatible with the rights of the citizen," etc., "and ought not to be sanctioned or allowed; . . .   people who have revolted and been overcome and subdued, must either be dealt with so as to induce them voluntarily to become friends or else they must be held by the absolute military power and devastated . . . which last-named policy is abhorrent to humanity and freedom."

March 2, 1867, Congress passed an act that "Whereas, no legal State Governments exist . . . in the rebel States . . .   said rebel States shall be divided into five military districts." Over each a Federal General was appointed; existing local governments were subject to him; he could reverse their decisions,

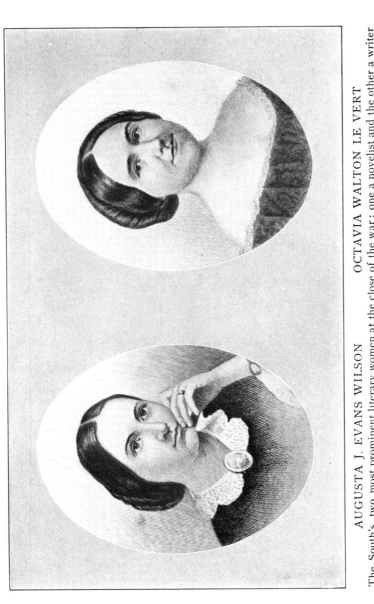

AUGUSTA J. EVANS WILSON   OCTAVIA WALTON LE VERT

The South's two most prominent literary women at the close of the war; one a novelist and the other a writer of translations and books of travel.

remove their officials and install substitutes; some commanders made radical use of power; others, wiser and kindlier, interfered with existing governments only as their position compelled. Upon the commanders Congress imposed the task of reconstructing these already once reconstructed States. Delegates to another convention to frame another Constitution were to be elected, the negroes voting. Of voters the test-oath was required, a provision practically disfranchising Southern whites and disqualifying them for office. Thaddeus Stevens, leader of the party forcing these measures, said of negro suffrage: "If it be a punishment to rebels, they deserve it."

Black and Tan Conventions met in long and costly sessions. That of Mississippi sat over a month before beginning the task for which convened, having passed the time in fixing per diems, mileages, proposing a bonus for negroes dismissed by employers, imposing taxes on anything and everything to meet the expenses of the convention; and badgering General Gillem, Commander of the District. The Blank and Tan Conventions framed constitutions which, with tickets for State and National officers, were submitted to popular vote, negroes, dominated by a few corrupt whites, determining elections. With these constitutions and officials, "carpet-bag rule" came into full power and States were plundered. The sins of these governments have been specified by Northern and Southern authorities in figures of dollars and cents. At first, Southern Unionists and Northern settlers joined issues with the Republican Party. Oppressive taxation, spoliation, and other evils drove all respectable citizens into coalitions opposing this party; these coalitions broke up Radical rule in the Southern States, the last conquest being in Louisiana and South Carolina in 1876. No words can present any adequate picture of the "mongrel" conventions and legislatures, but in the following chapter I try to give some idea of the absurdities of one, which may be taken as type of all.*

---

* See "History of the Last Quarter Century in the United States," by E. B. Andrews; "Reconstruction and the Constitution," by J. W. Burgess; "Destruction and Reconstruction," by Richard Taylor; "History of the American People; Reunion and Nationalism," by Woodrow Wilson; "A Political Crime," by A. M. Gibson; "The Lower South" and "History of the United States since the Civil War," by W. G. Brown; "Essays on the Civil War and Reconstruction" and "Reconstruction, Political and Economic," by W. A. Dunning; articles in "Atlantic Monthly" during 1901; Johns Hopkins University Studies and Columbia University Studies; Walter L. Fleming's "Documents Illustrative of the Reconstruction Period"; besides treating every phase of the subject, these "Documents" give a full bibliography; "A New South View of Reconstruction," Trent, "Sewanee Review," Jan., 1901; and other magazine articles.

THE BLACK AND TAN CONVENTION

CHAPTER XXIII

THE BLACK AND TAN CONVENTION: THE "MID-NIGHT CONSTITUTION"

THE Black and Tan Convention met December 3, 1867, in our venerable and historic Capitol to frame a new constitution for the Old Dominion. In this body were members from New York, Pennsylvania, Ohio, Maine, Vermont, Connecticut, Maryland, District of Columbia, Ireland, Scotland, Nova Scotia, Canada, England; scalawags, or turn-coats, by Southerners most hated of all; twenty-four negroes; and in the total of 105, thirty-five white Virginians, from counties of excess white population, who might be considered representative of the State's culture and intelligence. It was officered by foreigners and negroes; John C. Underwood, of New York, being President.

Capitol Square was garlanded with tables and stands; and the season was one of joy to black and yellow vendors of ginger-cakes, goobers, lemonade, and cheap whiskey. Early ornaments of the Capitol steps were ebony law-makers sporting tall silk hats, gold-headed canes, broadcloth suits, the coat always Prince Albert. Throughout the South this was the uniform of sable dignitaries as soon as emoluments permitted. The funny sayings and doings of negroes, sitting for the first time in legislative halls, were rehearsed in conversation and reported in papers; visitors went to the Capitol as to a monkey or minstrel show. Most of these darkeys, fresh from tobacco lots and corn and cotton fields, were as innocent as babes of any knowledge of reading and writing.

253

They were equally guileless in other directions.
Before the body was organised, an enthusiastic delegate
bounced up to say something, but the Chair nipped him
untimely in the bud: "No motion is in order until
roll is called.   Gentlemen will please remember parliamentary usage."   The member sank limp into his seat,
asking in awed whisper of his neighbour: "Whut in
de worl' is dat?"   Perplexity was great when a member rose to "make an inquiry." "Whut's dat?"
"Whut dat he gwi make?" was whispered round, the
question being settled summarily: "Well, it don' make
no diffunce.   We ain' gwi let him do it nohow case he
ain' no Radicule."   White constituents soon tried to
muzzle black orators.   Word was passed that white
"Radicules" would talk and black members keep silent
and vote as they were bid.   "Shew!   She-ew!"   "Set
down!" "Shut the door!" were household words, the
last ejaculation coming into request when scraps seemed
imminent and members wanted the sergeant-at-arms to
take each other, yet preferred that the public should
not be witness to these little family jars.

Black, white, and yellow pages flew around, waiting
on members; the blacker the dignitary, the whiter the
page he summoned to bring pens, ink, paper, apples,
ginger-cakes,   goober-peas.   And   newspapers.   No
sooner did darkeys observe that whites sent out and
got newspapers than they did likewise; and sat there
reading them upside down.

The gallery of coloured men and women come
to see the show were almost as diverting as the law-
makers.   Great were the flutterings over the seating of
John Morrissey, the "Wild Irishman," mistaken for
his namesake, the New York pugilist.   "Dat ain't de
man dat fit Tom Higher?" "I tell you it am!" "Sho
got muscle!" "He come tuh fit dem Preservatives

over dar." According to the happy darkey knack of
saying the wrong thing in the right place, a significant
version of "Conservative" was thus applied to the
little handful of representative white Virginians.
Great, too, were the flutterings when Governor "Plow-
pint" (so darkeys pronounced Pierpont) paid his visit
of ceremony; and when General Schofield and aide
marched in in war-paint and feathers: the Chair waved
the gavel and the convention rose to its feet to receive
the distinguished guests. The war lord was to pay
another and less welcome visit. The piety of neither
gallery nor convention could be questioned if the fervor
and frequency of "Amens!" interrupting the petitions
of the Chaplain (from Illinois) were an indication;
Dr. Bayne, of Norfolk, so raised his voice above the
rest that his colleagues became concerned lest that sea-
port were claiming for herself more than just proportion of religious zeal.

Curiosity was on tip-toe when motion was made that
a stenographer be appointed. "'Snographer?' What's
dat?" "Maybe it's de pusson whut takes down de
speeches befo' dee's spoken," explains a wise one. The
riddle was partly solved when a spruce, foreign individual of white complexion rose and walked to the
desk, vacated in his favour by a gentleman of colour.
"Dar he! dat's him!" "War's good close, anyhow!"
was pronounced of the new official; then the retired
claimed sympathy: "Whut he done?" "Whut dee
tu'n him out fuh?" "Ain't dee gwi give niggers
nothin'?" "Muzzling" was not yet begun; this occasion for eloquence was not to be ignored by the Honourable Lewis Lindsay, representing Richmond: "Mistah
Presidet, I hopes in dis late hour dat Ole Fuhginny
am imperilated, dat no free-thinkin' man kin suppose
fuh one minute dat we 'sires tuh misrippersint de idee

dat we ain' qualify de sability uh de sternogphy uh dis convention. I hopes, suh, dat we kin den be able tuh superhen' de principles uh de supposition."

Lindsay would always rise to an occasion if his coattails were not pulled too hard. Fortunately, his matchless oration on the mixed school question was not among gems lost to the world: "Mistah Presidet, de real flatform, suh. I'll sw'ar tuh high Heaven. Yes, I'll sw'ar higher dan dat. I'll go down an' de uth shall crumble intuh dus' befo' dee shall amalgamise my rights. 'Bout dis question uh cyarpet-bags. Ef you cyarpet-baggers does go back on us, woes be unto you! You better take yo' cyarpet-bags an' quit, an' de quicker you git up an' git de better. I do not abdicate de supperstition tuh dese strange frien's, lately so-called citizens uh Fuhginny. Ef dee don' gimme my rights, I'll suffer dis country tuh be lak Sarah. I'll suffer desterlation fus! When I blows my horn dee'll hear it! When de big cannons was thund'in, an' de missions uh death was flyin' thu de a'r, dee hollered: 'Come, Mr. Nigguh, come!' an' he done come! I'se here tuh qualify my constituents. I'll sing tuh Rome an' tuh Englan' an' tuh de uttermos' parts uh de uth—" "You must address yourself to the Chair," said that functionary, ready to faint. "All right, suh. I'll not 'sire tuh maintain de House any longer."

That clause against mixed schools was a rock upon which the Radical party split, white members with children voting for separate education of races; most darkeys "didn' want no sech claw in de law"; yet one declared he din't want his "chillun tuh soshate wid rebels an' traitors nohow"; they were "as high above rebels an' traitors ez Heaven 'bove hell!" Lindsay took occasion to wither white "Radicules" with criticism on colour distribution in the gallery. "Whar is de white Radicule members' wives an' chillun?" he asked, waving his hand towards the white section. "When dee comes here dee mos'ly set dar se'ves on dat side de House, whilst I brings mine on dis side," waving towards the black, "irregardless uh how white she is!"

Hodges, of Princess Anne, was an interesting member; wore large, iron-rimmed spectacles and had a solemn, owl-like way of staring through them. One day, he gave the convention the creeps: "Dar's a boy in dis House," he said with awful gravity, "whar better be outen do's. He's done seconded a motion." The House, following his accusing spectacles and finger, fixed its eye upon a shrivelling mulatto youth who had slipped into a member's chair. A coloured brother took the intruder's part. Lindsay threw himself into the breach: "Mistah Presidet, I hears de correspondence dat have passed an' de gemmun obsarves it have been spoken." "I seen him open his mouf an' I seen de words come outen it!" cried Hodges. The usurper, seizing the first instant Hodges turned his head another way, fled for his life, while somebody was making motion "to bring him before the bar."

The convention's thorn in the side was Eustace Gibson, white member from Giles and Pulaski, who had a knack for making the convention see how ridiculous it was. Negroes were famous for rising to "pints of order"; they laughed at themselves one day when two eloquent members became entangled and fell down in a heap in the aisle and Mr. Gibson, gravely rising to a point of order, moved that it was "not parliamentary for two persons to occupy the floor at one time." When questions of per diem arose, sable eloquence flowed like a cataract and Gibson's wit played like lightning over the torrents. Muzzling was difficult. "Mistah

Churman, ef I may be allowed tuh state de perquisi-
tion—" a member would begin and get no further
before a persuasive hand on his coat-tails would reduce
him to silence.   Dr. Bayne's coat-tails resisted force
and appeal.

"I wants $9, I does," he said.   "But den I ain' gwi
be dissatisfied wid $8.50.   Cose, I kin live widout dat
half a dollar ef I choose tuh.   But ef I don' choose
tuh?   Anybody got anything tuh say 'gins dat?   Hey?
Here we is sleepin' 'way f'om home, leavin' our wives
an' our expenses uh bode an' washin'.   Why, whut you
gwi do wid de po' delegate dat ain' got no expenses uh
bode an' washin'?   Tell me dat?   Why, you fo'ce
'em tuh steal, an' make dar constituen's look upon 'em
as po' narrer-minded fellers."   One member murmured
plaintively: "I ain' had no money paid me sence
'lection—"   "Shew!   She-ew!   Shew!" his coat-tails
were almost jerked off.   "You gwi tell suppin you ain'
got no business!"   "Mr. Churman, I adject.   De
line whar's his line, an' dat's de line I contain fuh—"
"Shew!   She-ew!   Set down!"   "What de Bible say
'bout it?" demanded a pious brother.   "De Bible it
say: 'Pay de labour' de higher.'   Who gwi 'spute de
Book?"   "This debate has already cost the State
$400," Mr. Gibson interposed wearily.

They finally agreed to worry along upon $8 a day—
a lower per diem than was claimed, I believe, in any
other State.   When the per diem question bobbed up
again, State funds were running low, but motion for
adjournment died when it was learned that of the
$100,000 in the treasury when the convention began
to sit, $30,000 remained.   Retrenchment was in order,
however, and the "Snographer's" head fell.   He was
impeached for charging $3.33 a page for spider-legs,
which he was not translating into English.   Mr.

Gibson showed that he had been drawing $200 a day
in advance for ten days; had drawn $2,000 for the
month of February, yet had not submitted work for
January. The convention began to negotiate a $90,000
loan on its own note to pay itself to sit longer, when our
war lord came to the front and gave opinion that it
had sat long enough to do what it had been called to
do, and that after ten days per diems must cease.
Another hurrying process was said to be at work.
Reports were abroad that the Ku Klux, having reached
conclusion that Richmond had been neglected, was on
the way. Solid reason for adjournment was death of
the per diem; but for which the convention might have
been sitting yet.

The morning of the last day, the sergeant-at-arms
flung wide the door, announcing General Schofield, who,
entering with Colonels Campbell, Wherry and Mallory,
of his Staff, was escorted to the Speaker's stand. He
came to protest against constitutional clauses disqualifying white Virginians. He said: "You cannot find in
Virginia a full number of men capable of filling office
who can take the oath you have prescribed. County
offices pay limited salary; even a common labourer could
not afford to come from abroad for the purpose of filling
them. I have no hesitation in saying that I do not
believe it possible to inaugurate a government upon that
basis." It was a business man's argument, an appeal to
patriotism and common sense. It failed. When he went
out, they called him "King Schofield," and retained those
clauses in the instrument which they ratified that night
when the hands on the clocks of the Capitol pointed
to twelve and the Midnight Constitution came to birth.

When General Schofield left in 1868 to become Secretary of War, the leading paper said: "General Schofield has been the best of all the military command-

ants placed over the Southern States. He has saved Virginia from much humiliation and distress that other States have suffered." What he did for Virginia, General Gillem, General Hancock and some other commanders tried to do for districts under their command. General Stoneman, who succeeded General Schofield, also fought the test-oath clauses.

When our Committee of Nine went to Washington to protest against those clauses, General Schofield appeared with them before President-elect Grant and one of General Grant's first acts as President was to arrange with Congress that Virginia should have the privilege of voting upon those clauses and the constitution separately, and that other States should have like privileges in regard to similar clauses in their constitutions.

Every American should study the history in detail of each Southern State during the period of which I write. He should acquaint himself at first hand with the attitude of the South when the war closed, and in this connection I particularly refer my reader to the address Governor Allen delivered to the people of Louisiana before going to Mexico, where he died in exile; and to the addresses of Perry, of South Carolina, and Throckmorton, of Texas.* He should compare the character and costs of the first legislatures and conventions assembling and the character and costs of the mongrel bodies succeeding them. He will then take himself in hand and resolve never to follow blindly the leadership of any party, nor attempt to put in practice in another man's home the abstract theories of speculative humanitarians.

---

* Phelps' "Louisiana," Perry's "Provisional Governorship," "Why Solid South," Hilary Herbert.

SECRET SOCIETIES

CHAPTER XXIV.

Secret Societies

Loyal League, White Camelias, White Brotherhood, Pale Faces, Ku Klux

PARENT of all was the Union or Loyal League, whose history may be briefly summarised: Organisation for dignified ends in Philadelphia and New York in 1862-3; extension into the South among white Unionists; formation, 1866, of negro leagues; admission of blacks into "mixed" leagues; rapid withdrawal of native whites and Northern settlers until leagues were composed almost wholly of negroes dominated by a few white political leaders. Churches, halls, schoolhouses, were headquarters where mystic initiation rites, inflammatory speeches, military drills, were in order. The League's professed object was the training of the negro to his duties as a citizen. It made him a terror and forced whites into the formation of counter secret societies for the protection of their firesides.

"To defend and perpetuate freedom and the Constitution, the supremacy of law and the inherent rights of civil and religious freedom, and to accomplish the objects of the organisation, I pledge my life, my fortune and my sacred honour." This was the oath in part. Members were sworn to vote only for candidates endorsed by the league. The ritual appealed to the negro's superstition. The catechism inculcated opposition to the Democratic Party, fealty to the Radical Republican, condemnation of Southern whites as trait-

263

ors. Candidates for membership were conducted to the Council Chamber; here, the Marshal rapped the league alarm, the Sentinel called, "Who comes under our signal?" Answer given, the door opens cautiously, countersign is demanded, and given in the "Four Ls"— the right hand pointing upward with the word, "Liberty," sinking to shoulder level with "Lincoln," dropping to the side with "Loyal," folding to the breast with "League." The Council receives the novitiates standing, as they march in arm in arm, singing, "John Brown's Body" and take positions around the altar before which the President stands in regalia.

The altar is draped with the flag, on which lies an open Bible, the Declaration of Independence, a sword, ballot-box, sickle, and anvil or other toy emblems of industry. At first the room may be in darkness with sounds of groans and clanking chains issuing from corners. The chaplain calls the league to prayer, invoking Divine vengeance on traitors. From a censer (sometimes an old stove vase) upon the altar blue flames, "fires of liberty," leap upward. The Council opens ranks to receive novitiates; joining hands, all circle round the altar, singing, "The Star-Spangled Banner" or other patriotic air. Novitiates lay hands upon the flag, kiss the Bible and swear: "I will do all in my power to elect true and loyal men to all offices of trust and profit." Instructions in pass-words, signals, etc., are given. Secret business is transacted.

Negroes were drilled, armed and marched about. Into League rooms social features were introduced, League literature was read aloud, feminine branches were formed. Leagues furnished a secret service bureau. Coloured servants told what happened in white houses. "My cook and I were children together," a friend tells me. "As we grew up, she made me read and write her letters.   One day, after freedom, she said, 'Miss, put 'tin dar fuh Jeems tuh write me suppin funny nex' time he do write.   We has to have all our letters read out in church an' when dere's anything funny, de folks laugh.'   Soon she ceased asking my services. Through this plan of having letters read out in church leagues and bureaus collected information of happenings in private homes from far and wide.   Such gleanings might be useful in revealing political or self-protective movements among whites, in hunting a man down; or serving his political or social enemy, or would-be robber."

In a South Carolina mansion, Mrs. Vincent and her daughter Lucy lived alone except for a few faithful ex-slaves.   A cabin on the edge of the plantation was rented to Wash, a negro member of the Loyal League, whose organiser was Captain Johnson, commander of a small garrison in a nearby town.   The captain was fond of imposing fines upon whites against whom negroes entered complaint.   There seemed nice adjustment between fines and defendants' available cash.   One day Wash, pushing past Lucy's maid into the Vincent parlor, said to Lucy's mother, "I'se come to cote Miss Lucy." "Leave the house!"   "I ain' gwi leave no such a thing! I'se gwi marry Lucy an' live here wid you." Lucy appeared.   "I'se come to ax you to have me. I'se de ve'y man fuh you to hitch up wid.   Dis here place b'long to me.   You b'long to me."   She whipped out a pistol and covered him.   "Run!   Run for your life!"   He ran.   When he was out of pistol-shot, he turned and yelled: "You d—d white she-cat!   I'll make you know!"   She caught up a musket and fired. Balls whistled past his head; he renewed his flight.

Next morning, as the ladies, pale and miserable, sat at breakfast, a squad of soldiers filed in, took seats,

helped themselves and ordered the butler around.   The
ladies rose and were arrested.   A wagon was at the
door.   "Please, marsters," said black Jerry humbly,
"lemme hitch up de kerridge an' kyar Mistiss an' Miss
Lucy in it.   'Taint fitten fuh 'em to ride in a waggin—
an' wid strange mens."   His request was refused.   The
ladies were arraigned before Captain Johnson on charge
that they had used insulting language to Mr. Washington Singleton Pettigru; and that Lucy, "in defiance of
law and morals and actuated by the devil," had "without provocation" fired on him with intent to kill.   A
fine of $1,000 or six months in jail was imposed.   "I
have not so much money!" cried Mrs. Vincent.   "Jail
may change your mind," said the captain.   They were
committed to a loathsome cell, their determination alone
preventing separation.

Lawyers flocked to their defense; the captain would
hear none.   Towards nightfall the town filled with white
men wearing set faces.   The captain sent for one of the
lawyers.   The lawyer said: "Unless you release those
ladies from the jail at once, no one can tell what may
happen.   But this I believe: you, nor a member of your
garrison, will be alive tomorrow."   They were released;
fine remitted; the captain left in haste.   An officer came
from Columbia to investigate "disorder in the district."
He condemned Johnson's course and tried to reassure
the community.   It came out that Johnson had received
information that Mrs. Vincent held a large, redeemable
note; he had incited Wash to "set up" to Miss Lucy,
urging that by marrying her he would become the plantation's owner: "Call in your best duds and ask her
to marry you.   If she refuses, we will find a way to
punish her."   Wash, it was thought, had fled the
country.   The negro body-servant of Lucy's dead
brother had felt that the duty of avenger devolved upon

him, and in his own way he had slain Wash and covered up the deed.

A white congregation was at worship in a little South Carolina church when negro soldiers filed in and began to take seats beside the ladies. The pastor had just given out his text; he stretched forth his hands and said simply: " Receive the benediction," and dismissed his people. A congregation in another country church was thrown into panic by balls crashing through boards and windows; a girl of fourteen was killed instantly. Black troops swung by, singing. Into a dwelling a squad of blacks marched, bound the owner, a prominent aged citizen, pillaged his house, and then before his eyes, bound his maiden daughter and proceeded to fight among themselves for her possession. " Though," related my informant with sharp realism, " her neck and face had been slobbered over, she stood quietly watching the conflict. At last, the victor came to her, caught her in his arms and started into an adjoining room, when he wavered and fell, she with him; she had driven a knife, of which she had in some way possessed herself, into his heart. The others rushed in and beat her until she, too, was lifeless. There was no redress."

In black belts, where such things happened and where negroes talked openly of killing out white men and taking white women for wives, the whites, few in number, poorly armed and without organisation, scattered over the country and leading themselves in no insignificant proportion the lives of the hunted, faced a desperate situation. Many who chanced to give offense to the ruling faction or who by force of character were considered obstacles to its advancement, found themselves victims of false charges, and, chased by troops, had to leave their families and dwell in swamps or other hiding-places. Compelled by necessity to labour in the field, white gentlemen going to their toil, let down gaps in surrounding fences so that they might fly at a moment's notice, and plowed with saddles on their horses' backs. Northerners, and Southerners who did not live in that day and in black belts, can form no conception of the conditions which gave rise to the white secret societies of which the most widely celebrated is the Ku Klux.

Larger in numbers and wider in distribution was the order of the Knights of the White Camelia, originating in Louisiana; small protective bodies consolidating May 23, 1867, in New Orleans, took this title. Extension over the United States was purposed. Its first article of faith was preservation of the integrity of the white race, and, in government, white supremacy. At the door of the Council Chamber the blindfolded candidate for initiation vowed: "The cause of our race must triumph;" and "We must all be united as are the flowers that grow on one stem." He swore "Never to marry any woman but of the white race." Mongrel legislatures were enacting laws about co-education and intermarriage of races; the whites were a "bewildered people." In Mississippi, the order of the Knights of the White Rose was modelled on the White Camelias; in Alabama, the White Brotherhood and the White League; there were Pale Faces, Union Guards, and others, all of which, with the White Camelias, may be included in the Ku Klux movement.

The Ku Klux originated near Pulaski, Tennessee, 1866, in something akin to a college boys' frolic. Some young ex-Confederates, of good families, finding time heavy on their hands after war's excitement, banded together in a fraternity, with initiation rites, signals, oaths of secrecy, and a name after the Greek, kyklos, a circle, corrupted into kuklos, kuklux, and adding klan. Their "den" was a deserted house near the town. They

From a portrait by Osgood, photographed by Reckling & Sons

MRS. DAVID R. WILLIAMS, OF SOUTH CAROLINA
(Daughter of Governor Miller)

rode at night in queer disguises; at first, without other object than diversion. Their fear and fame spread; branches were formed in other counties and States. In their pranks and negro superstition, whites found weapon for protection and defense. Through troubled neighbourhoods, white horsemen riding in noiseless procession, restored peace by parade and sometimes by sterner measures.

Notices left as warnings on doors or pinned to town-pumps or trees bore cross-bones and skull in red ink, and such inscriptions as:

K   K   K

The Raven Croaked
and we are come to Look on the Moon.
The Lion Tracks the Jackal
the Bear the Wolf
Our Shrouds are Bloody
But the Midnight is Black.

The Serpent and Scorpion are Ready.
Some Shall Weep and Some Shall Pray.
Meet at Skull
For Feast of the Wolf and
Dance of the Muffled Skeletons.

The Death Watch is Set
The Last Hour Cometh.
The Moon is Full.

Burst your cerements asunder
Meet at the Den of the Glow-Worm
The Guilty Shall be Punished.

I have felt defrauded of my rights because I never saw a Ku Klux; my native Virginia seems not to have had any. I have seen them abundantly, however, through the eyes of others. One of my cousins went, during K. K. days, to be bridesmaid to a Georgia cousin. One night, as she and the bride-elect sat on the piazza, there appeared in the circular driveway a white apparition of unearthly height, on a charger in white trappings. Behind came another and another, the horses moving without sound; they passed in silent review before the girls, each spectre saluting. With cold chills running down her spine, Sue asked, *"What* are they?" Her companion laughed. "Haven't you been saying you wanted to see the Ku Klux?" News enough next morning! A white man had been found tied to a tree, and over his head, pinned to the bark, a notice written in his blood, warning him to leave the county at once unless he desired to be carried out by a pathway to— a grave with headstone neatly drawn and showing epitaph with date of death, completed the sentence. He had been flogged and a scratch on his breast showed whence red ink had been drawn. As soon as untied, he left for parts unknown.

Neighbourhood darkeys had eyes big as saucers. Many quarters had been visited. Sable uncles and aunties shook their heads, muttering: "Jedgment Day 'bout tuh come. Gab'el gwi blow his ho'n an' sinners better be a-moanin' an' a-prayin'. Yes, my Lawd!" And: "'Tain't jes one Death a-ridin' on a pale horse! it's tens uv thousan's uv 'em is ridin' now. Sinner, you better go pray!" A few who had been making themselves seriously obnoxious observed terrified silence and improved demeanour. An expert chicken-thief had received a special notice in which skulls and cross-bones and chicken-heads and toes were tastefully intermixed. Others were remembered in art designs of the "All-Seeing Eye," reminder that they were being watched.

The white man was a receiver of stolen goods and instigator of barn-burnings; had been tried for some one of his offenses and committed to the penitentiary, only to be pardoned out by the State Executive. In a North Carolina case of which I heard, a negro firebug who could not be brought to justice through law, though the burning of two barns and a full stable were traced to him, disappeared as if the earth had swallowed him up after a night in which all the darkeys around smelled brimstone and saw fiery-eyed and long-tailed devils at large. People were hard put to it for protection against fire-fiends.

In a South Carolina newspaper a notice appeared from a man who gave warning that he would take vengeance into his own hands if incendiaries fired his property again.

The Ku Klux ruled its members with iron rod. Mr. M., of the order in Tazewell, N. C., was building a cabin on his place for a negro who had come under ban because of evil influence over other negroes; word had been passed that he was to be crowded out. A message reached Mr. M.: " Do not let this negro come on your place. K. K. K.", with due skull and cross-bones accompaniment. To close friends of the order Mr. M. said: "My rights shall not be abridged by the Klan." The cabin was finished on Saturday. Sunday he asked a visitor: "Let's take a stroll in the woods and a look at Henry's cabin." When they came to where the cabin had stood, Mr. M. exclaimed: "Why, what does this mean? Lo and behold, the cabin and everything is torn down and the logs scattered every which-a-way!" "And what's this?" his friend asked, pointing to three new-made graves with pine head-boards, inscribed respectively in epitaph to Mr. M., Henry, and Henry's wife, Mr. M.'s death dated the ensuing Sabbath. On a tiny hillock was a small gallows with grapevine attachment. As one of the order, Mr. M. knew enough to make him ill at ease. Friends begged him to leave the country for a time, and he went. " This may look like tyranny," said my informant, "but Mr. M. ought to have heeded the first message. The order could only do effective work through unfailing execution of sentence."

Between a young lady and the son of a house in which she was a guest, a tender passion arose. He had mysterious absences lasting half or all night, after which his horse would be found in the stables, lathered with foam. The family rallied him on his devotion to a fair demoiselle in an adjoining county. Though under cold treatment from the guest, he gave no other explanation until one day he conducted her and his sister into his room, locked the door, swore them to secrecy, drew from its hiding-place up the chimney a Ku Klux outfit and asked them to make duplicates for a new Klan he was forming. The lovers came to understanding; the girl reproached him: "Why did you not tell me before?" "I did not know if you could keep a secret. I have a public duty to perform; the liberty of my men can be imperiled by a careless word."

The widow of a Ku Klux captain tells me that one night, when her husband was absent on duty in a town where whites were in terror because the negroes were threatening to burn it, her own house was fired. She was in bed, her new-born baby at her side; stealthy steps were heard under her window. Her old black mauma was afraid to go to the window and look out. There was a smell of fire; the mauma ran to the door and shrieked alarm. A shout answered from the cellar, where a faithful negro man-servant was putting out flames. He had let the incendiaries go away thinking their purpose fulfilled. The returning husband, sorely perplexed, said: "I do not see how I can do my duty by my family and the public. I must give up my Klan." "No," she answered. "All have to take turns in leaving their own unprotected. I let you go into the army. Some one must lead, and your men will not follow and obey any one else as they will you." He had been their captain in the Confederate Army.

To a Loyal League jury or magistrate a prisoner on trial had but to give the League signal to secure acquittal. A convicted and sentenced criminal would be pardoned by a Loyal League Governor. Klans took administration of justice into their own hands because courts were ineffective. In a den, regularly established and conducted, a man would be tried by due process before judge and jury, with counsel appointed for defense; evidence would be taken, the case would be argued; the jury would render verdict; the judge would dismiss the case or pronounce sentence. The man on trial might or might not be present. A Ku Klux captain tells me that great effort was made to give fair trials; acquittals were more frequent than convictions. But when the court imposed sentence, sentence was carried out.

In the hill country of South Carolina, a one-armed ex-Confederate, a "poor white," made a scanty living for his large family by hauling. Once, on a lonely road when his load was whiskey, he was surrounded by negro soldiers, who killed him, took possession of the whiskey and drank it. Ring-leaders were arrested and lodged in jail; some were spirited away to Columbia and released; a plan was afoot to free the rest, among them the negro captain who had boasted of his crime, and flouted the whites with their powerlessness to punish him. The prison was surrounded one night by silent, black-robed horsemen on black-draped horses moving without sound; jailer and guards were overpowered; cells entered; prisoners tried—if proceedings interrupted by confessions and cries for mercy can be called trial. Sentences were pronounced. The black-robed, black-masked circle chanted "Dies Iræ, Dies Illa." The town awoke from a night of seeming peace and silence to behold dead bodies swinging from the trees.*

The Stevens Mystery, of Yanceyville, N. C., has never been unravelled; the $5,000 reward which President Grant offered for answer to the question, "Who killed Stevens?" was never won, though skilled detectives tried for it.   Stevens was a scalawag.   He achieved his sobriquet, "Chicken Stevens," through being chased out of his native county for stealing chickens.   One of his adherents, when quite drunk, said before an audience of two thousand negroes: "Stevens stole chickens; that elected him to the Legislature; if he steals turkeys, it will elect him to Congress."   The pleasantry was cheered to the echo.   Stevens was charged with instigating riots and barn-burnings.   He received a mystic warning to leave the country.   He did not go.

One day, while court was in full session, he was seen in the Court Room, in conversation with several people; was seen to leave in amicable company with a citizen who parted with him and went out by the street door, while Stevens entered a county office where clerks were busy; several persons recalled seeing and speaking to him here, but nobody could remember seeing him alive afterwards.   Yet hall and offices were thronged with his adherents.   He was soon missed by the negroes who set a guard around the building.   Next day he was found in the Grand Jury Room, sitting bolt upright, dead, strangled or with his throat cut, I forget which. This room opened on the hall through which a stream of people, white and black, had been passing all day; a negro cabin commanded a view of the window; a negro janitor held the key.

---

* This case was used by Celina E. Means in "Thirty-four Years." The Stevens case is misused by Tourgee in "A Fool's Errand."

Kirke's cut-throats, sent down by Governor Holden, arrested prominent citizens and carried them to Raleigh. No evidence for conviction could ever be found, and they were liberated. Stevens' death has been charged to Ku Klux; also, to his confederates, who, it is said, received instructions from headquarters to "kill off Stevens," meaning politically, which they construed literally. I have been told that one of the slayers is living and that at his death, a true statement will be published showing who killed Stevens and how.

These stories are sufficient to show the good and the evil of Ku Klux; there is public peril in any secret order which attempts to administer justice. Uniform and methods employed to justifiable or excusable ends by one set of people were employed to ends utterly indefensible by another. The Radicals were quick to profit by Ku Klux methods; and much was done under the name and guise that the Klan did not do. Yet, in its own ranks were men reckless, heedless, and wicked, avengers of personal grudges.

The Invisible Empire, as the Klan was called in its organisation in 1867 under the leadership of Grand Wizard, General Nathan Bedford Forrest, and with men like General Dudley Du Bose, of Georgia, for division commanders, had a code that might have served for Arthur's Round Table. Its first object was "To protect the weak, innocent and defenseless from the indignities, wrongs and outrages of the lawless, the violent and the brutal; to relieve the injured and oppressed, to succour the suffering and unfortunate, especially the widows and orphans of Confederate soldiers." Its second: "To protect and defend the Constitution of the United States and all laws passed in conformity thereto." Its third: "To aid and assist in the execution of all constitutional laws, and to pro-

tect the people from unlawful seizure and from trial
except by their peers in conformity to the laws of the
land."

"Unlawful seizure" was practiced in South Carolina,
Arkansas, Louisiana, Mississippi and other States, where
white men would be arrested on blank warrants or no
warrant at all; carried long distances from home, held
for weeks or months; and then, as happened in some
famous cases, be released without ever having been
brought to trial; in other instances, they were beaten;
in others, committed to penitentiaries; in others, it was
as if the earth had swallowed them up—they have never
been heard from. Some agency was surely needed to
effect ends which the Klan named as object of its existence; that the Klan was effective of these ends in great
degree no one conversant with facts will deny, nor will
they deny that "Tom-foolery" and not violence was its
most frequent weapon.

Where Ku Klux rode around, negroes ceased to ven-
ture out after dark. Some told tales of ghastly noc-
turnal visitors who plead for a drink of water, saying,
"Dee ain' had nay drap sence de Yankees killed 'em
at Gettysburg. An' den, suh, when you han' 'em er
gode-full, dee say: 'Kin you let me have de bucket?
I'se jes come f'om hell an' I'se scotchin' in my insides.'
An' den, mun, dat ar hant des drink down dat whole
bucket at a gulp, an' I hyern it sizzlin' down his gullet
des same ez you done flung it on de coals! I ain' gwi
fool longer nothin' lak dat! Some folks say it's white
folks tryin' tuh skeer we-all, but, suh, I b'lieve it's
hants—er Ole Satan one!" Terrible experience it was
when "A hant—or suppin nur—wid er hade mighty
nigh high ez er chimley ud meet a nigger in de road an'
say: 'I come f'om torment (hell) tuh shake han's wid
you!' An' de nigger—he didn' wanter do it, but he

feared tuh 'fuse—he tooken shuck han's wid dat ar hant, an' dat ar han' what he shuck was a skelumton's—de bones fa'r rattle!"

The regular Ku Klux costume was a white gown or sheet, and a tall, conical pasteboard hat; for the horse a white sheet and foot-mufflers. Black gown, mask and trappings, and red ones, were also worn; bones, skulls of men and beasts, with foxfire for eyes, nose and mouth, were expedients. A rubber tube underneath robe or sheet, or a rubber or leather bag, provided for miraculous consumption of water. In negro tales of supernatural appearances, latitude must be allowed for imagination. A Ku Klux captain tells me that one night as he rose up out of a graveyard, one of his negroes passed with a purloined gobbler in possession; he touched the negro on the shoulder. The negro dropped the turkey and flew like mad, and the turkey flew, too. Next morning, the darkey related the experience to his master (omitting the fowl). "How tall was that hant, George?" "Des high ez a tree, Marster! an' de han' it toch my shoulder wid burnt me lak fire. I got mutton-suet on de place." "I was about three feet taller than my natural self that night," says Captain Lea. George wore a plaster on his arm and for some time complained that it was "pa'lised."

Klans and Union Leagues came to an end conjointly when carpet-bag rule was expiring. The Invisible Empire was dissolved formally by order of the Grand Wizard, March, 1869. It had never been a close organisation, and "dens" and counterfeit "dens" continued in existence here and there for awhile, working good and evil. Ku Klux investigations instituted by State authorities and the Federal Government were travesties of justice. Rewards offered for evidence to convict caused innocent men to be hunted down, arrested, imprisoned, and on false accusation and suborned testimony, convicted and committed to State prisons or sent to Sing Sing. The jails of Columbia, at one time, overflowed with the first gentlemen of the state, thrown into filthy cells, charged with all manner of crimes.

The Union League incited to murder and arson, whipped negroes and whites. But I never heard of Union Leaguers being tried for being Union Leaguers as Ku Klux were tried for being Ku Klux. There are no Southerners to contend that the Klan and its measures were justifiable or excusable except on the grounds that the conditions of the times called for them; informed Northerners will concede that the evils of the day justified or excused the Klan's existence. For my part, I believe that this country owes a heavy debt to its noiseless white horsemen, shades of its troubled past.*

---

* See " Documents Illustrative of the Reconstruction Period," by Walter L. Fleming, Professor of History, West Virginia University; also articles in the " Atlantic Monthly."

THE SOUTHERN BALLOT-BOX

CHAPTER XXV

The Southern Ballot-Box

FREE negroes could vote in North Carolina until 1835, when a Constitutional Convention, not without division of sentiment, abolished negroid franchise on the ground that it was an evil. Thereafter, negroes first voted in the South in 1866, when the "Prince of Carpet-Baggers," Henry C. Warmouth, who had been dismissed from the Federal Army, conferred the privilege in a bogus election; he had a charity-box attachment to every ballot-box and a negro dropping a ballot into one had to drop fifty cents into the other, contributions paying Warmouth's expenses as special delegate to Washington, where Congress refused to recognize him. He returned to Louisiana and in two years was governor and in three was worth a quarter of a million dollars and a profitable autograph. "It cost me more," said W. S. Scott, "to get his signature to a bill than to get the bill through the Legislature"—a striking comparison, for to get a bill through this Legislature of which Warmouth said, "there is but one honest man in it," was costly process. Warmouth said of himself, "I don't pretend to be honest, but only as honest as anybody in politics."

Between the attitude of the army and the politicians on the negro question, General Sherman drew this comparison: "We all felt sympathy for the negroes, but of a different kind from that of Mr. Stanton, which was not of pure humanity but of politics. . . . I did not dream that the former slaves would be suddenly,

281

without preparation, manufactured into voters.   . . .
I doubted the wisdom of at once clothing them
with the elective franchise . . . and realised the
national loss in the death of Mr. Lincoln, who had long
pondered over the difficult questions involved."

April Fool's Day, 1870, a crowd clustered around
General Grant in the White House; a stroke of his pen
was to proclaim four millions of people, literate or
illiterate, civilised or uncivilised, ready or unready,
voters. When the soldier had signed the instrument
politicians had prepared for him, the proclamation
announcing that the Fifteenth Amendment had been
added to the Constitution of the United States by the
ratification of twenty-nine, some one begged for the
historic pen, and he silently handed it over. One who
was present relates: "Somebody exclaimed, 'Now
negroes can vote anywhere!', and a venerable old gentleman in the crowd cried out, 'Well, gentlemen, you
will all be d—d sorry for this!' The President's father-
in-law, Dent, Sr., was said to be the speaker." In
Richmond, the Dent family had seen a good deal of
freedmen. Negroes voted in 1867, over two years
prior to this, Congress by arbitrary act vesting them
with a right not conferred by Federal or State Constitutions. They voted for delegates to frame the new
State Constitutions; then on their own right to vote!—
this right forming a plank in said Constitutions.

The Southern ballot-box was the new toy of the Ward
of the Nation; the vexation of housekeepers and farmers, the despair of statesmen, patriots, and honest men
generally. Elections were preceded by political meetings, often incendiary in character, which all one's servants must attend. With election day, every voting
precinct became a picnic-ground, to say no worse.
Negroes went to precincts overnight and camped out.

Morning revealed reinforcements arriving. All sexes
and ages came afoot, in carts, in wagons, as to a fair
or circus. Old women set up tables and spread out
ginger-cakes and set forth buckets of lemonade. One
famous campaign manager had all-night picnics in the
woods, with bonfires, barrels of liquor, darkeys sitting
around drinking, fiddling, playing the banjo, dancing.
The instant polls opened they were marched up and
voted. Negroes almost always voted in companies. A
leader, standing on a box, handed out tickets as they
filed past. All were warned at Loyal Leagues to vote
no ticket other than that given by the leader, usually
a local coloured preacher who could no more read the
ballots he distributed than could the recipients. Fights
were plentiful as ginger-cakes. The all-day picnic
ended only with closing of polls, and not always then,
darkeys hanging around and carrying scrapping and
jollification into the night.

How their white friends would talk and talk the day
before election to butlers, coachmen, hoers and plowers,
on the back porch or at the woodpile or the stables;
and how darkeys would promise, "Yessuh, I gwi vote
lak you say." And how their old masters would return
from the polls next day with heads hung down, and the
young ex-masters would return mad, and saying, "This
country is obliged to go to the devil!"

There were a great many trying phases of the situation. As for example: Conservatives were running
General Eppa Hunton for Congress. Among the
General's coloured friends was an old negro, Julian,
his ward of pity, who had no want that he did not bring
to the General. Election day, he sought the General at
the polls, saying: "Mars Eppie, I want some shingles
fuh my roof." "You voted for me, Julian?" "Naw,
naw, Mars Eppie, I voted de straight Publikin ticket,

suh." He got the shingles. When "Mars Eppie" was elected, Julian came smiling: "Now, Mars Eppie, bein' how as you's goin' to Congress, I 'lowed you mought have a leetle suppin tuh gimme." A party of young lawyers tried to persuade their negro servant to vote with them. "Naw, naw," he said. "De debbul mought git me. Dar ain't but two parties named in de Bible—de Publikins an' Sinners. I gwi vote wid de Publikins."

In everything but politics, the negro still reposed trust in "Ole Marster;" his aches, pains, "mis'ries," family and business troubles, were all for "Ole Marster," not for the carpet-baggers. The latter feared he would take "Ole Marster's" advice when he went to the polls, so they wrought in him hatred and distrust. The negro is not to blame for his political blunders. It would never have occurred to him to ask for the ballot; as greatness upon some, so was the franchise untimely thrust upon him, and he has much to live down that would never have been charged against him else.

"Brownlow's armed cohorts, negroes principally," one of my father's friends wrote from Tennessee in 1867, "surround our polls. All the unlettered blacks go up, voting on questions of State interest which they do not in the least understand, while intelligent, tax-paying whites, who must carry the consequences of their acts, are not allowed to vote. I stayed on my plantation on election day and my negroes went to the polls. So it was all around me—white men at home, darkeys off running the government. Negro women went, too; my wife was her own cook and chambermaid—and butler, for the butler went."

Educated, able, patriotic men, eager to heal the breaches of war, anxious to restore the war-wrecked fortunes of impoverished States, would have to stand idly by, themselves disfranchised, and see their old and faithful negroes marched up to the polls like sheep to the shambles and voted by, and for the personal advancement of, political sharpers who had no solid interest in the State or its people, white or black. It would be no less trying when, instead of this meek, good-natured line, they would find masses of insolent, armed blacks keeping whites from the polls, or receive tragic evidence that ambushed guards were commanding with Winchesters all avenues to the ballot-box. Not only "Secesh" were turned back, but Union men, respectable Republicans, also; as in Big Creek, Missouri, when a citizen who had lost four sons in the Union Army was denied right to vote. "Kill him! kill him!" cried negroes when at Hudson Station, Virginia, a negro cast a Conservative ticket.

"This county," says a Southerner now occupying a prominent place in educational work for the negro, "had about 1,600 negro majority at the time the tissue ballot came into vogue. It was a war measure. The character and actions of the men who rode to power on the negro ballot compelled us to devise means of protection and defense. Even the negroes wanting to vote with us dared not. One of my old servants, who sincerely desired to follow my advice and example in the casting of his ballot, came to me on the eve of election and sadly told me he could not. 'Marster,' he said, 'I been tol' dat I'll be drummed outer de chu'ch ef I votes de Conserv'tive ticket.' A negro preacher said: 'Marse Clay, dee'll take away my license tuh preach ef I votes de white folks' ticket.' I did not cease to reproach myself for inducing one negro to vote with me when I learned that on the death of his child soon afterwards, his people showed no sympathy, gave no help, and that he had to make the coffin and dig the grave himself. I would have gone to his relief had I known, but he was too terrorised to come to me. I did not seek to influence negro votes at the next election; I adopted other means to effect the issue desired."

"If the whites succeed at the polls, they will put you back into slavery. If we succeed, we will have the lands of the whites confiscated and give every one of you forty acres and a mule." This scare and bribe was used in every Southern State; used over and over; negroes only ceased to give credence when after Cleveland's inauguration they found themselves still free. On announcement of Cleveland's election, many negroes, prompt to choose masters, hurried to former owners. The butler of Dr. J. L. M. Curry (administrator of the Peabody Education Fund), appeared in distress before Dr. Curry, pleading that, as he now must belong to some one, Dr. Curry would claim him. An old "mammy" in Mayor Ellyson's family, distracted lest she might be torn from her own white folks and assigned to strangers, put up piteous appeal to her ex-owners.

From the political debauchery of the day, men of the old order shrank appalled. Even when the test-oath qualification was no longer exacted and disabilities were removed, many Southerners would not for a time touch the unclean thing; then they voted as with averted faces, not because they had faith in or respect for the process, but because younger men told them the country's salvation demanded thus much of them. If a respectable man was sent to the Legislature or Congress, he felt called upon to explain or apologise to a stranger who might not understand the circumstances. His relatives hastened to make excuse. "Uncle Ambrose is in the Legislature, but he is honest," Uncle Ambrose's nieces and nephews hurried to tell before the suspicious "Honourable" prefixed to his name brought judgment on a good old man who had intended no harm, but had got into the Legislature by accident rather than by design— who was there, in fact, by reason of circumstances over which he had no control. The few representative men who got into these mixed assemblies had difficulty in making themselves felt. Judge Simonton, of the United States Circuit Court (once President of the Charleston Library Association, Chairman of the Board of School Commissioners, bearer of many civic dignities besides), was member of a reconstruction legislature. He has said: "To get a bill passed, I would have to persuade a negro to present it. It would receive no attention presented by me."

Negroes were carried by droves from one county to another, one State to another, and voted over and over wherever white plurality was feared. Other tricks were to change polling-places suddenly, informing the negroes and not the whites; to scratch names from registration lists and substitute others. Whites would walk miles to a registration place to find it closed; negroes, privately advised, would have registered and gone. When men had little time to give to politics, patriotism was robust if it could devote days to the siege of a Registration Board, trying to catch it in place in spite of itself.

The Southerner's loathing for politics, his despair, his inertia, increased evils. "Let the Yankees have all the niggers they want," he was prone to say. "Let them fill Congress with niggers. The only cure is a good dose!" But with absolute ruin staring him in the face, he woke with a mighty awakening. Taxpayers' Conventions issued "Prayers" to the public, to State Governments, to the Central Government; they raised out of the poverty of the people small sums to send committees to Washington; and these committees were forestalled by Radical State Governments who, with open State Treasuries to draw upon, sent committees ahead, prejudicing the executive ear and closing it to appeal.

The most lasting wrong reconstruction inflicted upon the South was in the inevitable political demoralisation of the white man.   No one could regard the ballot-box as the voice of the people, as a sacred thing.   It was a plaything, a jack-in-the-box for the darkeys, a conjurer's trick that brought drinks, tips and picnics.   It was the carpet-bagger's stepping-stone to power.   The votes of a multitude were for sale.   The votes of a multitude were to be had by trickery.   It was a poor patriot who would not save his State by pay or play. Taxation without representation, again; the tissue ballot—a tiny silken thing—was one of the instruments used for heaving tea—negro plurality—into the deep sea.

"As for me," says a patriot of the period, "I bless the distinguished Virginian who invented the tissue ballot.   It was of more practical utility than his glorious sword.   I am free to say I used many tissue ballots. My old pastor (he was eighty and as true and simple a soul as ever lived) voted I don't know how many at one time, didn't know he was doing it, just took the folded ballot I handed him and dropped it in, didn't want to vote at all."   Others besides this speaker assume that General Mahone invented the tissue ballot, but General Mahone's intimates say he did not, and that to ask who invented the tissue ballot is to ask who struck Billy Patterson.   Democrats waive the honour in favor of Republicans, Republicans in favor of Democrats; nobody wants to wear it as a decoration.   For my part, I think it did hard work and much good work, and quietly what else might have cost shedding of blood.

"We had a trying time," one citizen relates, "when

negroes gained possession of the polls and officered us. Things got simply unendurable; we determined to take our town from under negro rule. One means to that end was the tissue ballot. Dishonest? Will you tell me what honesty there was, what reverence for the ballot-box, in standing idly by and seeing a horde of negroes who could not read the tickets they voted, cram our ballot-boxes with pieces of paper ruinous to us and them? We had to save ourselves by our wits. Some funny things happened. I was down at the precinct on Bolingbrook Street when the count was announced, and heard an old darkey exclaim: ' I knows dat one hunderd an' ninety-seben niggers voted in dis distric', an' dar ain' but th'ee Radicule ballots in de box! I dunno huccum dat. I reckon de Radicule man gin out de wrong ones. I knows he gin me two an' I put bofe uv 'em in de box.' "

Tissue ballots were introduced into South Carolina by a Republican named Butts, who used them against Mackey, another Republican, his rival for Congressional honours; there was no Democratic candidate. Next election Democrats said: " Republicans are using tissue ballots; we must fight the devil with fire." A package arrived one night at a precinct whereof I know. The local Democratic leader said: " I don't like this business." He was told: " The Committee sent them up from the city; they say the other side will use them and that we've got to use them."

According to election law, when ballots polled exceeded registration lists, a blindfolded elector would put his hand in the box and withdraw until ballots and lists tallied. Many tissue ballots could be folded into one and voted as a single ballot; a little judicious agitation after they were in the box would shake them apart. A tissue ballot could be told by its feel; an elector would withdraw as sympathy or purchase ran. Voting over at the precinct mentioned, the box was taken according to regulations into a closed room and opened. Democrats and Republicans had each a manager. The Republican ran his hand into the box and gave it a stir; straightway it became so full it couldn't be shut, ballots falling apart and multiplying themselves. The Republican laughed: "I have heard of self-raising flour. These are self-raising ballots! Butts' own game!" That precinct went Democratic.

So went other precincts. Republicans had failed on tissues. A Congressional Committee, composed of Senators McDonald of Indiana, Randolph of New Jersey, and Teller of Colorado, came down to inquire into elections. Republicans charged tissue ballots on Democrats. But, alas! one of the printers put on the stand testified that the Republicans had ordered many thousand tissue ballots of him, but he had failed to have them on time!

There were other devices. Witness, the story of the Circus and the Voter. "A circus saved us. Each negro registering received a certificate to be presented at the polls. Our people got a circus to come through and made a contract with the managers. The circus let it be known that registration certificates would be accepted instead of admission tickets, or entrance fees, we agreeing to redeem at admission price all certificates turned over to us. The arrangement made everybody happy— none more than the negroes, who got a better picnic than usual and saw a show besides. The circus had tremendous crowds and profited greatly. And one of the most villainous tickets ever foisted upon a people was killed quietly and effectually."

An original scheme was resorted to in the Black Belt of Mississippi in order to carry the day. An important local election was to be held, and the whites felt that they could not afford to lose. But how to keep out the black vote was a serious question. Finally, a bright young fellow suggested a plan. For a week preceding election, he collected, by paying for it, negro hair from barbers serving negroes, and he got butchers to save waste blood from slaughter-pens. The night before the election, committees went out about a mile on every road and path leading to the town, and scattering wool and blood generously, "pawed up the ground" with foot-tracks and human body imprints. Every evidence of furious scuffle was faithfully carried out. The day dawned beautiful and bright, but not a black vote was cast—not a negro was to be seen. Hundreds had quit farm-work to come to vote, but stopped aghast at the appalling signs of such an awful battle, and fled to their homes in prompt and precipitate confusion.

I heard a good man say, with humour and sadness, "I have bought many a negro vote, bought them three for a quarter. To buy was their terms. There was no other way. And we couldn't help ourselves." "There were Federal guards here and they knew just what we were doing," another relates, "knew we were voting our way any and everybody who came up to vote, had seen the Radicals at the same thing and knew just what strait we were in. I voted a dead man knowingly when some one came up and gave his name. I did the same thing unknowingly. I heard one man ask of a small funeral procession, 'Who's dead?' 'Hush!' said his companion, 'It's the man that's just voted!'" "I never voted a dead man," a second manager chimes in, "but I voted a man that was in Europe. His father was right in front of the ballot-box, telling about a letter just received from his son, when up comes somebody in that son's name and votes. The old man was equal to the occasion. 'Why, my dear boy!'—had never seen the other before—'so glad you got back in time to cast your vote!' and off they walked, arms around each other."

"The way we saved our city," one says, "was by buying the Radical manager of the election. We were standing right under the statue of George Washington when we paid the $500 he demanded. These things are all wrong, but there was no other way. Some stood off and kept clean hands. But a thing had to be done, and we did it, not minding the theoretical dirt. The negroes were armed with ballots and bayonets, and the bayonets were at our breasts. Our lands were taxed until we were letting our homes go because we could not pay the taxes, while corrupt officials were waxing fat. We had to take our country from under negro rule any way we could." It was not wounds of war that the Southerner found it hard to forget and forgive, but the humiliation put upon him afterward, and his own enforced self-degradation.

I do not wish to be understood as saying that the Southerner re-won control of local government by only such methods as described; I emphasize the truth that, at times, he did use them and had to use them, because herein was his deep moral wound. He employed better methods as he could; for instance, when every white man would bind himself to persuade one negro to vote with him, to bring this negro to the polls, and protect him from Radical punishment. Also, he availed himself of weak spots in the enemy's armour. Thus in Hancock County, Georgia, in 1870, Judge Linton Stephens challenged voters who had not paid poll-tax, and, when election managers would not heed, had them arrested and confined, while their places were supplied and the election proceeded. The State Constitution, framed by the Radicals themselves, called for this poll-tax—a dollar a head—and its application to "educational purposes." The extravagant Radical regime, falling short of bribing money, remitted the poll-tax in lieu thereof. Judge Stephens caught them. Governor Bullock disapproved his action; United States Marshal Seaford haled him before United States Commissioner Swayze. The Federal Grand Jury ignored the charge against him, and that was the end of it. The Judge had, however, been put to expense, trouble, and loss of time.

THE WHITE CHILD

CHAPTER XXVI

The White Child

Upon the Southern white child of due age for schooling the effects of war fell with cruel force.

The ante-bellum planter kept a tutor or governess or both for his children; his neighbours' children sometimes attended the school which he maintained for his own. Thus, were sons and daughters prepared for academy and college, university, finishing school. Private schools were broken up quite generally by the war. It became quite the custom for the mother or an elder sister to fill the position of instructor in families on big plantations. Such schooling as this was none too plentiful in rural Dixie just after the war. Sisters of age and capacity to teach did not stay in one family forever. Sometimes they got married; though many a beautiful and brilliant girl sacrificed her future for little brothers and sisters dependent upon her for mental food. The great mass of Southern women had, however, to drop books for broomsticks; to turn from pianos and guitars and make music with kettles and pans. Children had to help. With labour entirely disorganised, in the direst poverty and the grasp of such political convulsions as no people before them had ever endured, the hour was strenuous beyond description, and it is no wonder if the claims of children to education were often overlooked, or, in cruel necessity, set aside.

Sometimes neighbours clubbed together and opened an "old field school," paying the teacher out of a common fund subscribed for the purpose; again, a man

297

who could teach went around, drummed up pupils at so much a head, opened a school and took chances on collection of dues.   Many neighbourhoods were too poor for even such expedients; to get bread itself was a struggle to which children must lend labour.   The seventies found few or no rural districts without a quota of half-grown lads and lassies unable to read and write. It was no strange thing to see little white boys driving a plow when they were so small they had to lift their hands high to grasp the handles; or little white girls minding cows, trotting to springs or wells with big buckets to fill, bending over wash-tubs, and working in the crops.

The public school system was not put in operation at once, and if it had been, could not have met conditions of the hour.   Planters lived far apart; roads in some sections long unworked, in others lately plowed by cannons or wagon-trains, were often impassable for teams—if people were so fortunate as to have teams; and much more so for little feet; then, too, the reign of fear was on; highways and by-ways were infested by roving negroes; many were harmless; would, indeed, do a child a kindness; but some were dangerous; the negro, his own master now, was free to get drunk at other times than Christmas and corn-shucking.   An argument against the success of the public as of the "old field" school, lay in the strong spirit of caste animating the high-born Southerner.   It was against his grain to send his children—particularly his daughters—to school with Tom, Dick and Harry; it did not please him for them to make close associates of children in a different walk of life—the children of the "poor white trash." This spirit of exclusiveness marks people of position today, wherever found.   Caste prejudice was almost inoperative, however, having small chance to pick and choose. Gaunt poverty closed the doors of learning against the white child of the South, while Northern munificence was flinging them wide to the black.

Soon as war ended, schools for negroes were organised in all directions with Government funds or funds supplied by Northern charity; and under Northern tutelage—a tutelage contributing to prejudice between the races. These institutions had further the effect of aggravating the labour problem—a problem so desperate for the Southern farmer that he could not turn from it to give his own child a chance for intellectual life.

He was not pleasantly moved by touching stories that went North of class-rooms where middle-age, hoary-head and pickaninny sat on the same bench studying the same page, all consumed with ambition to master the alphabet. It did not enter into these accounts that the plows and hoes of a sacked country had been deserted for the A B C book. He resented the whole tendency of the time, which was to make the negro despise manual labour and elevate book-learning above its just position. Along with these appealing stories did not go pictures of fields where white women and children in harness dragged plows through furrows; the artists did not portray white children in the field wistfully watching black children trooping by to school; had such pictures gone North in the sixties and seventies, some would have said, so bitter was the moment, " Just retribution for the whites," but not the majority. The great-hearted men and women of the North would have come to the rescue.

"There were two reasons for Northern indifference to the education of the Southern white child," an embittered educator says; "natural prejudice against the people with whom they had been at war, and the feeling that the negro had been persecuted—had been 'snatched from his happy home in Africa' (they forgot they had done more than a full share of the snatching) ; brought over here and sold into slavery (they forgot they had done more than a full share of the selling), and thereby stripped of all his brilliant opportunities of life in Africa and the advancement he might else have had; the Southern white man, instead of sending him to college, had made him work in the fields; to even up matters now, the negro must go to college and the white man work in the fields. This was the will of Providence and they its executors."

The two reasons given—undue prejudice against the Southern white and overweening pity for the negro— were the grand disposing cause of Northern indifference to the white child and abnormal sensibility about everything concerning the black. But at the bottom was ignorance of actual conditions here. The one story was put before them, the other was not. It was not to the interests of Freedmen's Bureau agents to let the other be known; and, of course, the business of teachers and missionaries was to make out the strongest case possible in order to draw funds for negro education. The negro's ignorance, in a literary sense, could hardly be exaggerated, nor his poverty; but he was a laborer and an artisan and held recuperative power in his hands.

It was not in the thought of the proud old planter to cry for help; it was his habit to give, not take; he and his wife and children made as little parade as possible of their extremities to their nearest neighbour; such evidences as would not down were laughed over with a humour inherent as their spirit of independence.

In 1867, Mrs. Sarah Hughes said: "Since leaving Kentucky last December, I have travelled many thousand miles in the South; I have seen spreading out before me in sad panorama solitary chimneys, burned buildings, walls of once happy homes, grounds and gardens grown with weeds and briers; groups of sad human faces; gaunt women and children; old, helpless men; young men on crutches, and without arms, sick, sad, heart-broken. Words cannot describe the destitute condition of the orphaned children. It excites my deepest commiseration. The children of the dead soldiers are wandering beggars, hand in hand with want. Except in large cities, there are no schools or homes for the fatherless. An attractive academy has been built near Atlanta by citizens of Northern cities for the children of the freedmen; and it is in a flourishing condition," etc. An editorial in a newspaper of the day reads: "The white children of the South are growing up in pitiful neglect, and we are wrong to permit it."

General Pope, commanding Georgia, Alabama, Mississippi and Florida, wrote General Grant, April 14, 1867: "It may be safely said that the remarkable progress made in the education of these people (the negroes), aided by noble charitable institutions of Northern societies and individuals, finds no parallel in the history of mankind. If the white people exhibit the same indisposition to be educated that they do now, five years will have transferred intelligence and education so far as the masses are concerned, to the coloured people of the district." Does it not seem incredible that an Anglo-Saxon should regard with complacency a situation involving the supreme peril of his race, should consider it cause of congratulation? The state of affairs was urged as argument that the negro was or quickly would be qualified for exercise of the franchise with which he had been invested and his late master deprived.

The Sunday School acquired new interest and significance. I remember one that used to be held in summer under the trees near a blacksmith's shop, in which Webster's Spelling Book divided attention with the New Testament.   The school was gotten up by a planter in kindly effort to do what he could for the poor children in the neighbourhood.   There were grown girls in it who spelled out rather than read Bible verses.   On weekdays, the planter's daughter received and taught free of charge a class of poor whites.   A Georgia friend, who was a little boy at the close of the war, tells me: "The Sunday Schools made more impression upon me than any other institution of the period. There were, I suppose, Sunday Schools in plenty before and during the war, but somehow they seemed a new thing thereafter."

This movement was at once an expression of a revival of religious sentiment (there was a strong revival movement at the time), the desire for social intercourse, and an effort to advance the educational interests of the young, who in countless instances were deprived of ordinary means of instruction.   Hon Henry G. Turner wrote of the conditions of that day : "Cities and great tracts of country were in ashes.   Colleges and schools were silent, teachers without pupils, pupils without teachers.   Even the great charities and asylums were unable to take care of lunatics, the deaf and the blind . . . Repudiation by States of bonds, treasury notes, and other obligations issued during the war reduced to penury thousands of widows and orphans, and many people too old to start life over again." Congress demanded this repudiation at the point of the bayonet.

The South was not unmindful of her orphans; there were early organised efforts such as the land was capable of making; the churches led in many of these.   And there were efforts of a lighter order, such as the bazaar which the Washington and Lee Association held in Norfolk. The Baltimore Society for the Liberal Education of Southern Children was a notable agency. Individual effort was not lacking. Few did more according to their might than Miss Emily V. Mason, who provided for many orphans gravitating towards her at a time when she was paying for her nieces' board with family silver, a spoon or a fork at a time. One of her most sympathetic aides was a Miss Chew, of the North, with whom during the entire war she had maintained an affectionate correspondence begun in times of peace. Illustrative of a rather odd form of relief is this extract from a letter by Mrs. Lee to Miss Mason:

"My dear Miss Em, did I ever write you about a benevolent lady at the North who is anxious to adopt two little 'rebel' children, five or six years old—of a Confederate officer—and she writes General Lee to recommend such a party to her. She wants them of gentle blood. I have no doubt there are a great many to whom such an offer would be acceptable. Do you know of any?" In regard to Baltimore's work, she says: "How can we ever repay our kind friends in Baltimore for all they have done for us?" When the Confederate General, John B. Hood, died, he left a number of very young children in poor circumstances; one of their benefactors was the Federal General McClellan, I have heard.

Doubtless many hands were outstretched from the North in some such manner as is indicated in Mrs. Lee's letter. Thousands would have extended help in every way had the truth been known. What the Southern white child really needed, however, was the removal of an oppressive legislation which was throttling his every chance in life, and a more temperate view on the part of the dominant section of the negro question—a question that was pressing painfully at every point upon his present and future. He had a right to an equal chance in life with the negro.

That quality in Northern people which made them pour out money for the freedmen, would have stirred their sense of justice to the white child had the situation been clear to them. One of the earliest homes for orphans of Confederate soldiers was established at Macon by William H. Appleton, of New York, at the suggestion of his friend, Bishop Beckwith, of Georgia. Vanderbilt and Tulane Universities, the Seney benefactions to Emory and Wesleyan Colleges, and other evidences of awakening interest in the South's white youth, will occur at once to my readers. Chief of all was the Peabody Fund, in which white and black had share. Dr. Sears, of Boston, first administrator, was sharply blamed by William Lloyd Garrison and others because he did not make mixed schools a condition of bestowal upon whites; his critics grew quiet when shown that, under the terms of the gift, such a course would divert the whole fund to white children.

To illustrate white need: Late as 1899, I heard, through Miss Sergeant, Principal of the Girls' High School, Atlanta, of a white school in the Georgia mountains where one short shelf held all the books—one grammar, one arithmetic, one reader, one history, one geography, one spelling-book. Starting at the end of the first bench, a book would pass from hand to hand, each child studying a paragraph. There are schools of scrimped resources now, where young mountaineers make all sorts of sacrifices and trudge barefoot seemingly impossible distances to secure a little learning. Nobody in these communities dreams of calling for outside help and sympathy, and when help is tendered, it must be with the utmost circumspection and delicacy,

Photograph by Vianelli, Italy

MISS EMILY V. MASON

or native pride is wounded and rejects. Appalachia is a region holding big game for people hunting chances to do good.

The various Constitutional Conventions adopted public school systems for their commonwealths. In Virginia, it was not to go into operation until 1871, after which there was to be as rapid extension as possible and full introduction into all counties by 1876. The convention made strenuous efforts, as did that of every other State, to force mixed schools, in which, had they succeeded, the white child's chance of an education would have suffered a new death.

Early text-books used in public schools grated on the Southerner; they were put out by Northern publishing houses and gave views of American history which he thought unjust and untrue. The "Southern Opinion" printed this, August 3, 1867: "In a book circulating in the South as history, this occurs: 'While the people of the North were rejoicing because the war was at an end, President Lincoln, one of the best men in the world, was cruelly murdered in Washington by a young man hired by the Confederates to do the wicked deed.' It calls Lee 'a perjured traitor;' says 'Sherman made a glorious march to the sea;' prints 'Sheridan's Ride' as a school recitation." To comprehension of the Southern mind as it was then and is now in some who remember, it is essential that we get its view of the "Ride" and the "March."

"Have you seen a piece of poetry," a representative Southern woman wrote another in the fall of 1865, "called 'Sheridan's Ride'? If you can get it, do send it to me. I want to see if there isn't some one smart enough to reply to it and give a true version of that descent of armed ruffians upon store-rooms, stables, hen-roosts and ladies' trunks—even tearing the jewelry from their persons—even robbing the poor darkies of their watches and clothing. Not a single Confederate soldier did they encounter. They ought to live in history! My Vermont friend, Lucy Adams, says these things 'are not true, no one at the North believes them, they are impossible.' But we know they are true. I was very anxious to send you Sherman's speech at Cincinnati— perhaps you have seen it—in which he unblushingly sanctions all the outrages committed by his men. I really think some notice ought to be taken of it, but our papers, you see, are all ruined now; and in New York, only 'The News' dares publish anything true. . . . I have found a copy, but this says at 'Lancaster, Ohio'; perhaps he said the same thing twice; it was at the close of a grand speech: 'Soldiers, when we marched through and conquered the country of the rebels, we became owners of all they had; and I don't want you to be troubled in your consciences for taking, while on our great march, the property of the conquered rebels— they had forfeited their right to it.'"

"For several years since the nineties it has been my privilege to serve a large charitable institution here," a Southern friend writes me from a Northern city. "On the Fourth of July I join with as much fervor as anybody in the flag salute, in singing 'America' and all the other patriotic songs, until they come to 'Marching Through Georgia.' That takes the very heart out of me! Sometimes it is all I can do to keep from bursting into tears! Then again I feel as if I must stand up and shout: 'We should not teach any American child to sing that song!' You know the home of one of my dearest friends was in the way of that march; it was burned to the ground and she, a little girl, and her aged grandfather wandered homeless in the night. I wonder, O, I wonder, if our soldiers in the Philippines,

Northern and Southern boys, are giving grounds for any such songs as that! I'd rather we'd lose the fight!"

A cause operating against education of both races remains to be cited. The carpet-bag, scalawag and negroid State Governments made raids on educational funds. In North Carolina, $420,000 in railroad stock belonging to the Educational Fund for the Benefit of Poor Children were sold for $158,000, to be applied in part payment of extended per diems of legislators. These legislators gave at State expense lavish entertainments, and kept a bar and house of prostitution in the Capitol; took trips to New York and gambled away State funds by thousands; war had left a school fund, taxation increased it; but for two years no child, white or black, received benefits. There was money enough for the Governor to raise and equip two regiments, one of negroes, for intimidation of whites, but none for education. Of Georgia's public school fund of $327,000, there seems not to have been a penny left to the State when her million-dollar legislature adjourned in 1870

Louisiana's permanent school fund for parishes vanished with none to tell where it went. Attention was called to its disappearance by W. E. Brown, the negro State Superintendent of Education. When Warmouth, was inaugurated (1868), the treasury held $1,300,500 for free schools. "Bonds representing this," states Hon. B. F. Sage, "the most sacred property of the State, were publicly auctioned June, 1872, to pay warrants issued by Warmouth." Warmouth, like Holden of North Carolina, and Scott and Moses of South Carolina, raised and maintained at State expense a black army. In 1870, the Radical Governor of Florida made desperate efforts to lay hands on the Agricultural Land

Scrip, property of the Agricultural College of that State; to save it from his clutches C. T. Chase, President of Public Instruction, asked President Grant's intervention. A forger, embezzler and thief presided over Mississippi's Department of Education. In every State it was the same story of public moneys wasted by nefarious tricksters who had ridden to power on the negro ballot; the widow and the orphan robbed, the gray-beard and the child; the black man and the white.

SCHOOLMARMS AND OTHERS

CHAPTER XXVII

SCHOOLMARMS AND OTHER NEWCOMERS

MANY good people came down to do good to us and the negroes; we were not always so nice to these as we ought to have been. But very good people can try other very good people sorely sometimes. Besides, some who came in sheep's clothing were not sheep, and gave false ideas of the entire flock.

Terms of professional philanthropy were strange in the Southerner's mouth. It never occurred to the men, women and maidens who visited all the poor, sick, old and feeble negroes in their reach, breaking their night's rest or their hours of recreation or toil without a sense of sacrifice—who gave medicines, food, clothing, any and everything asked for to the blacks and who ministered to them in neighbourly ways innumerable—that they were doing the work of a district or parish visitor. Southerners have been doing these things as a matter of course ever since the negroes were brought to them direct from Africa or by way of New England, making no account of it, never organizing into charitable associations and taking on corresponding tags, raising collections and getting pay for official services; the help a Southerner gave a darkey he took out of his own pocket or larder or off his own back; and that ended the matter till next time.

Yet, here come salaried Northerners with "Educator," "Missionary," or "Philanthropist" marked on their brows, broidered on their sleeves; and as far as credit for work for darkeys goes, "taking the cake" from the Southerner, who had no warm welcome for the avalanche of instructors pouring down upon him with the "I am holier than thou" expression, and bent as much upon teaching him what he ought to have been doing as upon teaching the negro to struggle indecorously for the semblance of a non-existent equality.

Newcomers were upon us like the plagues of Egypt. Deserters from the Federal Army, men dismissed for cause, followers in its wake, political gypsies, bums and toughs. Everybody in New York remarked upon the thinning out of the Bowery and its growing orderliness during enlistments for the Spanish-American War; and everybody knew what became of vanishing trampdom; it joined the army. The Federal Army in the sixties was not without heavy percentage of similar element; and, when, after conquest, it returned North, it left behind much riff-raff. Riff-raffs became politicians and intellectual and spiritual guides to the negroes. From these, and from early, unwise, sometimes vicious Freedmen's Bureau instructors, Southerners got first ideas of Yankee schoolmasters and schoolmarms.

"Yankee schoolmarms" overran the country. Their spirit was often noble and high as far as the black man's elevation—or their idea of it—was concerned; but towards the white South, it was bitter, judicial, unrelenting. Some were saints seeking martyrdom, and finding it; some were fools; some, incendiaries; some, all three rolled into one; some were straight-out business women seeking good-paying jobs; some were educational sharps.

Into the Watkins neighbourhood came three teachers, a male preacher and two women teachers. They went in among the negroes, ate and slept with them, paraded the streets arm-in-arm with them. They were disturbed to perceive that, even among negroes, the familiarity that breeds contempt is not conducive to usefulness; and that they were at a disadvantage in the eyes of the negroes because white people failed to recognise them. Mr. Watkins, master of the manor, was a shining light to all who knew him. In summer his verandah, in winter his dining-room, was crowded Sunday afternoons with negroes on his invitation: "I will be glad to have you come to sing and pray with me." He would read a chapter from the Bible, lead the opening prayer, then call upon some sable saint to lead, himself responding with humble "Amens." White and black would sing together. When the newcomers found how things were, they felt aggrieved that they had not his countenance.

He had seen one of them walk up to his ex-hostler and lay her hand on his coat-collar, while she talked away archly to him. I hardly believe a gentleman of New York, Boston or Chicago would conclude that persons making intimates of his domestic force could desire association with his wife and daughters or expect social attentions from them; I hardly believe he would urge the ladies of his family to call upon these persons. Mr. Watkins did not send his women-kind to see the newcomers; at last, the newcomers took the initiative and came to see his family. His daughters did not appear, but Mrs. Watkins received them politely. They went straight to the point, lodging complaint against the community.

"We had no reason to suppose," said she, quietly, "that you cared for the coöperation of our white people. You acted independently of us; you did not advise with us or show desire for affiliation. We would have been forcing ourselves upon you. I will be as frank as you have been. Had you started this work in a proper spirit and manner, my husband for one would have responded to the limit of his power to any call you made upon him."

They dragged in the social equality business and found her adamant. When they charged "race prejudice," she said promptly: "Were I to visit relatives in Boston, the nice people there would, I doubt not, show me pleasant attentions. Were I to put myself on equal terms with their domestics, I could hardly expect it. The question is not altogether one of race prejudice, but of fitness of things." "But we are missionaries, not social visitors." "We do not feel that you benefit negroes by teaching them presumption and to despise and neglect work and to distrust and hate us."

A garrulous negress was entertaining one of these women with hair-raising accounts of cruelties practiced upon her by whites when, as a slave, she cooked for them. The schoolmarm asked: "Why didn't you black people poison all the whites and get your freedom that way? You're the most patient people on earth or you would have done so." A "mammy" who overheard administered a stinging rebuke: "Dat would ha' been a sin even ef our white folks wuz ez mean ez Sukey Ann been tellin'. Mine wuz good tuh me. Sukey Ann jes been tellin' you dem tales tuh see how she kin wuk you up." Perhaps the school-teacher had not meant to be taken more literally than Sukey Ann deserved to be.

Until freedom, white and black children could hardly be kept apart. Boys ran off fishing and rabbit-hunting together; girls played dolls in the garret of the great house or in a sunny corner of the woodpile. They rarely quarrelled. The black's adoration of the white, the white's desire to be allowed to play with the black, stood in the way of conflict. An early result of the social equality doctrine was war between children of the races. Such strife was confined almost wholly to white and black schools in towns, where black and white children were soon ready to "rock" each other. A spirit of dislike and opposition to blacks, which their elders could hardly understand, having never experienced it, began to take possession of white children. The following story will give some idea of these dawning manifestations of race prejudice:

Negro and white schools were on opposite sides of the street in Petersburg, the former a Freedmen's Bureau institution, the latter a private school taught by a very youthful ex-Confederate, Captain M., who, though he looked like a boy himself, had made, after a brilliant university course, a shining war record. The negro boys, stimulated by the example of their elders who were pushing whites off the sidewalks, and excited by ill-timed discourses by their imported white pedagogue, "sassed" the white boys, contended with them for territory, or aggravated them in some way. A battle ensued, in which the white children ran the black off the street and into their own schoolhouse, the windows of which were damaged by rocks, the only serious mischief resulting from exchange of projectiles.

In short order six Federal soldiers with bayonets fixed marched into the white schoolhouse, where the Captain was presiding over his classes, brought by this time to a proper sense of penitence and due state of order, their preceptor being a military disciplinarian. The invading squad came to capture the children. The Captain indignantly protested, saying he was responsible for his boys; it was sufficient to serve warrant on him, he would answer for them; it was best not to make a mountain out of a mole-hill and convulse the town with a children's quarrel. The sergeant paid him scant courtesy and arrested the children. The Captain donned his old Confederate overcoat, than which he had no other, and marched down the street with his boys to the Provost's office.

The Provost, a soldier and a gentleman, after examining into the case and considering the small culprits, all ranged in a terrified row and not knowing but that they would be blown next moment into Paradise or the other place, asked the Captain if he would guarantee that his children would keep the peace. The Captain assured him that he could and would if the teacher of the coloured boys would keep his charges in bounds, adding that he would have the windows repaired at his expense. The Provost accepted this pledge, and with a withering look at the pedagogic complainant, said to the arresting officer: "Sergeant, I am sorry it was necessary to send six armed men to arrest these little boys." This happened at ten o'clock in the morning. Before ten that night the Provost was removed by orders from Washington. So promptly had complaint been entered against him that he was too lenient to whites, so quickly had it taken effect! Yet his course was far more conservative of the public peace than would have been the court-martialing of the children of prominent citizens of the town, and the stirring-up of white and black parents against each other.

"It's no harm for a hungry coloured man to make a raid on a chicken-coop or corn-pile," thus spoke Carpet-Bagger Crockett in King William County, Virginia, June, 1869, in the Walker-Wells campaign, at a meeting opened with prayer by Rev. Mr. Collins, Northern missionary. Like sentiment was pronounced in almost the same words by a carpet-bag officer of state, a loud advocate of negro education, from the steps of the State House in Florida. Like sentiment was taught in direct and indirect ways by no small number of preceptors in negro schoolhouses.

A South Carolina schoolmarm, after teaching her term out at a fat salary, made of her farewell a "celebration" with songs, recitations, etc.; the scholars passed in procession before the platform, she kissed each, and to each handed a photograph of herself for $1. She carried off a harvest. Various other small ways of levying tribute were practiced by the thoughtless or the unscrupulous; and negroes pilfered to meet demands. Schoolmarms and masters did not always teach for sweet charity's sake. With moving stories some drew heavily upon the purse of the generous North for contributions which were not exactly applied to the negro's relief or profit. In order to attract Northern teachers to Freedmen's schools in Mississippi salaries were paid out of all proportion to their services or to the people's ability to pay. "Examinations for teachers' licenses were not such as to ascertain the real fitness of applicants or conduce to a high standard of scholarship," says James Wilford Garner in "Reconstruction in Mississippi." "They were asked a few oral questions by the superintendent in his private office and the certificate granted as a matter of course."

"While the average pay of the teachers in Northern schools is less than $300 a year, salaries here range from $720 to $1,920," said Governor Alcorn to the Mississippi Legislature in 1871. The old log schoolhouses were torn down by the reconstructionists, new and costly frame and brick ones built; and elegant desks and handsome chairs, "better suited to the academy than the common school," displaced equipments that had been good enough for many a great American's intellectual start in life. In Monroe County, schoolhouses which citizens offered free of charge were rejected and new ones built; teachers' salaries ranged from $50 to $150 a month; schools were multiplied; heavy special taxes were levied. In Lowndes, a special tax of $95,000 over and above the regular tax for education was levied. Taxpayers protested in formal meetings. The Ku Klux whipped several male teachers, one an ex-Confederate, and warned a schoolmarm or two to leave. Expenses came down.

What was true of one Southern State was true of others where costly educational machinery and a peculative system covering "deals" and "jobs" in books, furniture, schoolhouse construction, etc., were imposed. Whippings with which Ku Klux visited a few male teachers and school directors here and there, and warnings to leave served upon others of both sexes, were, in most cases, protests—and the only effective protests impoverished and tax-ridden communities could make—against waste of public funds, peculation, subordination of the teacher's office to that of political emissary, Loyal League organizer, inculcator of social equality doctrines and race hatred. Some whippings were richly deserved by those who got them, some were not; some which were richly deserved were never given. It was not always Ku Klux that gave the whippings, but their foes, footing up sins to their account. It became customary for white communities to assemble and condemn violence, begging their own people to have no part in it.

I have known many instances where Southern clergy maintained friendly relations with schoolmarms, aiding them, operating with them, lending them sympathy, thinking their methods often wrong, but accepting their earnestness and devotion and sacrifice at its full value. I have heard Southerners speak of faculties of certain institutions thus: "Those teachers came down here in the spirit that missionaries go to a foreign land, expect-

ing persecution and ostracism, and prepared to bear it."
I have deeply respected the lovely and exalted character
of some schoolmarms I have personally known, who
suffered keenly the isolation and loneliness of their position; to missionaries and teachers of this type, I have
seen the Southern attitude change as their quality was
learned.   I have seen municipal boards helping with
appropriations Northern workers among negroes, while
these workers were ungraciously charging them with race
prejudice.   And I have seen the attitude of such workers
gradually change towards their white neighbours as they
understood our white and black people better.

Early experiments must have sometimes perplexed the
workers.   Negroes had confused ideas of education.
Thus, a negress who did not know the English alphabet,
went to a teacher in Savannah and demanded to be
taught French right off.   Others simply demanded "to
know how to play de pianner."   The mass were eager
for "book-learnin'."   Southerners who had been trying
to instruct indifferent little negroes beheld with curiosity
this sudden and intense yearning when "education" was
held up as a forbidden fruit of the past.

It has been said that Southern whites would not at
first teach in the negro schools.   "Rebels" were not
invited and would not have been allowed to teach in
Bureau schools.   Reconstructionists preferred naturally
their own ilk.   Certainly all Southerners were not
opposed *per se* to negro schools, for we find some so
influential as the Bishop of Mississippi advising planters
in 1866 to open schools for their negroes.   Leading
journals and some teachers' conventions in 1867 advocated public schools for negroes, with Southern whites
as teachers.   It has been said, too, that Northern
teachers who came to teach the negroes could not secure
board in respectable white families, and, therefore, had

no choice but to board in black.   I think this may be wholly true.   The Southerner firmly believed that the education given the negro was not best for him or the country; and he was deeply prejudiced against the Northern teacher and all his or her ways.   The efforts of Black and Tan assemblies to force mixed schools upon the country was a ground of prejudice against teachers and the schools; so, too, the course of some teachers in trying to compel this.

How could rational people, with the common welfare at heart, advocate mixed schools when such feelings were in evidence at outset as the captain and the pedagogue incident and many similar ones in many States proved existent?   Such feelings were not and are not limited to the South.   Only a year or two ago the mixed school question caused negroes to burn a schoolhouse near Boston.   Many white and black educators at the North seem to agree that it is not best to mix the races there. Prominent negroes are now asserting that it is not best for the negro child to put him in schools with whites; he is cowed as before a superior or he exhibits or excites antipathy.   Besides, he casts a reflection upon his own race in insisting upon this association.

If white Southerners at first objected to teaching negroes, this objection speedily vanished before the argument: "We should teach the negroes ourselves if we do not wish them influenced against us by Yankees," and, "We should keep the money at home," and the all-compelling "I must make a living."   As the carpet-bag governments went out of power, Northern school-teachers lost their jobs and Southern ones got them.   As negroes were prepared, Southern whites appointed negroes to teach negroes, which was what the blacks themselves desired and believed just.

School fights between the races ceased as Southern

whites or Southern negroes came in charge of schools for blacks, and as Northern people who came South to work in charitable enterprises understood conditions better. Those who had unwittingly wrought ill in the first place had usually meant well. The missionary of the sixties and seventies was not as wise as the missionary of today, who knows that he must study a people before he undertakes to teach and reform them, and that it is all in the day's work for him not to run counter heedlessly to established social usages or to try to uproot instantly and with violence customs centuries old. A reckless reformer may tear up more good things in a few weeks than he can replant, or substitute with better, in a lifetime.

THE CARPET-BAGGER

CHAPTER XXVIII

The Carpet-Bagger

THE test-oath was invitation to the carpet-bagger. The statements of Generals Schofield and Stoneman show how difficult it was to find in the South men capable of filling office who could swear they had "never given aid or comfort" to a Confederate. Few or no decent people could do it. In the summer of 1865, President Johnson instructed provisional governors to fill Federal offices of mail, revenue and customs service with men from other States, if proper resident citizens—that is, men who could take the test-oath—could not be found. Office-seekers from afar swarmed as bees to a hive.

The carpet-bagger was the all-important figure in Dixie after the war; he was lord of our domain; he bred discord between races, kept up war between sections, created riots and published the tale of them, laying all blame on whites. Neither he nor his running mate the scalawag or turn-coat Southerner, was received socially. Sentence fell harder upon the latter when old friends insulted him and the speaker on the hustings could say of him no word too bitter. His family suffered with him. The wife of the native Radical Governor of one Southern State said when her punishment was over: "The saddest years of my life were spent in the Executive Mansion. In a city where I had been beloved, none of my old friends, none of the best people, called on me." In times of great poverty, temptations were great; men, after once starting in politics, were drawn further than they had dreamed possible. Again, men with State welfare at heart, urged compromises as the only way to secure benefits to the State; on being irritated, urged unwisely; on being ostracized, out-Heroded Herod. Our foreign office-holders were not all bad men or corrupt. We will not call these carpet-baggers. The carpet-bagger has been defined: "A Yankee, in a linen duster and with a carpet-bag, appearing suddenly on a political platform in the South, and calling upon the negroes to vote him into office." I give portraits of two types.

In the wake of Sherman's Army which passed through Brunswick, Virginia, toward Washington, came and stopped two white men, Lewis and McGiffen. They were desperadoes and outlaws, carried Winchester rifles and were fine shots; said they hailed from Maine; to intimates, the leader, Lewis, boasted that he had killed his step-father and escaped the hangman by playing crazy. They leased the farm of a "poor white," Mrs. Parrish. Lewis opened a negro school and a bank, issuing script for sums from twenty-five cents to five dollars; he organized a Loyal League, collecting the fees and dues therefrom. He armed and drilled negroes and marched them around to the alarm of the people. Court House records show lawful efforts of whites at self-protection. August 8, 1868, Lewis was tried before William Lett, J. P., for inciting negroes to insurrection, when, under pretense of preaching the Gospel to them, he convened them at Parrish's. He was sentenced to the penitentiary for seven years. The State was under military rule, and the decision of the civil court was set aside and Lewis left at large. John Drummond was a witness against Lewis.

Lewis soon had the negroes well organised; he established a system of signal stations from the North Carolina line to Nottoway and Dinwiddie. By the firing of signal guns, they would receive notice to congregate. Suddenly, all hands on a man's plantation would stop work and say: "Got orders, suh, tuh go tuh de Cote House." And all at once roads would be lined with negroes from every direction bound for the Court House. In a few hours the little town would fill with darkeys, a thousand or more on the streets. They would collect thus from time to time, and hold secret or public political meetings, Lewis, McGiffen and other speakers working them up to a state of great excitement.

At one meeting, a riot occurred in which several men were killed or wounded. Mr. Freeman Jones, later Sheriff of the County, gave me a version of it. He said: "Meade Bernard (afterwards Judge Bernard) and Sidney Jones were set upon. Negroes knocked the last-named gentleman senseless, continuing chastisement until he was rescued by the Freedmen's Bureau officer. When Bernard was attacked, his old coloured nurse, Aunt Sally Bland, rushed into the melée, crying: 'Save my chile! save my chile!' Sticks were raining blows on his head when she interfered, pleading with them to desist until they stopped. These white men had shown all their lives, only kindness to negroes. When set upon they were doing nothing to give offense, they were simply listening to the speeches. One negro, observing their presence, cried out: 'Kill the d—d white scoundrels!' Others took up the cry.

"The whites, a little handful, retreated towards the village, followed by at least a thousand negroes, yelling intention to sack and fire the town. The road passed through a very narrow lane into Main Street. Here they were blocked and confronted by Mr. L. G. Wall, carrier of the United States Mail, who, as a Government official, halted them, telling them he had right of way and that they were obstructing Government service;

he ordered them to move back and make room; they would not; he drew his pistol and fired five or six times. I believe every shot took effect. Several negroes were desperately wounded. The mob retired and Wall went on. In the suburbs the negroes held an angry meeting, but they had got enough of mob violence." Which was fortunate. The normal white male population of the village did not exceed forty or fifty. White men went to the polls soon after not knowing what to expect, and found everything quiet. Negroes had come, voted early and gone. They had learned a salutary lesson.

Lewis claimed to be an officer duly commissioned, and went about making arrests, selecting some prominent men. One of his victims was William Lett, an old and wealthy citizen, and the justice before whom Lewis had been brought to trial. A complaint by Mr. Lett's cook was the ostensible ground of Lewis' call upon Mr. Lett; the real purpose was robbery. The outlaws had seduced into their service John Parrish, an unlettered boy who liked to hunt with them, and who, boy-like, was pleased with their daredevil ways. He composed the third in the "team" that went around arresting people. He recently gave me the next chapter in the Lewis story.

"I was jes a little boy an' I done what I was ordered to. I was goin' out sqir'l huntin', an' I see Dr. Lewis, an' he had a paper in his han', an' he say: 'Johnny, I want you to go with me this evenin'.' I says: 'I wants to go squir'l huntin'.' He says: 'I summons you to go wid me to serve a warrant on Mr. Lett.' An' I lef' my dawgs at my sister's an' I taken my little dollar-an'-a-half gun along. He says: 'Johnny, people tell me this ole man is mighty hot-headed. If he comes out of his house an' I tell you to shoot, shoot.' Dr. Lewis called Mr. Lett out to de gate, an' read de warrant to him. An' Mr. Lett said he wouldn' be arrested by him, an' Dr. Lewis grabbed at his coat collar, an' Mr. Lett broke loose, an' hollered for somebody to han' him his gun outer de house. An' he went into de house an' got a gun an' shot Lewis, an' Lewis stepped behin' de gate-pos', an' he called to me: 'D— him! where is he?' An' I said: 'Jes behin' de winder.' An' I stepped behin' de corner, an' Dr. Lewis called me, an' I stepped out, an' I thought I see a gun or pistol pointin' my way f'om de winder, an' I thought I heard Lewis say 'Shoot!' an' I shot. It warn't nothin' but a little bitter dollar-an'-a-half bird gun. But dem shot went through de weather-bo'din'. I heard Mr. Lett's gun when it fell an' I heard him when he fell. Lewis was standin' behin' de gate-pos'. The cook-woman hollered: 'Here he is! here he is, going out at de back door!' And thar was a little chicken-house. An' Lett shot Lewis with bird-shot."

Mr. Freeman Jones summed it up simply thus: "When the gang came to capture Mr. Lett, the old man attempted a defense, ordering them off his place, and barricading himself behind the nearest thing at hand, which happened to be a chicken-coop. Lewis shot and nearly killed him; the old man lingered some time between life and death." Mr. Lett, it seems, was shot by both. "They toted Lewis away," concludes Parrish, "to de house of a feller named Carroll, an' he stayed thar. They sent for de military soldiers an' they came, an' I stated de case well as I could, an' they discharged me." Lewis was tried in the civil court, sentenced to a term in the penitentiary, was carried by the sheriff to that institution and pardoned next day by Governor Wells, military appointee of General Schofield; he got back to the county almost as soon as the sheriff.

The people became more and more incensed at
repeated outrages. Dr. Powell, whose assassination
was attempted, tells me that the immediate cause of the
final tragedies was that Lewis ordered Carroll to
leave home. John B. Drummond, volunteering, was
appointed special constable to arrest Lewis. He met
Lewis and his gang in a turn of the road and halted
them, telling Lewis he had a warrant for him. Lewis
fired, killing him instantly. The temper of the public
was now such that Lewis and McGiffen fled the State,
enticing Parrish along. They sought asylum in North
Carolina and sent Parrish back for some property. A
reward was offered for them. In a little one-horse
wagon which Parrish brought with Lewis' pony, they
travelled by night to Charleston, South Carolina. Here
Lewis opened a school and Parrish hired himself out.
They staid there two years. McGiffen married again.
He had taken his little child from his Brunswick wife;
now he concluded to carry it back to her.

"I went with him," says Parrish. "We come near
a village an' we stopped at a man's house. He mis-
trusted something wrong." (Naturally! Dr. Powell
says he saw his guests moulding bullets, ordered them
out, and they defied him, declaring they would spend
the night.) "He sent out an' got two men an' they
come in thar wid thar guns an' staid all night. When
we got up in de little town nex' mornin', thar come out
twenty men wid guns in thar han's, an' de Mayor he
was thar, an' McGiffen tole 'em to stop; an' they
stopped. He tole 'em thar couldn' but one or two come
near. They suspicioned about our having the little chile
along. You see, thar was trouble 'bout dat time 'bout
children bein' kidnapped an' carried off to de Dismal
Swamp. I see ten or thirteen men on de railroad, an'
they comin' pretty close. McGiffen hollered out for

'em to stop, or he would certainly shoot. An' they stopped. Then somebody hollered 'Close up!'
"I had de little boy in my lap. To keep him f'om gittin' hurt, I set him down by de roadside. McGiffen an' me had been ridin' one horse, takin' turns, de one ridin' carryin' de baby. A feller kep' comin' closer, an' I hollered, 'Stop, sir, or I'm goin' to shoot you!' an' I shot him him in de han'. He kep' hollerin' I had killed him, an' de other fellers sorter scattered, an' that give McGiffen chance to git away. An' I got away. Had to leave de baby settin' thar side de road. An' they follered me up an' got me, an' they got McGiffen. After they captured us, they heard about thar bein' three strangers down whar we had come f'om, an' they suspicioned we was de men dat had been advertised for because of de trouble in Brunswick. An' they sent after Lewis. It was one night. He had unbuckled his pistols an' laid 'em on his bureau, an' some visitors come to see him; an' he was talkin' to them, an' eight or ten men stepped up behin' him an' that's how they got him. An' they had de three of us. An' Governor Walker sent Bill Knox, de detective, an' Dr. Powell he was sent to identify us. An' we were carried to Richmond, an' then we were carried to Greensville, an' we were tried. De little boy was sent back to his mother. I was sent to de penitentiary for eight years, but I got out sooner for good behaviour; an' I learned a good trade thar. But I don't think they ought to ha' sent me, because I was jes a boy an' I done what I was ordered to do when I shot Mr. Lett—that what's they sent me for. An' de military soldiers had said I warn't to blame. Lewis he played off crazy like he done befo', an' they sent him to de asylum, an' he escaped like he done befo'. De superintendent was a member of de Loyal League. An' McGiffen was hung, an' I never thought he ought to ha'

been hung." Military rule was at an end and Virginia was back in the Union when the fugitives were captured.

There was another flutter of the public pulse in this county when, perhaps, the one thing that saved the day was the confidence of the negroes in Sheriff Jones. Court was in session when several people ran into the court room, shouting: "Sheriff! Sheriff! they are killing the negroes out here!" Sheriff Jones ran out and saw a crowd of five or six hundred negroes, some drunk, in the street, and in their midst two drunken white men. A few other whites were lined up against a fence, their hands on their pistols, not knowing what a moment would bring forth. People cried out: "Don't go into that crowd, Sheriff! You're sure to get shot!" "Here, boys!" called the Sheriff to some negroes he knew, "take me into that crowd." Two negroes made a platform of their hands, and on this the officer was carried into the mob, his bearers shouting as they went: "Lis'n to de sheriff! Hear what de sheriff say!" He called on everybody to keep the peace, had no trouble in restoring quiet, and arrested everybody he thought ought to be arrested. "But our coloured people soon became orderly and well-behaved after the carpet-baggers left us," says Sheriff Jones.

In several Southern States at this period, such a termination to the last incident would have been almost impossible. Here, the officer was a representative native white; he understood the people and all elements trusted him; the interest of the community was his own. With an outsider in position, the case must have been quite different; the situation more difficult and the sequel probably tragic, even conceding to the officer sincere desire to prevent trouble, a disposition carpet-baggers did not usually betray. Riots in the South were breath of life to carpet-bag governments. July 25, 1870, Governor Smith, Republican, of Alabama, said over his signature, of a politician who had criticised him for not calling out negro militia to intimidate whites: "My candid opinion is that Sibley does not want the law executed, because that would put down crime, and crime is his life's blood. He would like very much to have a Ku Klux outrage every week, to assist him in keeping up strife between whites and blacks, that he might be more certain of the latter's votes. He would like to have a few coloured men killed weekly to furnish semblance of truth to Senator Spencer's libels against the State."

In quiet country places where people did not live close enough for mutual sympathy and protection, the heavy hand was often most acutely felt. Such neighbourhoods were shortened, too, of ways to make oppression known at headquarters; it cost time and money to send committees to Washington, and influence to secure a hearing. When troubles accumulated, some hitherto peaceful neighbourhood, hamlet or town would suddenly find unenviable fame thrust upon it. There was, for instance, the Colfax Riot, Grant Parish, Louisiana, where sixty-three lives were lost. Two tickets had been announced elected. Governor Kellogg, after his manner of encouraging race wars, said, "Heaven bless you, my children!" to both, commissioned the two sets of officers, and told them to "fight it out," which they did with the result given and the destruction of the Court House by fire. Negroes had been called in, drilled, armed and taught how to make cannon out of gas-pipe.

And now for the portrait of a carpet-bagger of whom all who knew him said: "He is the most brilliant man I ever met." I can only give fictitious names. Otherwise, innocent people might be wounded.

A young lieutenant, discharged from the Federal Army, located in Roxmere, a college town. His first move was to pose as a friend to whites, and to insinuate himself into nice families. When there was trouble— which he stirred up—between the races, he would assume the authority—none was given him by the Government—to interfere and settle it. For instance, he would undertake to punish negroes for impertinence. He began to practise law. He married a young lady of the section, of means but not a daughter of the aristocracy; she had owned many negroes; he made out a list, which he kept, expecting the Government to pay for them. He said his father was an English clergyman, and he spoke beautifully and feelingly of his early life. When it became apparent that the negro was to be made a voter, Yankee Landon (as Roxmere called him), changed tactics; he organized Union Leagues, drilled negroes and made incendiary speeches.

One day, Judge Mortimer, hurrying into the Court House, said: "Yankee Landon is on the hustings making a damnable speech to the negroes!" Landon's voice could be heard and the growls of his audience. The whites caught these words ringing clear and distinct: "We will depopulate this whole country of whites. We have got to do it with fire and sword!" Some one else, much excited, came in, saying, "A movement's on foot to lynch Landon." The old Judge hastened up the street. He met some stern-faced men and stopped them. "We know what Landon is saying," they told him, "and we intend to swing him." He tried to turn them from their purpose, but they declared: "There is no sense in waiting until that scoundrel has incited the negroes to massacre us." Another cool-headed jurist sought to stay them. "Do you realise what you are going to do?" he asked. "We are going to hang Yankee Landon." "That will not do!" "We've got to do it. The safety of our homes demands it." The combined efforts of conservative men stayed summary action. Landon got wind of what was brewing, and for a time was more prudent of tongue; then, concluding that the people were afraid to molest him, broke forth anew.

In the Union League season, there was a tremendous negro crowd on the streets; whites had hardly room to walk; they got very sick of it all. Roxmere's college men decided to take a hand and disposed themselves for action. "Don't give way one inch to these old slavocrats!" Landon was shouting from a goods-box, when they sent Cobb Preston out. Cobb, in a dressing-gown trailing four feet, walked into the crowd. He placed a chip on his hat. "Will some one step on my dressing-gown or knock this chip off?" he asked loudly and suavely. Everybody gave him room to trail around in. Nobody stepped near the tail of that dressing-gown! No hand approached within yards of that chip! Any sudden turn he made was a signal for fresh scatterings which left wide swath for his processional. Did he flirt around quickly, calling on somebody to step on his gown or knock off his chip, darkeys fell over each other getting out of his way. Landon understood. He knew if the college boys succeeded in starting a row he would be killed. After that, whites could use sidewalks without being shoved off. Landon was adept in pocketing insults. Men cast fearful epithets in his teeth. "I have heard Vance McGregor call him a dog, a thief—and he would take it," says a lawyer who practised in the same courts with him.

He and a negro "represented" the county in the Black and Tan Convention. He came back a much richer man. Nobody visited his family. One day,

Rev. Dr. Godfrey encountered on the street a little girl, who asked: "Have you seen my papa?" "Who is your papa, little one?" "Yan-kee Landon!" she piped. He led her to the corner and tenderly directed her way. Rev. Dr. Godfrey did not hesitate to arraign Landon from his pulpit. One Sunday, when Landon and his wife sat in the front pew, and the conversion of Zaccheus happened to be his subject, the congregation was electrified to hear him draw comparisons between Zaccheus and carpet-baggers, to the great disparagement of the latter. He spoke of the fine horses, wines and cigars of modern Mr. Zaccheus, and of Mrs. Zaccheus' silks and jewels. "Zaccheus of old could say," he cried, "'If I have taken anything from any man, I restore him fourfold! Not so Zaccheus of today," and he looked straight in Landon's face. Landon's contribution was equal to that of all the other people in the church put together. The Landons gave up their pew, and attended worship elsewhere, but presently came back to Dr. Godfrey's, the "swell" church. He spared them not. But he went to see Landon's wife and sent his wife to see her. "Mrs. Landon is a young mother, my dear," he said, "you should go."

Twice Landon represented the district in the Legislature, first in the House, then in the Senate. While Commonwealth's Attorney, he made a startling record; he ran a gambling saloon, a thing it was his sworn duty to ferret out and prosecute. Hazard, chuck-a-luck and other games of chance were played there. It was a new departure in a quiet, religious town; the college boys were drawn in. Judge Mortimer's little son trotted into it at the heels of a grown-up relative, and going home innocently told his father about "the funny little things they play with; when they win, they take the money; when Mr. Landon wins, he takes it." In

modern parlance, the old judge "pulled" that saloon
next evening, bagging thirty of the nicest young fellows
in the community.   They were indicted for gambling
and Landon for keeping a gambling saloon.   Landon
prosecuted everybody but himself, convicting the last
one; then resigned, and McGregor conducted the case
against him.   His sentence was $100 fine and four
months in jail.   While in jail he studied law and
acquired more knowledge of it than in all the years of
his freedom; he had known little about it, shrewdness
and sharpness standing him in place of knowledge.   A
hog-drover was put in the cell with him one night and
he won $150 out of him at poker.   The Governor par-
doned him out at three months.   He ran for Commonwealth's Attorney and was elected; he made an able
and efficient officer.   He would prosecute unswerv-
ingly his closest friend.   His political ally built the new
jail, Landon getting him the job.   "I wonder who will
be the first fool to get in here," he said to Landon.
He was; Landon convicted him.   Men who despised
his principles admired his intellect.   In court-room
repartee he could take the wind out of McGregor's
sails, and McGregor was past master in the art.   He
was able, brilliant, unscrupulous, without a moral conscience, but with a keen intellectual one.   He was no
spendthrift in rascality, economised in employment of
evil means, using them no farther than self-interest
required.   He could show kindness gracefully; ceased
to stir up negroes when it ceased to pay.   A neighbour
who was civil when others snubbed him, went to Washington when Landon, at his zenith, was there in a high
Government position, and opened a law office.   Landon
threw work his way.

One day McGregor, Governor of his State, got a
letter from Landon; a great foreign dignitary, visiting

this country, was to be entertained at Landon's palace; would McGregor lend the old State flag to be draped with the Stars and Stripes and the foreigner's flag over the end of the room where Landon and the dignitary would stand while receiving? McGregor sent it. In the little town in which he tricked and won his way, court was never paid to Landon on account of his wealth and power, but people gradually came to treat him less coldly as he changed with the times. Reconstruction tried men's souls and morals; a man who went to pieces under temptation sometimes came out a gentleman, or something like it, when temptation was over. Landon won favors of all parties. Cleveland gave him a position. A committee waited upon Mr. McKinley, asking appointment for Landon. Mr. McKinley demurred: "I understand that in the South, Mr. Landon is not considered a gentleman." "We promised him this if he would render the party the service which he has rendered." The President had to yield. Roosevelt, who came to the Presidency without election, turned this man down with a firm hand.

THE DEVIL ON THE SANTEE

CHAPTER XXIX

THE DEVIL ON THE SANTEE

(A Rice-Planter's Story)

BETWEEN the plantation where harmony and industry still prevailed and that in which was complete upheaval of the old order, were thousands showing its disintegration in intermediate grades. On the James River, in Virginia, and on waterways in rice and cotton lands up which Federal gunboats steamed, and on the Sea Islands, plantations innumerable furnished parallel cases to that set forth in the following narrative, which I had from Captain Thomas Pinckney, of Charleston, South Carolina. When Captain Pinckney went down to El Dorado, his plantation on the Santee, in 1866, he found things "in a shocking condition and the very devil to pay." The night before reaching his place he spent at the house of an English neighbour, who had had oversight of his property. He received this report:

"Your negroes sacked your house, stripped it of furniture, bric-a-brac, heirlooms, and divided these among themselves. They got it into their heads that the property of whites belongs to them; and went about taking possession with utmost determination and insolence. Nearly all houses here have been served the same way. I sent for a United States officer and he made them restore furniture—the larger pieces, which are much damaged. Small things—mementoes which you value as much or more—are gone for good. There was but one thing they did not remove—the mirror in the

341

wall." *   "The negroes have been dancing shin-digs in
your house," the Englishman went on.   "They have
apportioned your land out among themselves."

Yet the Captain was not fully prepared for the deso-
lation that met his eyes when he went home next day.
Ever before, he had been met with glad greetings.
Now, instead of a merry crowd of darkeys rushing out
with shouts of "Howdy do, Marster!"   "Howdy do,
Boss!", silence reigned and no soul bade him welcome
as he made his way to his own door.   Within the house
one faithful servant raised her voice in lonely and
pathetic notes of joy.   "Where are the others?" he
asked.   "Where are the men?"   "Don' know, Marster."   "Tell any you can find to come here."   She
returned from search to say none could be found.
Dinner-hour passed.   The men kept themselves invisible.   He said to her: "I will be back tomorrow. Tell
the men I must see every one of them then."   He
returned armed.   It was his known custom as a hunts-
man to carry a gun; hence he could carry one now
without betraying distrust.   "Indeed, I felt no fear
or distrust," he says; "these were my own servants,
between whom and myself the kindest feelings had
always existed.   They had been carefully and conscien-
tiously trained by my parents; I had grown up with
some of them.   They had been glad to see me from
the time that, as a little boy, I accompanied my mother
when she made Saturday afternoon rounds of the quarters, carrying a bowl of sugar, and followed by her little

---

* This mirror had been built into the wall when the house was
erected by the Captain's grandfather, General Thomas Pinckney, of
the Revolution, soon after his return from the Court of St. James,
where he served as United States Minister by Washington's appointment.   It was Charles Cotesworth, brother of this Thomas, who
threw down the gage to France in the famous words: "The United
States has millions for defense but not one cent for tribute!'"

handmaidens bearing other things coloured people liked. At every cabin that she found swept and cleaned, she left a present as an encouragement to tidiness. I could not realise a need of going protected among my own people, whom I could only remember as respectful, happy and affectionate."

He bade the woman summon the men, and he waited under the trees. They came, sullen, reluctant, evincing no trace of old-time cordiality; addressed him as "you" or "Cap'n"; were defiant; brought their guns. "Men," he said, "I know you are free. I do not wish to interfere with your freedom. But I want my old hands to work my lands for me. I will pay you wages." They were silent. "I want you to put my place in order, and make it as fruitful as it used to be, when it supported us all in peace and plenty. I recognise your right to go elsewhere and work for some one else, but I want you to work for me and I will on my part do all I can for you."

They made answer short and quick: "O yes, we gwi wuk! we gwi wuk all right. De Union Ginruls dee done tell us tuh come back f'om follin arter de army an' dig greenbacks outer de sod. We gwi wuk. We gwi wuk fuh ourse'ves. We ain' gwi wuk fuh no white man." "Where will you go?" "We ain' gwine nowhar. We gwi wuk right here on de lan' whar we wuz bo'n an' whar belongs tuh us." Some had not been born on the land, but had been purchased during the war by Captain Pinckney, in the kindness of his heart, to prevent family division in the settlement of an estate. One of this lot, returning from a Yankee gunboat, swaggered to conference under the trees, in a fine uniform, carrying a handsome rifle, and declared he would work or not as he pleased, come and go as he pleased and consider the land his own. He went to his cabin, stood in the door, looked the Captain in the eye, brought his gun down with a crash, and said: "Yes, I gwi wuk right here. I'd like tuh see any man put me outer dis house!"

Captain Pinckney, after waiting for the men to think over the situation, assembled them again. Their attitude was more insolent and aggressive. He gave them ten days longer for decision; then all who would not work must go. His neighbours were having similar experiences. In a section where a few years before perfect confidence had existed between white and black, all white men went armed, weapons exposed to view. They were few, the blacks many. After consultation, they reported conditions to General Devens at Charleston, and suggested that he send down a representative. He sent a company under an officer whom the planters carried from plantation to plantation. Negroes were called and addressed: "I have come to tell you people that these lands belong to these planters. The Government has not given these lands to you; they do not belong to the Government to give. You are free to hire out to whom you will, or to rent lands. But you must work. You can't live without work. I advise you to make contracts quickly. If crops are not made, you and your families will suffer."

This Federal visitation was not without wholesome effect. Yet the negroes would not work till starvation drove them to it. The Captain's head-plower came confessing: "Cap'n, I 'clar' 'fo' Gawd, suh, I ain' got no vittles fuh my wife an' chillun. I ain' got a day's rations in my cabin." "It's your own fault. You can go to work any minute you want to." "Cap'n, I'se willin'. I been willin' fuh right smart while. I ain' nuvver seed dis way we been doin' wuz zackly right. I been 'fused in my min'. But de other niggers dee won' let me wuk. Dee don' want me tuh wuk fuh you, suh. I'se feared." The Captain was sorely tempted to give rations without conditions, but realised that he must stand his ground. In a day or two the head-plower reappeared. "Cap'n, I come tuh ax you tuh lemme wuk fuh you, suh." "All right. There's your plow and mule ready. You can draw rations ahead." One by one all came back. They had suffered, and their ex-master had suffered with them.

Many planters had severer trials than the Captain and his immediate neighbours. Down on the coast, negroes demanded possession of plantations, barricaded them and shot at owners. They pulled up bridges so owners could not reach their homes, and in this and other ways kept the whites out of property. Many planters never recovered their lands. When the time came that they might otherwise have done so, they were unable to pay accumulated taxes, and their home-steads passed forever out of their keeping.

In making contracts, Captain Pinckney's negroes did not want money. "We don' trus' dat money. Maybe it git lak Confeddick money." In rice they saw a stable value. Besides a share in the general crop, the Captain gave each hand a little plot on which to grow rice for family consumption. When the general crop was divided into shares, they would say, after retaining a "sample": "Keep my part, suh, an' sell it wid yo's." They knew he could do better for them than they could for themselves. In business and in the humanities, they looked to him as their truest friend. If any got sick, got out of food and clothes, got into a difficulty or trouble of any sort, they came or sent for him; sought his advice about family matters wherein they would trust no other man's counsel; trusted him in everything except politics, in regard to which they would rely upon the word of the most unprincipled stranger did he but appear under the title "Republican," "Radical," "Union Leaguer."

Carpet-baggers told them: "If the whites get into power, they will put you back in slavery, and will not let your wives wear hoop-skirts. If we win the election we will give you forty acres and a mule." "I know for a fact," Captain Pinckney assured me, "that at Adam's Run negroes came to the polls bringing halters for mules which they expected to carry home."

The excitement of the election of 1876, when native whites strained every nerve to win the negro vote, was fully felt on the Santee. The morning news reached El Dorado of Hampton's election, the Captain, according to custom, walked down to his wharf to give orders for the day. He found his wharf foreman sitting on an upturned canoe, his head hung down, the picture of dejection. "William," the Captain said, "I have good news." "Whut is it, suh?" "General Hampton is elected." Silence. Presently the negro half lifted his face, and looking into the eyes of the white man with the saddest, most hopeless expression in his own, asked slowly: "Well—Cap'n—*whut you goin' tuh do wid we, now?*" The master's heart ached for him! Remanded back to slavery—that was what negroes were taught to look for—to slavery not such as they had known, but in which all the follies and crimes to which they had been incited since freedom should be charged up to them. They did not, could not, realise how their old owners pitied, condoned, forgave.

Next election the struggle was renewed. After a hopeful barbecue, the Captain's hands were threshing his rice crop. He called the foreman behind the stacks, and asked: "Well, Monday, what are you people going to do at the polls tomorrow?" "Dee gwi vote

From a painting photographed by Reckling & Sons, Columbia, S. C.

MRS. WADE HAMPTON
(Daughter of Governor McDuffie, of South Carolina.)

de 'Publican ticket, suh.   Ef dee tells you anything else, dee's lyin'.   I gwi vote de 'Publican ticket, suh.   I got it tuh do.   I b'lieve all what you white gent'muns been tellin' us at de barbecues.   I knows myse'f dat dis way we niggers is a-doin' an' a-votin' ain' de bes' way fuh de country—anybody kin see dat.   But den I got tuh vote de 'Publican ticket, suh.   We all has.   Las' 'lection I voted de Democrack ticket an' dee killed my cow. Abum, he vote de Democrack ticket; dee killed his colt."   Monday counted off the negroes who had voted the "Democrack" ticket, and every one had been punished.   One had been bombarded in his cabin; another's rice crop had been taken—even the ground swept up and every grain carried off, leaving him utterly destitute.   "I tell you, suh," said Monday, "I got tuh do it on my 'count, an' on yo' 'count.   You make me fo'man an' ef I didn' vote de 'Publican ticket, I couldn' make dese niggers wuk.   I couldn' do nothin' 'tall wid 'em."

The night before an election the Democratic Club was in session at McClellanville when Mr. McClellan came in and said there would be trouble next day.   He had heard on the river that negroes were buying up ammunition and were coming armed to the polls.   He had gone to stores and given orders that sale should be stopped.   Whites now tried to buy but found stock sold out.   They collected available arms and ammunition in village and neighbourhood, and concealed these under a hay-wagon, which appeared next day near the polls, one of many of similar appearance.   Squads were detailed for duty near polls and wagon.

Blacks came armed, and, demurring, stacked muskets at the cross-roads which marked the hundred-yard limit prescribed by election ruling; all day they were in terrible humour.   "I heard my own servants," Captain Pinckney tells, "between whom and myself the kind-

liest feelings had existed, say in threatening tones:
'We's here tuh stan' up fuh our rights. We ain' gwi
leave dese polls. None our colour got tuh leave dese
polls 'fo' dee close.'"

Whites preserved a front of unconcern they were far
from feeling. Seventy-five whites and 500 blacks voted
at this precinct. Guns once in the hands of the blacks,
and turned against this little handful of whites, God
help all concerned! Whites had begun to hope the day
would end smoothly, when a trifling incident seemed to
precipitate conflict. Two drunken white men rode
hallooing along the road. The negroes, taking this as
a pretext for a fight, rushed for their muskets. An old
trial justice, Mr. Leland, sprang on a box and called
loudly: "Come here! Come here!" They looked
back. "I am the Peace Officer!" he yelled. "Come,
listen to me!" Threatening, curious, sullen, they came
back some paces with an air of defiance, of determination suspended for the moment. "I don't like the looks
of things," said the old trial justice, "and I am going
to call on the most influential men in the community to
act as my constabulary force and help me maintain
order. Pinckney!" The gunboat desperado stepped
forward. "Calhoun! De Saussure! Huger! Horry!
Porcher! Gaillard!" So the wily old justice went on,
calling names famous in the annals of South Carolina,
and black men answered. "Line up there! Take the
Oath of Office! Hold up your hands and swear that,
so help you God, you will help me maintain the laws
and preserve the peace and dignity of the State of
South Carolina!" He happened to have in his pocket
a dozen old badges of office, and swift as he swore the
men in, he pinned badges on them. He made them a
flighty, heroic little speech and the face of events was
changed.

He had picked off ring-leaders in mischief for justices of the peace.   Whites found it difficult to pocket smiles while beholding them strutting around, proud as pea-cocks, and reducing to meekness inoffensive negroes who would never have made any disturbance in the first place but for the prodding of these same new "limbs of the law."   It was trying in a different way to see a peace-able, worthy negro knocked about incontinently by bullies "showing off."   Yet the matter in hand was to get the day over without bloodshed.   And this end was achieved.

Avoidance of bloodshed was not attained at all public meetings, as students of reconstruction history know too well.   "And all sorts of lies went North about us," says the Captain, "the Radicals and their paid allies sending them; and sometimes, good people writing about things they did not understand or knew by hearsay only. I stopped reading Northern papers for a long time— they made me mad.   The 'Tribune's' false accounts of the Ellenton Riot exasperated me beyond endurance. It got its story from a Yankee schoolmarm who got it from a negro woman.   I was so aggravated that I sat down and wrote Whitelaw Reid my mind.   I told him I had subscribed to the 'Tribune' for years, but now it was so partisan it could not tell the truth; its reports were not to be trusted and I could not stand it any longer; and he would oblige me by never sending me another copy; he could give the balance of my sub-scription to some charity.   I directed his attention to the account of the Ellenton Riot in the 'New York Herald' and reminded him that the truth was as accessible to one paper as the other.   Reid did not answer my letter except through an editorial dealing with mine and similar epistles."   He said in part, to the best of the Captain's memory:

"We have received indignant letters from the South in regard to recent articles in this paper. A prominent South Carolinian writes: 'I can't stand the "Tribune" any longer!' One party from Texas says: 'Stop that d—d paper!' Now, all this for reasons which can be explained in a few words. When the 'Tribune' is exposing Republican rascalities, the Southerners read it with pleasure. But when it exposes Democratic rascalities, they write: 'Stop that d—d paper!'"

BATTLE FOR THE STATE HOUSE

CHAPTER XXX

BATTLE FOR THE STATE-HOUSE

SOUTH CAROLINA'S first Governor under her second reconstruction was General R. K. Scott, of Ohio, ex-Freedmen's Bureau Chief. His successor was Franklin J. Moses, Jr., scalawag, licentiate and débauché, four years Speaker of the House, the " Robber Governor." Moses' successor was D. H. Chamberlain, a cultivated New Englander, who began his public career as Governor Scott's Attorney General. A feature of the Scott-Moses administration was a black army 96,000 strong, enrollment and equipment alone costing over a half-million dollars, $10,000 of which, on Moses' admission, went into his own pocket as commission on purchases. The State's few white companies were ordered to surrender arms and disband.

The State House was refurnished on this scale: $5 clocks were replaced by $600 ones; $4 looking-glasses by $600 mirrors; $2 window curtains by $600 to $1,500 ones; $4 benches by $200 sofas; $1 chairs by $60 chairs; $4 tables by $80 tables; $10 desks, $175 desks; forty-cent spittoons, $14 cuspidors, etc. Chandeliers cost $1,500 to $2,500 each. Each legislator was provided with Webster's Unabridged, a $25 calendar inkstand, $10 gold pen; railroad passés and free use of the Western Union Telegraph were perquisites. As " Committee Rooms," forty bed-rooms were furnished each session; legislators going home, carried the furniture. At restaurant and bar, open day and night in the State House, legislators refreshed themselves and friends at

353

State expense with delicacies, wines, liquors, cigars, stuffing pockets with the last. Orders for outside entertainments, given through bar and restaurant, were paid by the State. An incident of Radical rule: "Hell Hole Swamp," purchased by the Benevolent Land Commission as site for homes for homeless negroes. Another: Moses lost $1,000 on a horse race; next day the House of Representatives voted him $1,000 as "gratuity." The order on the Treasurer, signed by Moses as Speaker, to pay this "gratuity" to Moses is on file in Columbia.

Bills made by officials and legislators and paid by the State, reveal a queer medley! Costly liquors, wines, cigars, baskets of champagne, hams, oysters, rice, flour, lard, coffee, tea, sugar, suspenders, linen-bosom shirts, cravats, collars, gloves (masculine and feminine, by the box), perfumes, bustles, corsets, palpitators, embroidered flannel, ginghams, silks, velvets, stockings, chignons, chemises, gowns, garters, fans, gold watches and chains, diamond finger-rings and ear-rings, Russia-leather workboxes, hats, bonnets; in short, every article that can be worn by man, woman or infant; every article of furniture and house furnishing from a full parlour-set to a baby's swinging cradle; not omitting a $100 metallic coffin.

Penitentiary bills display in abundant quantities fine liquors, wines, delicacies and plain provisions; yet convicts nearly starved; bills for the coloured Orphan Asylum, under coloured General Senator Beverly Nash's direction, show silks, satins, corsets, kid gloves, all manners of delicacies and substantials for the table, yet it came out that orphans got at "breakfast, hominy, mackerel and bean coffee—no milk. At dinner, a little bacon or beef, cornbread and hominy, sometimes a little baker's bread; at supper, a slice of baker's bread and

RADICAL MEMBERS OF THE LEGISLATURE
OF SOUTH CAROLINA.

These are the photographs of sixty-three members of the "reconstructed" Legislature of South Carolina. Fifty of them were Negroes or Mulattos; thirteen were white men. Of the twenty-two among them who could read and write only eight used the vernacular grammatically. Forty-one made their mark with the help of an amanuensis. Nineteen were taxpayers to an aggregate of $146.10. The other forty-four paid no taxes, and yet this body was empowered to levy on the white people of the state taxes amounting to $4,000,000.

black molasses, each child dipping a slice into a saucer passed around." The State-paid gardener worked Senator Nash's garden; coal and wood bought " for the Asylum " was delivered at Senator Nash's; ditto lumber and other supplies. The matron sold dry goods and groceries. I have mentioned trifles. For big " steals " and " hauls," Railroads, Bond and Printing Ring swindles, consult the Fraud Reports.

The State University was negroised, adult white and black men matriculating for the express purpose; its scholastic standard was reduced below that of an academy. Attempt to negroise the Deaf and Dumb Asylum closed it. At the Insane Asylum the tact and humanity of Dr. J. F. Ensor, Superintendent, made the situation possible to whites.*

South Carolinians beheld Franklin J. Moses, Jr., owner of the beautiful and historic Hampton-Preston home; at receptions and fêtes the carriages of a ring-streaked, striped and speckled host rolled up gaily to ancient gateways hitherto bars exclusive to all that was not aristocratic and refined. One-time serving-maids sat around little tables under the venerable trees and luxuriant vines and sipped wine in state. A Columbian tells me she used to receive a condescending bow from her whilom maid driving by in a fine landau. Another maid, driving in state past her ex-mistress's door, turned her head in shame and confusion. One maid visited her ex-mistress regularly, leaving her carriage a square or two off; was her old, respectful, affectionate self, and said these hours were her happiest. " I'se jes myse'f den." A citizen, wishing to aid his butler, secured letters of influence for him and sent him among rulers of the land. George returned: " Marster, I have asso-

---

* See " Reconstruction in South Carolina," by John S. Reynolds, in the Columbia " State."

ciated with gentlemen all my life. I can't keep comp'ny with these folks. I'd rather stay with you, I don' care how poor we are."

One night when Rev. William Martin's family were asleep, there came a knocking at the door. Miss Isabella Martin answered. Maum Letty stood outside weeping: "Miss Isabella, Robert's (her son) been killed. He went to a party at General Nash's an' dee all got to fightin'. I come to ax you to let me bring 'im here." Permission was given. A stream of negroes flowed in and out of the basement rooms where the dead was laid. And it was, "The General says this," "The General says that." Presently the General came. "Good morning, Beverly," said Miss Martin. "Good morning, Miss Isabella;" he had been a butler and had nice manners. "This is a sad business, Beverly." "Yes, Miss Isabella. It happened at my house, but I am not responsible. There was a party there; all got to fighting—you know how coloured people will do—and this happened." It is law for the coroner to see a corpse, where death has occurred from violence, before any removal or change is made. The coroner did not see Robert until noon. General Nash had gotten the body out of his house quickly as possible.

Belles of Columbia were Misses Rollins, mulattoes or quadroons. Their drawing-room was called "Republican Headquarters." Thick carpets covered floors; handsome cabinets held costly bric-a-brac; a $1,000 piano stood in a corner; legislative documents bound in morocco reposed with big albums on expensive tables. Jewelers' and other shops poured treasures at Misses Rollins' feet. In their salon, mingling white and dusky statesmen wove the destinies of the old Commonwealth. Coloured courtezans swept into furniture emporiums, silk trains rustling in their wake, and gave orders for "committee rooms"; rode in fine carriages through the streets, stopped in front of this or that store; bareheaded white salesmen ran out to show goods or jewels. Judge M. (who went over to the Radicals for the loaves and fishes and ever afterward despised himself) was in Washington with a Black and Tan Committee, got drunk, and for a joke took a yellow demi-mondaine, a State official's wife, on his arm and carried her up to President and Mrs. Grant and introduced her at a Presidential reception.

Black Speaker Elliott said ("Cincinnati Commercial," Sept. 6, 1876): "If Chamberlain is nominated, I shall vote for Hampton." A member of the Chamberlain Legislature tells me this is how the Chamberlain-Elliot split began. Mrs. Chamberlain was a beautiful woman, a perfect type of high-born, high-bred, Anglo-Saxon loveliness, noble in bearing, lily-like in fairness. She brought a Northern Governor, his wife, and other guests to the State House. They were standing near my informant in the "white part" of the House, when Elliott, black, thick-lipped, sprang down from the Speaker's chair, came forward and asked a gentleman in attendance for introduction. This gentleman spoke to Alice Chamberlain. The lily-white lady lifted her eyes toward Elliott, shivered slightly, and said: "No!" Elliott did not forgive that.

If the incident were not on good authority, I should doubt it. At Chamberlain's receptions, the black and tan tide poured in and out of his doors; he entertained black legislators, and presumably Elliott, at dinners and suppers. But all men knew Chamberlain's rôle was repugnant to him and his exquisite wife. What she suffered during the hours of his political successes, who can tell? Tradition says she was cut to the quick when a black minister was called in by her husband to perform the last rites of the church over her child. Any white clergyman of the city would have responded on call. There were many to say Chamberlain turned to political account even so sacred a thing. Others to say that if white ministers had shown him scant attention he was right not to call upon them. And yet I cannot blame the white clergy for having stood aloof, courting no favours, of the foreigner who fraternised with and was one of the leaders of the State's spoilers, whether he was a spoiler himself or no.

Governor Chamberlain was fitted for a better part than he had to play; he won sympathy and admiration of many good citizens. He was a gentleman; he desired to ally himself with gentlemen; and the connections into which ambition and the times forced him was one of the social tragedies of the period. He began his administration denouncing corruption within his own party and promising reforms. At first, he investigated and quieted race troubles, disbanding negro militia, and putting a stop to the drilling of negroes. He bestowed caustic criticisms on "negrophilists," which Elliott brought against him later. He was at war with his legislature; when that body elected W. J. Whipper, an ignorant negro gambler, and ex-Governor Moses to high judicial positions, he refused to commission them.

Of that election he wrote General Grant: "It sends a thrill of horror through the State. It compels men of all parties who respect decency, virtue, or civilisation, to utter their loudest protests." He prophesied immediate "reorganization of the Democratic Party as the only means left, in the judgment of its members, for opposing solid and reliable front to this terrible *crevasse* of misgovernment and public debauchery." There was then no Democratic party within the State; Democrats had been combining with better-class Republicans in

ɔromise tickets.   To an invitation from the New
ɪnd Society of Charleston, to address them on
fathers' Day," he said: " If there was ever an
hour when the spirit of the Puritans, the spirit of undy-
ing, unconquerable enmity and defiance to wrong ought
to animate their sons, it is this hour, here, in South
Carolina.   The civilisation of the Puritan and the Cavalier, the Roundhead and the Huguenot, is in peril."

A new campaign was at hand.   Chamberlain's name
was heard as leader of a new compromise ticket.   He
had performed services that seemed inspired by genuine
regard for the old State and pride in her history.   He
was instrumental in having the Washington Light
Infantry, of Charleston, at Bunker Hill Centennial, and
bringing the Old Guard, of New York, and the Boston
Light Infantry to Fort Moultrie's Centennial, when he
presented a flag to the Washington Light Infantry and
made a speech that pleased Carolinians mightily.   He
and Hampton spoke from the same platform and sat at
the same banquet.   He was alive to South Carolina's
interest at the Centennial in Philadelphia.   The State
began to honour him in invitations to make addresses
at college commencements and on other public occasions.

A Democratic Convention in May came near nominat-
ing him.   Another met in August.   Between these he
shook confidence in his sincerity.   Yet men from the low
country said: " Let's nominate him.   He has tried
to give honest government."   Men from the up country: " He can not rule his party, his party may rule
him."   Men from the low country: " We cannot elect
a straight ticket."   Men from the up country: " We
have voted compromise tickets the last time.   We are
not going to the polls unless we have a straight, clean
white ticket."   They sent for Hampton and nominated him.   His campaign reads like a tale of the old

Crusades. To his side came his men of war, General Butler, General Gary and Colonel Haskell. At his name the people lifted up their hearts in hope.

Governor Chamberlain had denounced the rascalities of Elliott, Whipper's election in the list. He was nominated by the Blacks and Tans, on a ticket with R. H. Cleaves, mulatto; F. L. Cardoza, mulatto; Attorney General R. B. Elliott, black, etc. He walked into the convention arm in arm with Elliott. Soon he was calling for Federal troops to control elections, charging all racial disorders to whites; ruling harsh judgments against Red Shirts and Rifle Clubs; classing the Washington Light Infantry among disorderly bodies, though he had been worthily proud of this company when it held the place of honour in the Bunker Hill parade and, cheered to the echo, marched through Boston, carrying the battle-flag of Colonel William Washington of the Revolution.

That was a picturesque campaign, when every county had its "Hampton Day," and the Red Shirts rode, and ladies and children raised arches of bloom and scattered flowers in front of the old cavalry captain's curvetting steed. Barbecues were spread for coloured brethren, and engaging speakers tried to amuse, instruct and interest them.

The Red Shirts, like the Ku Klux, sprang into existence almost as by accident. General Hampton was to speak at Anderson. The Saturday before Colonel R. W. Simpson proposed to the Pendleton Club the adoption of a badge, suggesting a red shirt as cheap and conspicuous. Pickens men caught up the idea. Red store supplies ran out and another club donned white ones. The three clubs numbered a body of three hundred or more stalwart, fine-looking men of the hill-country, who had nearly all seen service on battlefields, and who rode like centaurs. Preceded by the Pendleton Brass Band, they made an imposing procession at the Fair Grounds on the day of the speaking, and were greeted with ringing cheers. The band-wagon was red; red flags floated from it and from the heads of four horses in red trappings; the musicians wore red garments; instruments were wrapped in red. The effect was electrical. In marching and countermarching military tactics were employed with the effect of magnifying numbers to the eyes of the negroes, who had had no idea that so many white men were alive.

The red shirt uniform idea spread; a great red-shirted army sprang into existence and was on hand at public meetings to see that speakers of the White Man's Party had equal hearing with the Black Republicans. The Red Shirts rode openly by day and by night, and where they wound their scarlet ways women and children felt new sense of security. Many under its protection were negroes. Hampton strove hard to win the negro vote. He had been one of the first after the war to urge qualified suffrage for them. In public speeches he declared that, if elected, he would be "the governor of all the people of South Carolina, white and black." He got a large black vote. Years after, when he lay dying, friends bending to catch his last words, heard him murmur: "God bless my people, white and black!"

Mrs. Henry Martin tells me of some fearful days following the pleasant ones when her father, Professor Holmes, entertained the Old Guard in his garden among the roses and oleanders. "One night, my brother, after seeing a young lady home from a party, was returning along King Street with Mr. Evaugh, when they encountered a crowd of negro rowdies and ran into a store and under a counter. The negroes threw cobble-stones—the street was in process of paving—on them. My brother was brought home in a wagon. When our mother removed his shirt, the skin came wholly from his back with it; he lived several years, but never fully recovered from his injuries. My father cautioned us to stoop and crawl in passing the window on the stairway to his room. In other houses, people were stooping and crawling as they passed windows; a shadow on a curtain was a target for a rock or a bullet. Black women were in arms, carrying axes or hatchets in their hands hanging down at their sides, their aprons or dresses half-concealing the weapons." "There are 80,000 black men in the State who can use Winchesters and 200,000 black women who can light a torch and use a knife," said "Daddy Cain," ex-Congressman and candidate for reëlection, in his paper, "The Missionary Record," July, 1876, and in addressing a large negro gathering, when Rev. Mr. Adams said, "Amen!"

Northern papers were full of the Hamburg and Ellenton riots, some blaming whites, some blacks, some distributing blame impartially. Facts at Cainhoy blazed out the truth about that place, at least. The whites, unarmed except for pistols which everybody carried then, were holding peaceable meeting when fired into from ambush by negroes with muskets, who chased them, continuing to fire. A youth of eighteen fell, with thirty-three buckshot in him; another, dying, wrote his mother that he had been giving no trouble. A carpenter and a shoemaker from Massachusetts, and an aged crippled gentleman were victims.

"Kill them! Kill them all! Dis town is ours!" Old Charlestonians recall hearing a hoarse cry like this from negro throats (Sept. 6, 1876), recall seeing Mr. Milton Buckner killed while trying to protect negroes from negroes. They recall another night of unforgettable horror, when stillness was almost as awful as tumult; frightened blacks were in-doors, but how long would they remain so? Rifle Clubs were protecting a meeting of black Democrats. Not a footfall was heard on the streets; not a sound broke the stillness save the chiming of St. Michael's bells. Women and children and old men listened for the alarm that might ring out any moment that the negroes had risen *en masse* for slaughter. They thanked God when presently a sound of careless footsteps, of talk and laughter, broke upon the night; the Rifle Club men were returning in peace to their firesides.

General Hunt, U. S. A., reported on the Charleston riot, November, 1876, when white men, going quietly to places of business, were molested by blacks, and young Ellicott Walker was killed. The morning after the election General Hunt "walked through the city and saw numbers of negroes assembled at corners of Meeting and Broad Streets," and was convinced there would be trouble, "though there was nothing in the manner of the whites gathered about the bulletin board to provoke it." Surgeon De Witt, U. S. A., told him "things looked bad on King and other streets where negroes insisted on pushing ladies off the sidewalks."

When Walker was killed, and the real trouble began, General Hunt hurried to the Station House; the Marshal asked him for assistance; reports came in that negroes were tearing up trees and fences, assailing whites, and demanding arms of the police. General Hunt found at the Station House "a number of gentlemen, young and old," who offered aid. Marshal Wallace said, "But these are seditious Rifle Clubs." Said General Hunt, "They are gentlemen whom I can trust and I am glad to have them." Pending arrival of his troops, he placed them at the Marshal's disposal. The general relates: "They fell in with his forces; as I was giving instructions, he interposed, saying the matter was in his hands. He then started off. I heard that police were firing upon and bayonetting quiet white people. My troops arrived and additional white armed citizens. One of the civil authorities said it was essential the latter be sent home. I declined sending these armed men on the streets, and directed them to take position behind my troops and remain there, which direction they obeyed implicitly."

With the Mayor and other Radical leaders General Hunt held conference; the negro police was aggravating the trouble, he proposed that his troops patrol streets; the mayor objected. "Why cannot the negroes be prevailed upon to go quietly home?" the General asked. "A negro has as much right to be on the streets armed as a white man." "But I am not here to discuss abstract rights. A bloody encounter is imminent. These negroes can be sent home without difficulty by you, their leaders." "You should be able to guarantee whites against the negroes, if you can guarantee negroes against the whites." "The cases are different. I have no control over the blacks through their reason or intelligence. They have been taught that a Democratic victory will remand them to slavery. Their excited fears, however unfounded, are beyond my control. You, their leaders, can quiet and send them home. The city's safety is at stake." The Mayor said he must direct General Hunt's troops; Hunt said he was in command. The Mayor wired Chamberlain to disband the Rifle Clubs "which were causing all the mischief." Hunt soon received orders to report at Washington.

"Hampton is elected!" the people rejoiced. "Chamberlain is elected!" the Radicals cried, and disputed returns. The Radical Returning Board threw

THE SOUTHERN CROSS   Photograph by Reckling & Sons, Columbia, S. C.

General Hampton, while Governor, built this, his residence, with his own hands and with the assistance of his faithful negroes. The men in the picture, from left to right, are: Hon. LeRoy F. Youmans, General Hampton, Judge McIver, Hon. Joseph D. Pope, General James McGowan.

out the Democratic vote in Laurens and Edgefield and made the House Radical. The State Supreme Court (Republican) ordered the Board to issue certificates to the Democratic members from these counties. The Board refused; the Court threw the Board in jail; the United States Court released the Board. The Supreme Court issued certificates to these members. November 28, 1876, Democrats organised in Carolina Hall, W. H. Wallace, Speaker; Radicals in the State House, with E. W. Mackey, Speaker, and counting in eight Radical members from Laurens and Edgefield. The Democratic House sent a message to the Radical Senate in the State House that it was ready for business. Senate took no notice. On Chamberlain's call upon President Grant, General Ruger was in Columbia with a Federal regiment.

November 29, the Wallace House marched to the State House, members from Edgefield and Laurens in front. A closed door, guarded by United States troops, confronted them. J. C. Sheppard, Edgefield, began to read from the State House steps a protest, addressed to the crowd around the building and to the Nation. The Radicals, fearful of its effect, gave hurried consent to admission. Each representative was asked for his pistol and handed it over. At the Hall of Representatives, another closed and guarded door confronted them. They saw that they had been tricked and quietly returned to Carolina Hall.

The people were deeply incensed. General Hampton was in town, doing his mightiest to keep popular indignation in bounds. He held public correspondence with General Ruger, who did not relish the charge that he was excluding the State's representatives from the State House and promised that the Wallace House should not be barred from the outer door, over which he had control. But its members knew they took their lives in their hands when they started for the Hall. A committee or advance guard of seven passed Ruger's guard at the outer door. Col. W. S. Simpson (now President of the Board of Directors of Clemson College), who was one of the seven, tells me:

"On the first floor was drawn up a regiment of United States troops with fixed bayonets; all outside doors were guarded by troops. Upstairs in the large lobby was a crowd of negro roughs. Committee-rooms were filled with Chamberlain's State constables. General Dennis, from New Orleans, a character of unsavoury note, with a small army of assistants, was Doorkeeper of the Hall. Within the Hall, the Mackey House, with one hundred or more sergeants-at-arms, was assembled, waiting Mackey's arrival to go into session." The seven dashed upstairs and for the door of the Hall. The doorkeepers, lolling in the lobby, rushed between them and the door and formed in line; committee presented certificates; doorkeepers refused to open the door.

"Come, men, let's get at it!" cried Col. Alex. Haskell, seizing the doorkeeper in front of him. Each man followed his example; a struggle began; the door parted in the middle; Col. Simpson, third to slip through, describes the Mackey House, "negroes chiefly, every man on his feet, staring at us with eyes big as saucers, mouths open, and nearly scared to death." Meanwhile, the door, lifted off its hinges, fell with a crash. The full Democratic House marched in, headed by Speaker Wallace, who took possession of the Speaker's chair. Members of his House took seats on the right of the aisle, negroes giving way and taking seats on the left.

Speaker Wallace raised the gavel and called the

House to order. Speaker Mackey entered, marched up and ordered Speaker Wallace to vacate the chair. Speaker Wallace directed his sergeant-at-arms to escort Mr. Mackey to the floor where he belonged. Speaker Mackey directed his sergeant-at-arms to perform that office for General Wallace. Each sergeant-at-arms made feints. Speaker Mackey took another chair on the stand and called the House to order. There was bedlam, with two Speakers, two clerks, two legislative bodies, trying to conduct business simultaneously! The "lockout" lasted four days and nights. Democrats were practically prisoners, daring not go out, lest they might not get in. Radicals stayed in with them, individual members coming and going as they listed, a few at a time.

The first day, Democrats had no dinner or supper; no fire on their side of the House, and the weather bitterly cold. Through nights, negroes sang, danced and kept up wild junketings. The third night Democrats received blankets through windows; meals came thus from friends outside; and fruit, of which they made pyramids on their desks. Two negroes came over from the Mackey side; converts were welcomed joyously, and apples, oranges and bananas divided. The opposition was enraged at defection; shouting, yelling and rowdyism broke out anew. Both sides were armed. The House on the left and the House on the right were constantly springing to their feet, glaring at each other, hands on pistols. Wallace sat in his place, calm and undismayed; Mackey in his, brave enough to compel admiration; more than once he ran over to the Speaker's stand, next to the Democratic side, and held down his head to receive bullets he was sure were coming. Yet between these armed camps, small human kindnesses and courtesies went on; and they joined in laughter at the comedy of their positions. Between Speakers, though, there was war to the knife, there was also common bond of misery.

The third afternoon Democrats learned that their massacre was planned for that night. Negro roughs were congregating in the building; the Hunkidory Club, a noted gang of black desperadoes, were coming up from Charleston. A body of assassins were to be introduced into the gallery overlooking the floor of the Hall; here, even a small band could make short work its own way of any differences below. Chamberlain informed Mackey; Mackey informed Wallace. Hampton learned of the conspiracy through Ruger; he said: "If such a thing is carried out, I cannot insure the safety of your command, nor the life of a negro in the State." The city seethed with repressed anxiety and excitement. Telegrams and runners were sent out; streets filled with newcomers, some in red shirts, some in old Confederate uniforms with trousers stuffed in boots, canteens slung over shoulders. Hampton's soldiers had come.

Twenty young men of Columbia contrived, through General Ruger, it is said, to get into the gallery, thirty into the Hall, the former armed with sledge-hammers to break open doors at first intimation of collision. The Hook and Ladder Company prepared to scale the walls. The train bringing the Hunkidory Club broke down in a swamp, aided possibly by some peace-loving agency. The crowding of Red Shirt and Rifle Clubs into the city took effect. The night passed in intense anxiety, but in safety. Next day, Speaker Wallace read notification that at noon the Democrats, by order of President Grant, would be ejected by Federal troops if, before that time, they had not vacated the State House; in obedience to the Federal Government, he and the other Democratic members would go, protesting, however, against this Federal usurpation of authority. He adjourned the House to meet immediately in Carolina Hall. Blankets on their shoulders, they marched out. A tremendous crowd was waiting. Far as the eye could reach, Main Street was a mass of men, quiet and apparently unarmed.

I have heard one of Hampton's old captains tell how things were outside the State House. "The young men of Columbia were fully armed. Clerks in our office had arms stowed away in desks and all around the rooms; we were ready to grab them and rush on the streets at a moment's notice. It was worse than war times. We had two cannon, loaded with chips of iron, concealed in buildings, and trained on the State House windows and to rake the street. We marched to the State House in a body. General Hampton had gone inside. He had told us not to follow him. He and General Butler, his aide, had been doing everything to keep us quiet. He knew we had come to Columbia to fight if need be. 'I will tell you,' he said, 'when it is time to fight. You have made me your governor, and, by Heaven, I will be your governor!' Again and again he promised that. Usually, we obeyed him like lambs. But we followed him to the State House.

"Federal troops were stationed at the door. What right had they there? It was our State House! Why could roughs and toughs and the motley crowd of earth go in, on a pass from Doorkeeper Dennis, a Northern rascal imported by way of New Orleans, while we, the State's own sons and taxpayers, could not enter? We pressed forward. We were told not to. We did not heed. We were ready not to heed even the crossed bayonets of the guard. Things are very serious when they reach that pass. The guard in blue used the

utmost patience. Federal soldiers were in sympathy
with us. Colonel Bomford,* their officer, ran up the
State House steps, shouting: 'General Hampton!
General Hampton! For God's sake come down and
send your men back!' In an instant General Hampton
was on the steps, calmly waving back the multitude:
'All of you go back up the street. I told you not to
come here. Do not come into collision with the Federal
troops. I advise all, white and black, who care for the
public welfare to go home quietly. You have elected
me your Governor, and by the eternal God, I will be
your Governor! Trust me for that! Now, go back!'
We obeyed like children. On the other side of the
State House a man ran frantically waving his hat and
shouting: 'Go back! go back! General Hampton says
go back!' This man was ex-Governor Scott, who a
few years before had raised a black army for the intimidation and subjugation of South Carolina!"

The Wallace House sat, until final adjournment, in
South Carolina Hall, the Mackey House in the State
House. Governor Chamberlain, with the town full of
Rifle Clubs supposed to be thirsting for his gore, rode
back and forth in his open carriage to the State House
and occupied the executive offices there, refusing to
resign them to General Hampton. He was inaugurated inside the "Bayonet House"; General Hampton
in the open streets. General Hampton conducted the
business of the State in two office-rooms furnished with
Spartan simplicity. The Wallace House said to the
people: "Pay to tax collectors appointed by Governor
Hampton, ten per cent of the tax rate you have been
paying Governor Chamberlain's tax collectors, and we
will run your Government on it." So the people paid

---

* I think this was General Ruger or Colonel Black, but I let the
name stand as my informant gave it.

their tax to Hampton's collectors and to no others. Without money, the Chamberlain Government fell to pieces.

Northern sentiment had undergone change. Tourists had spread far and wide the fame of Black and Tan Legislatures. Mr. Pike, of Maine, had written "The Prostrate State." In tableaux before a great mass-meeting and torchlight procession in New York, South Carolina had appeared kneeling in chains before the Goddess of Liberty. The North was protesting against misuse of Federal power in the South. General Sherman said: "I have always tried to save our soldiers from the dirty work. I have always thought it wrong to bolster up weak State Governments by our troops." "Let the South alone!" was the cry. One of Grant's last messages reflected this temper. President Hayes was exhibiting a spirit the South had not counted on. He sent for Hampton and Chamberlain to confer with him in Washington. The old hero's journey to the National Capital and back was an ovation. Soon after his return, Chamberlain resigned the keys and offices of the State House. Chamberlain was bitter and felt that the Federal Government had played him false.

With Governor Nicholls established in Louisiana and Governor Hampton in South Carolina, the battle between the carpet-baggers and the native Southerners for their State Houses was over. The Federal soldiers packed up joyfully, and the Southerners cheered their departure.

Louisiana had been engaged in a struggle very similar to South Carolina's. For three months she had two governors, two legislatures, two Supreme Courts. Again and again was her Capitol in a state of siege. Once two Republican parties faced each other in battle array for its possession—as two Republican parties had faced each other in Little Rock contending for Arkansas's Capitol. One morning, Louisianians woke to find the entrance commanded by United States Artillery posted on the "Midnight Order" of a drunken United States District Judge. Once a thousand negroes, impressed as soldiers, lived within the walls, eating, drinking, sleeping, until the place became unspeakably filthy and small-pox broke out. More than once for its possession there was warfare on the levees, bloodshed in barricaded streets. Once the citizens were marching joyfully to its occupation past the United States Custom House, and the United States soldiers crowded the windows, waved their caps and cheered. Once members were ejected by Federal force; Colonel de Trobriand regretting that he had the work to do and the Louisianans bearing him no grudge; it was, " Pardon me, gentlemen, I must put you out." " Pardon us, that we give you the trouble."

These corrupt governments had glamours. Officials had money to burn. New Orleans was like another Monte Carlo for one while. Gambling parlours stood open to women and minors. Then was its twenty-five-year charter granted the Louisiana State Lottery. At a garden party in Washington not long ago, a Justice of the Supreme Court said in response to some question I put: " It would take the pen of a Zola to describe reconstruction in Louisiana! It is so dark a chapter in our national history, I do not like to think of it." A Zola might base a great novel on that life and death struggle between politicians and races in the land of cotton and sugar plantations, the swamps and bayous and the mighty Mississippi, where the Carpet-Bag Governments had a standing army, of blacks chiefly, with cavalry, infantry, artillery, and navy of warships going up and down waterways; where prominent citizens were arrested on blank warrants, carried long distances, held for months; where women and children listened for the tramp, tramp, of black soldiers on piazzas, the crash of a musket on the door, the demand for the master or son of the house!

Dixie after the war is a mine for the romancer, historian, ethnologist. Never before in any age or place did such conditions exist. The sudden investiture of the uncivilised slave with full-fledged citizenship wrought tragedy and comedy not ready to Homer's, Shakespeare's or Cervantes's pen. The strange and curious race-madness of the American Republic will be a study for centuries to come. That madness took a child-race out of a warm cradle, threw it into the ocean of politics—the stormiest and most treacherous we have known—and bade it swim for its own life and the life of the nation!

CRIME AGAINST WOMANHOOD

CHAPTER XXXI

CRIME AGAINST WOMANHOOD

THE rapist is a product of the reconstruction period. In the beginning he commanded observation North less by reason of what he did than by reason of what was done unto him. His chrysalis was a uniform; as a soldier he could force his way into private homes, bullying and insulting white women; he was often commissioned to tasks involving these things. He came into life in the abnormal atmosphere of a time rife with discussions of social equality theories, contentions for coeducation and intermarriage.

General Weitzel, resigning his command, wrote from La Fourche and La Teche to Butler in New Orleans: "I can not command these negro regiments. Women and children are in terror. It is heartrending." * General Halleck wrote, April, 1865, to General Grant of a negro corps: "A number of cases of atrocious rape by these men have already occurred. Their influence on the coloured people is reported bad. I hope you will remove it." Similar reports were made by other Federal officers. Governor Perry, of South Carolina, says: "I continued remonstrances to Secretary Seward on the employment of negro troops, gave detail of their atrocious conduct. At Newberry . . . (Crozier's story). At Anderson, they protected and

---

* See Sherman-Halleck correspondence in Sherman's "Memoirs" on "the inevitable Sambo." Also, W. T. Parker, U. S. A., on "The Evolution of the Negro Soldier,". N. Amer. Rev., 1899. Lincoln disbanded the troops organised by General Hunter.

carried off a negro who had wantonly murdered his master. At Greenville, they knocked down citizens in the streets without slightest provocation. At Pocotaligo, they entered a gentleman's house, and after tying him, violated the ladies." Mr. Seward wrote that Northern sentiment was sensitive about negro troops. When Governor Perry handed Generals Meade and Gillmore the Pocotaligo report, General Meade said he was opposed to negro troops and was trying to rid the army of them, but had to exercise great caution not to offend Northern sentiment. General Gillmore had some offenders executed. Federal commanders largely relieved the South of black troops, but carpet-bag officials restored them in the form of militia.

I have told elsewhere Crozier's story. Let me contrast his slayers with a son of industry it was my honour to know, Uncle Dick, my father's coachman. During the war, when my father had occasion to send a large sum in gold coin through the country, Uncle Dick carried it belted around his body under his shirt. My father's ward was attending the Southern Female College in Danville when the President and his Cabinet, fleeing from Richmond, reached that place. Knowing that Danville might become a fighting center, Mr. Williams T. Davis, Principal, wrote my father to send for Sue. The way to reach Danville was by private conveyance, seventy miles or more. Uncle Dick, mounted high on his carriage-box, a white-headed, black-faced knight-errant of chivalry, set forth. Nobody knew where the armies were. He might have to cut his horses loose from his carriage, mount Sue on one, himself take the other, and bring her through the forest. In due time the carriage rolled into our yard, Uncle Dick proud and happy on his box, Sue inside wrapped in rugs, sound asleep, for it was midnight. That is the way we could trust our black men.

The following account by an ex-Confederate captain shows how General Schofield handled a case of the crime which is now under discussion: "A young white girl on her way to Sunday School was attacked by a negro; 'attempted' assault, the family said; it is usually put that way; 'consummated' nails the victim to a stake. Our people were in a state of terror; they seemed paralysed; they were inured to dispossession and outrage. No one seemed to know what to do. I picked up several young men and trailed down the ruffian. Then I sent a letter to General Schofield (with whom I had some acquaintance, as we had met each other hunting), asking instructions. He sent two detectives and a file of soldiers, requesting that I call for further assistance if occasion demanded. I wrote full statement of facts, had the girl's testimony taken in private; evidence was laid before General Schofield; the negro was sent to the penitentiary for eighteen years. The promptness of his action inspired people here with hope. We had no Ku Klux in Virginia— one reason, I have always thought, was the swiftness with which punishment was meted out in that case."

I have, as I believe, from Judge Lynch himself particulars of another case in which, the law being inactive, citizens took justice into their own hands:

"Two young girls, daughters of a worthy German settler, were out to bring up cows, when attacked by a negro tramp; they ran screaming, but were overtaken; he seized the older; the younger, about ten years old, continued to run. Some passers on the nearest road, a private and lonely one, rushed to the relief of the older girl, who was making such outcry as she could. We found her prostrate, the negro having her pinioned with one knee on either arm. His jack-knife open, was held between his teeth, and he was stuffing his handkerchief in her mouth to stifle her cries. We rescued her, took him prisoner, carried him to the nearest magistrate, a carpet-bag politician, who committed him to jail to await the action of the grand jury. He made his escape a few days afterward, was recaptured and relodged in jail. Ten days later a band was organised among respectable citizens in and around our town; a Northern settler was a member. One detachment set out about dark for the rendezvous where they met a score more of resolute, armed men, some with masks, some without. They effected entrance into the jail, but their way was arrested when they found the prisoner in a casemated cell, which other negroes readily pointed out, one offering a lamp; a railroad section hand procured crow-bars with which the casemate was crushed in; the prisoner was taken in charge. He stood mute; seemed calm and unmoved; was put in a close carriage, the purpose being to drive him to the exact spot of his crime, but it coming on day, the company thought best to execute him at once. He was placed upon a mule; a rope attached to his neck was tied to the limb of a tree about ten feet above. The leader now learned of an intention to riddle his body with bullets when the drop occurred. Each member had pledged obedience to orders; each had been pledged to take no liquor for hours before, or during this expedition—pledges so far rigidly observed. The leader addressed them: 'We are here to avenge outrage on a helpless child, and to let it be well known that such crime shall not go unpunished in this community. But mutilation of this fiend's remains will be a reflection upon ourselves and not a dispensation of justice.'

"The negro, seeing his end surely at hand, broke down, pleading for mercy; confessed that he had appreciated in advance the great peril in which his crime might place him, but had argued that, as a stranger, he would not be liable to identification, and that as the country was thickly wooded, he was sure of escape. ' But, fo' Gawd, gent'mun, ef a white man f'om de Norf hadn't put't in my hade dat a white 'oman warn' none too good fuh—'

"Word was given, and he dropped into eternity. It was broad daylight when the party got back to town. They overtook several negro men going to work who knew full well what they had been about. But there was no sign of protest or demur. The Commonwealth's Attorney made efforts to ascertain the perpetrators of the deed, but as the company entered the town and jail so quietly and left it with so little disturbance that only one person in the village had knowledge of their coming and going, no one was discovered who could name a single member of the party or who had any idea of whence they came or whither they went. So of course no indictment could be found." This was in 1870; since then till now no similar crime has occurred in that community. Within the circumscribed radius of its influence, lynching seems to eradicate the evil for which administered.

The moderation marking this execution has not always accompanied lynching. Reading accounts of unnecessary tortures inflicted, of very orgies of vengeance, people remote from the scenes, Southerners no less than others, have shuddered with disgust, and trembled with concern for the dignity of their own race. Only people on the spot, writhing under the agony of provocation, comprehended the fury of response to the crime of crimes. Vigilants meant to make their awful vengeance effective deterrent to the crime's repetition. No other crime offers such problems to relatives and officers of justice and to the people among whom it occurs; it is so outside of civilisation that there seem no terms for dispassionate discussion, no fine adjustment of civil trial and legal penalty.

Listen to this out of the depths of one Southern woman's experience: "I stood once with other friends, who were trying to nurse her back to life and reason, by the bedside of a girl—a beautiful, gentle, high-born creature—who had been outraged. We were using all the skill and tact and tenderness at our command. It seemed impossible for her to have one hour's peaceful sleep. She would start from slumber with a shriek, look at us with dilated eyes, then clutch us and beg for help. But the most unspeakable pity of it all was her loathing for her own body; her prayers that she might die and her body be burned to ashes. I heard her physician say to an officer who came to take her deposition: 'I would be signing that girl's death warrant if I let you in there to make her tell that horrible story over again.' When a grim group came with some negroes they wanted to bring before her for identification, her brothers and her lover said: 'Only over our dead bodies.'"

Lynching is inexcusable, even for this crime, which is comparable to no other, and to which murder is a trifle. So we may coolly argue when the blow has not fallen upon ourselves or at our own door. When it has, we think there's a wolf abroad and we have lambs. Those to whom the wrecked woman is dear are quiveringly alive to her irreparable wrong. The victim has rights, they argue; if, unhappily for herself, she survive the outrage, she is entitled to what poor remnants of reason may be left her; it is naturally their whole care to preserve her from memories that sear and craze, and from rehearsal before even the most private tribunal, of events that the merciful, even if not of her blood, must wish her to forget. Under such strain, men see as the one thing imperative the prompt and informal removal from existence of the offender, whom they look upon, not as man, but beast or fiend.

The " poor white " is the most frequent sufferer from assault; the wife of the small farmer attending household ·duties in her isolated home while her husband is in the fields or otherwise absent about his work; or the small farmer's daughter when she goes to the spring for water, or to the meadow for the cows, or trudges a lonely road or pathway to school; these are more convenient material than the lady of larger means and higher station, who is more rarely unattended. In cases on record the ravished and slain were children, five, six, eight years old; in others, mothers with babies at their breasts, and the babies were slain with the mothers. Here is a case cited by Judge M. L. Dawson: A negro raped and slew a farmer's five-year-old child. Arrested, tried, convicted, appealed, sentence reversed, reappealed (on insanity plea) ; people took him out and hung him.

In full-volumed indignation over lynching, the usual course of the Northern press was to almost lose sight of the crime provoking it. It was a minor fact that a woman was violated, that her skull was crushed or that she sustained other injuries from which she died or which made her a wreck for life—particulars too trivial to be noted by moulders of public opinion writing eloquent essays on " Crime in the South." Picking up a paper with this glaring headline, one would have a right to expect some outburst of indignation over the ravishment and butchering of womanhood. But there would be editorial after editorial rife with invectives against lynching and lynchers, righteous with indignation over "lawlessness in the South," and not one word of sympathy or pity for the white victim of negro lust! The fact that there was such a victim seemed lost sight of; the crime for which the negro was executed would often escape everything but bare mention, sometimes that. What deductions were negroes to draw from such distinctions, except that lynching was monstrous crime, rape an affair of little moment, and strenuous objection to it only one feature of damnable "Race Prejudice in the South"?

"They do not care, the men and women of the North," I have heard a Southern girl exclaim, "if we are raped. They do not care that we are prisoners of fear, that we fear to take a ramble in the woods alone, fear to go about the farms on necessary duties, fear to sit in our houses alone; fear, if we live in cities, to go alone on the streets at hours when a woman is safe anywhere in Boston or New York."

From the Northern attitude as reflected in the press and in the pulpit, negroes drew their own conclusions. Violation of a white woman was no harm; indeed, as a leveler of social distinctions, it might almost be construed into an act of grace. The way to become a hero in the eyes of the white North and to win the crown of martyrdom for oneself and new outbursts of sympathy for one's race was to assault a white woman of the South. This crime was a development of a period when the negro was dominated by political, religious and social advisers from the North and by the attitude of the Northern press and pulpit. It was practically unknown in wartime, when negroes were left on plantations as protectors and guardians of white women and children.

"There was only one case,* as far as the writer can ascertain, of the negro's crime against womanhood during all the days of slavery," said Professor Stratton in the "North American Review" a few years ago, "while his fidelity and simple discharge of duty during the Civil War when the white men were away fighting against his liberty have challenged the admiration of the world; but since he has been made free, his increase in crime and immorality has gone side by side with his educational advancement—and even in greater ratio." The Professor gave figures, as others have done, which proved his case, if figures can prove anything. Considered with reference to the crime under discussion, it is difficult to see how purely intellectual training tends to its increase, if there is any truth in the doctrine that brain development effects a reduction of animal propensities. Only in moral education, however, rests any real security for conduct. Negroes educated and negroes uneducated, in a technical sense, have committed this crime.†

The rapist is not to be taken as literal index to race character; he is an excrescence of the times; his crime is a horror that must be wiped out for the honour of

---

*In Boston, 1676. I suppose this is the case meant as it rests on court records. "The Nation," 1903, published letters showing four specific cases from slavery's beginning to 1864; that just cited, one mentioned in Miss Martineau's "Society in America"; one reported in "Leslie's Weekly," 1864; one reported in a periodical not named. In the earliest days of slavery, laws enacted against negro rape (the penalty was burning) seem to show that the crime existed or that the Colonists feared it would exist. The fact that during the War of Secession, Southern men left their families in negro protection is proof conclusive that this tendency, if inherent, had been civilised out of the race.

† For other reasons for rape than I have given see "The Negro; The Southerner's Problem," by Thomas Nelson Page, p. 112, and "The American Negro," by William Hannibal Thomas (negro), pp. 65, 176-7, 223.

the land, the security of womanhood, the credit of our negro citizenhood. The weapon for its destruction is in the hands of Afro-Americans; overwhelming sentiment on their part would put an end to it; they should be the last to stand for the rapist's protection; rather should they say to him: "You are none of us!" They should be quick to aid in his arrest, identification and deliverance to the law. Such attitude would be more effective than any other one force that can be brought to bear upon this crime and that of lynching. I chronicle here as worthy of record, that in June, 1870, William Stimson, rapist, was tried before a negro jury, convicted on negro evidence, and hung November 4. This happened in North Carolina during negro rule.

The negro guilty of this hideous offense has committed against his race a worse crime than lynching can ever be. By the brutish few the many are judged— particularly when the many in vociferous condemnation of the penalty visited upon the criminal seem to condone his awful iniquity against themselves. Black men who have been and will be womanhood's protectors outnumber the beasts who wear like skins as many thousands to one; and it is not fair to themselves that they pursue any course, utter any sentiment, which causes them to be classed in any way whatever with these. Black men are seeing this and are setting their faces towards stamping out the crime which causes lynching. Utterances from some of their pulpits and resolutions passed by some of their religious bodies indicate this.

The occurrence of rapes, lynchings and burnings in the North and West has had beneficial influence upon the question at large. It has led white people of other sections to understand in some degree the Southern situation and to express condemnation of the crime that leads to lynching. The attitude of the Northern press has

undergone great change in recent years, change effective
for reform, in that while lynching is as severely under
the ban as ever—which it should be—the companion
crime goes with it.   Southern sentiment is against lynching; I recall seven governors—Aycock of North Carolina, Montague of Virginia, Heyward of South Carolina, Candler and Terrell of Georgia, Jelks of
Alabama, Vardaman of Mississippi—who have so
placed themselves conspicuously on record.   All our
newspapers have done so, I believe, from the "Times-
Dispatch" of Richmond, the Charlotte "Observer,"
the "Constitution" and the "Journal" of Atlanta, the
"State" of Columbia, the Charleston "News-Courier,"
the Savannah "News," to the "Times-Democrat" of
New Orleans, and "Times-Union" of Jacksonville.

One hope and promise of the new constitutions
with which Southern States lately replaced the Black
and Tan instruments is the eradication of this
method of procedure.   Soon after Virginia adopted
hers, three negro rapists in that State received
legal trial and conviction and not over hasty execution.   On motion of District Attorney E. C. Goode,
reprieve was granted after conviction that a case
in Mecklenburg might be looked into more fully.   Such
deliberation has not been exceeded—if, indeed, it has
been equaled—north of Mason & Dixon's line.   But
as long as rapes are committed, so long will there be
danger of lynchings, not only in the South, but anywhere else.   In the presence of this worse than savage
crime the white race suffers reversion to savagery.

RACE PREJUDICE

CHAPTER XXXII

RACE PREJUDICE

As LATE as 1890, Senator Ingalls said: "The use of the torch and dagger is advised. I deplore it, but as God is my judge, I say that no people on this earth have ever submitted to the wrongs and injustice which have been put upon the coloured men of the South without revolt and bloodshed." Others spoke of the negro's use of torch and sword as his only way to right himself in the South. When prominent men in Congressional and legislative halls and small stump speakers everywhere fulminated such sentiments, the marvel would have been if race prejudice had not come to birth and growth. Good men, whose homes were safe, and who in heat of oratory or passion for place, forgot that other men's homes were not, had no realisation of the effect of their words upon Southern households, where inmates lay down at night trembling lest they wake in flames or with black men shooting or knifing them.

But for a rooted and grounded sympathy and affection between the races that fierce and newly awakened prejudice could not kill, the Sepoy massacres of India would have been duplicated in the South in the sixties and seventies. Under slavery, the black race held the heart of the white South in its hands. Second only in authority to the white mother on a Southern plantation, was the black mammy; hoary-headed white men and women, young men and maidens and little children, rendered her reverence and love. Little negroes and little white children grew up together, playing together and form-

391

ing ties of affection equal to almost any strain. The servant was dependent upon his master, the master upon his servant. Neither could afford to disregard the well-being of the other. No class of labour on earth today is as well cared for as were the negroes of the Old South. Age was pensioned, infancy sheltered. There was a state of mutual trust and confidence between employer and employee that has been seen nowhere else and at no time since between capital and labour.

Had the negro remained a few centuries longer the white man's dependant, often an inmate of his home, and his close associate on terms not raising questions and conflicts, his development would have proceeded. Through the processes of slavery, the negro was peaceably evolving, as agriculturist, shepherd, blacksmith, mechanic, master and mistress of domestic science, towards citizenship—inevitable when he should be ready for it; citizenship all the saner, because those who were training him were unconscious of what they were doing and contemplated making no political use of him. They were intent only on his industrial and moral education. His evolution was set back by emancipation.

Yet, if destruction of race identity is advancement, the negro will advance. The education which he began to receive with other Greek gifts of freedom has taught him to despise his skin, to loath his race identity, to sacrifice all native dignity and nobility in crazy antics to become a white man. "Social equality!" those words are to be his doom. It is a pity that the phrase was ever coined. It is not to say that one is better than the other when we say of larks and robins, doves and crows, eagles and sparrows, that they do not flock together. They are different rather than unequal. Difference does not, of itself, imply inequality. To ignore a difference inherent in nature is a crime against nature and is punished accordingly by nature.

The negro race in America is to be wiped out by the dual process of elimination and absorption. The negro will not be eliminated as was the Indian—though the way a whole settlement of blacks was made to move on a few years ago in Illinois, looks as if history might repeat itself in special instances. Between lynchings and race riots in the North and West and those in the South there has usually been this difference: in the former, popular fury included entire settlements, punishing the innocent with the guilty; in the latter, it limited itself to the actual criminal. Another difference between sectional race problems. I was in New York during Subway construction when a strike was threatened, and overheard two gentlemen on the elevated road discussing the situation: "The company talks of bringing the blacks up here." "If they do, the tunnel will run blood! These whites will never suffer the blacks to take their work." I thought, "And negroes have had a monopoly of the South's industries and have scorned it!" I thought of jealous white toilers in the slime of the tunnel; and of Dixie's greening and golden fields, of swinging hoes and shining scythes and the songs of her black peasantry. And I thought of her stalwart black peasants again when I walked through sweat-shops and saw bent, wizened, white slaves.

The elimination of the negro will be in ratio to the reduction of his potentiality as an industrial factor. Evolutionary processes reject whatever has served its use. History shows the white man as the exponent of evolution. There were once more Indians here than there are now negroes. Yet the Indian has almost disappeared from the land that belonged to him when a little handful of palefaces came and found him in their way. Had he been of use, convertible into a labourer, he would have been retained; he was not so convertible, and other disposition was made of him while we sent to Africa for what was required. The climate of the North did not agree with the negro; he was not a profitable labourer; he disappeared. He was a satisfactory labourer South; he throve and multiplied. He is not now a satisfactory labourer in any locality. What is the conclusion if we judge the white man's future by his past?

The white man does not need the negro as *littérateur*, statesman, ornament to society. Of these he has enough and to spare, and seeks to reduce surplus. What he needs is agricultural labour. The red man would not till the soil, and the red man went; if the black man will not, perhaps the yellow man will. Sporadic instances of exceptional negroid attainments may interest the white man—in circumscribed circle—for a time. But the deep claim, the strong claim, the commanding claim would be that the negro filled a want not otherwise supplied, that the negro could and would do for him that which he cannot well do for himself—for instance, work the rice and cotton lands where the negro thrives and the white man dies.

The American negro is passing. The mulatto, quadroon, octoroon, strike the first notes in the octave of his evolution—or his decadence, or extinction, or whatever you may call it. The black negro is rare North and South. Negroes go North, white Northerners come South. In States sanctioning intermarriage, irregular connections obtain as elsewhere between white men and black women; and, in addition, between black men and white women of most degraded type or foreigners who are without the saving American race prejudice. Recent exposure of the "White Slave Syndicate" in New York which kidnapped white girls for negro bagnios, is fresh in the public mind.

Under slavery many negroes learned to value and to practice virtue; many value and practice it now; but the freedwoman has been on the whole less chaste than the bond. With emancipation the race suffered relapse in this as in other respects. The South did not do her whole duty in teaching chastity to the savage, though making more patient, persistent and heroic struggle than accredited with. The charge that under slavery miscegenation was the result of compulsion on the part of the superior race finds answer in its continuance since. Because he was white, the crying sin was the white man's, but it is just to remember that the heaviest part of the white racial burden was the African woman, of strong sex instincts and devoid of a sexual conscience, at the white man's door, in the white man's dwelling.*

In 1900, negroes constituted 20.4 per cent. of the population of Texas, the lowest rate for the Southern States; in Mississippi, 58.6, the highest. In Massachusetts, they were less than two per cent. Questions of social intermingling can not be of such practical and poignant concern to Massachusetts as to Mississippi, where amalgamation would result in a population of mulatto degenerates. Prohibitions are protective to both races. Fortunately, miscegenation proceeds most slowly in the sections of negro concentration, the sugar and cotton lands of the lower South. In these, it is also said, there is lower percentage of negro crime of all kinds than where negroes are of lighter hue.

Thinkers of both races have declared amalgamation an improbable, undesirable conclusion of the race ques-

---

* "The Negro in Africa and America," J. A. Tillinghast. On miscegenation see "The Color Line," W. B. Smith; also A. R. Colquhoun, N. Amer. Rev., May, 1903.

tion; that it would be a propagation of the vices of both races and the virtues of neither. In a letter (March 30, 1865) to the Louisville "Courier-Journal," recently reproduced in "The Outlook," Mr. Beecher said: "I do not think it wise that whites and blacks should mix blood . . . it is to be discouraged on grounds of humanity." Senator Ingalls said: "Fred Douglas once said to me: 'The races will blend, coalesce, and become homogeneous.' I do not agree with him. There is no affinity between the races; this solution is impossible. . . . There is no blood-poison so fatal as the adulteration of race."

At the Southern Educational Conference in Columbia, 1905, Mr. Abbott, in one of the clearest, frankest speeches yet heard from our Northern brotherhood, declared the thinking North and South now one upon these points: the sections were equally responsible for slavery; the South fought, not to perpetuate slavery, but on an issue "that had its beginning before the adoption of the Federal Constitution;" racial integrity should be preserved. In one of the broadest, sanest discussions of the negro problem to which the American public has been treated, Professor Eliot, of Harvard, has said recently: "Northern and Southern opinion are identical with regard to keeping the races pure—that is, without admixture of the one with the other . . . inasmuch as the negroes hold the same view, this supposed danger of mutual racial impairment ought not to have much influence on practical measures. Admixture of the two races, so far as it proceeds, will be, as it has been, chiefly the result of sexual vice on the part of white men; it will not be a wide-spread evil, and it will not be advocated as a policy or method by anybody worthy of consideration."

"It will not be a wide-spread evil!" The truth stares

us in the face. Except in the lower South the black negro is now almost a curiosity. In any negro gathering the gamut of colour runs from ginger-cake to white rivaling the Anglo-Saxon's; and according as he is more white, the negro esteems himself more honourable than his blacker fellow; though these gradations in colour which link him with the white man, were he to judge himself by the white man's standard, would be, generally speaking, badges of bastardy and shame.

In Florida, a tourist remarked to an orange-woman: "They say Southerners do not believe in intermingling of the races. But look at all these half-white coons!" "Well, Marster," she answered, "don't you give Southern folks too much credit fuh dat. Rich Yankees in de winter-time; crap uh white nigger babies in de fall. Fus' war we all had down here, mighty big crap uh yaller babies come up. Arter de war 'bout Cuba, 'nother big crap come 'long. Nigger gal ain' nuvver gwi have a black chile ef she kin git a white one!" Blanch, my negro hand-maiden, is comely, well-formed, black; the descendant of a series of honest marriages, yet feels herself at a disadvantage with quadroons and octoroons not nearly her equals in point of good looks or principle. "I'd give five hundred dollars ef I had it, ef my ha'r was straight," she tells me with pathetic earnestness; and "I wish I had been born white!" is her almost heart-broken moan.* She would rather be a mulatto bastard than the black product of honest wedlock.

The integrity of the races depends largely upon the virtue of white men and black women; also, it rests *on the negroid side upon the aspiration to become white,* acknowledgment in itself of inferiority and self-loathing.

---

* Fakirs, taking advantage of the general racial weakness, are selling "black skin removers," "hair straighteners," etc.

The average negress will accept, invite, with every wile she may, the purely animal attention of a "no-count white man" in preference to marriage with a black. The average mulatto of either sex considers union with a black degradation. The rainbow of promise spanning this gloomy vista is the claim that the noble minority of black women who value virtue is on the increase as the race, in self-elevation, recognises more and more the demands of civilisation upon character, and that dignity of racehood which will not be ashamed of its own skin or covet the skin of another. The virtuous black woman is the Deborah and the Miriam of her people. She is found least often in crowded cities, North and South; most often in Southern rural districts. Wherever found, she commands the white man's respect.

Hope should rest secure in the white man. If the faith of his fathers, the flag of his fathers, the Union of his fathers, are worthy of preservation, is not the blood of his fathers a sacred trust also? Besides, before womanhood, whatever its colour or condition, however ready to yield or appeal to his grosser senses, the white man should throw the ægis of his manhood and his brotherhood.

The recent framing of State Constitutions in the South to supersede the Black and Tan creations revived the charge of race prejudice because their suffrage restrictions would in great degree disfranchise the negro. As compared with discussion of any phase of the race issue some years ago, the spirit of comment was cool and fair. "The Outlook" led in justifying the South for protecting the franchise with moderate property and educational qualifications applying to both races, criticising, however, the provision for deciding upon educational fitness—a provision which Southerners admit needs amendment. One effect of these restrictions will be to stimulate the negro's efforts to acquire the necessary education or the necessary three hundred dollars' worth of property. Another effect will be decrease of the white farmer's scant supply of negro labour; this scarcity, in attracting white immigrants, provides antidote for Africanisation of the South.

As to whether negro ownership of lands improves country or not, I will give a Northern view. I met in 1903 at the Jefferson Hotel in Richmond, a wealthy Chicagoan and his wife (originally from Massachusetts), who were looking for a holiday residence in Tidewater Virginia. They made various excursions with land agents, and one day reported discovery of their ideal in all respects but one. "The people around are ruining property by selling lands to negroes. A gentleman at whose house we stopped, a Northerner, had just bought, as he told us, at much inconvenience, a plantation adjoining his own to make sure it would not be cut up and sold by degrees to negroes." I hear Southern farmers in black belts say: "I had much rather have a quiet, orderly negro for neighbour than a troublesome white." But the fact remains that negro ownership of property reduces value of adjoining lands. Besides the social reason, the average negro exhausts and does not improve lands.

"Why don't the negroes live up North?" one is asked; "they go up there and make a little money and come back and buy lands."

"Land is cheap here. It is almost beyond their reach there. The climate here appeals. Then, this is home." Thus I answered in 1902, in Southside, Virginia. After further travel, I amend: Negroes do not wish to work for white land-owners; they wish to remain in the South or to return to the South, as land-owners. They are acquiring considerable property. But, generally speaking, they are thinning out. One may journey miles along Southern railroads and see but few in fields where once were thousands. In Northern cities and pleasure resorts negroes increase. The race problem is broadening, changing territory.

The daughter of an Ohioan gave me a glimpse of this changing base. " Columbus negroes—those born there or who came there long ago, are very different from Southern negroes. They will have nothing to do with the negroes coming direct. The Southern negroes have nice, deferential manners; the Northern negroes hate them for it. Columbus negroes—why, they will push white ladies off the streets!" In a New York store in 1904, I observed two negresses in a crowd near a window where articles of baggage were on check. They pushed their way to the front and demanded belongings without the courteous "please" which any Southerner, or which Northern gentlefolks, would have used; the young white girl in charge—it was a hot day and she looked faint—was doing her cheerful best to meet the noon rush, but was not quick enough for the coloured persons; they hurried and reproved her; as she turned about within, confused by their descriptions and commands, they exclaimed: "That's it! Right befo' you! Don't you see that case right there? What a fool!" She never thought of resenting; came up humbly, loaded with their property, glad to have found it. Their manners would have scandalised a black aristocrat of the Old South.

We cannot afford to wrong this race as we wronged the Indian. We must aid the negro's advancement in the right direction. But we should not discriminate against the white race. Educational doors are open to the negro throughout the land; the South is rich in noble institutions of learning for him; in black belts Southerners are paying more to educate black children than white. In black belts, in white belts, in the mountains, white children are put into fields and factories when they ought to be going to school. Educational odds are against the white children. In regard to schools of manual training, to limit the negro to these and these to the negro is to put a stigma on manual labor in the eyes of white youth and to continue the negro's monopoly of a field which he does not appreciate. We should do more educationally for the white child and not less for the negro. The negro pays small percentage of the Southern educational tax and enjoys full benefits. The negro needs to realize that if the white man owes him a debt, he owes the white man one; and that he cannot safely despise the school of service in house and field which white people from Europe and yellow people from the Orient are eager to enter.

I would close no door of opportunity to the negro. But I must say my affection is for the negro of the old order. I owe reverence to the memory of a black mammy and a debt to negroes generally for much kindness. The real negro I like, the poet of the veldt and jungle, the singer in field and forest, the tiller of the soil, the shepherd of the flocks, the herdsman of the cattle, the happy, soft-voiced, light-footed servitor. The negro who is a half-cut white man is not a negro, and it can be no offense to the race to say that he is unattractive when compared with the dear old darkey of Dixie who was worth a million of him! At Fort Mill, S. C., hard by a monument to a forgotten people, the Catawba Indians, stands a monument to the " Faithful Slaves of the Confederacy," type of a memorial many hearts yet hold. The new negro, in reaching out for higher and better things than the old attained, will be wise not to sacrifice those qualities which told in his ancestor in spite of all shortcomings. The one true plane of equalisation is that of mutual service, each race doing for the other all it can. The old negro and the white man stood more surely on this plane than do their descendants, yet not more surely than all must wish their descendants to stand. My regard for the negro, my pride in what he has really accomplished under the hammering of civilisation, call, in his behalf, for a race pride and reserve in him which shall match the Anglo-Saxon's. There are negroes who have it and who deplore efforts placing them in the position of postulants for a social intermingling which they do not consider essential to their dignity or happiness.* Between blacks and whites South we constantly see race pride maintained on one side as on the other while humanities are observed in manifold exchanges of kindness and courtesy that make a bond of brotherhood.* Whatever position the white Southerner takes theoretically on manufactured race issues, he will usually fight rather than see his inoffensive black neighbour or employe maltreated; his black neighbour or employe will often do as much for him. This attitude is sometimes an expression of the clan habit surviving the destruction of clan-life (old plantation-life in which the white man was Chief and his negroes his clansmen); also, it exists in the recognition of a common bond of humanity more than skin deep. Upon this rock the future may be builded.* As a useful, industrious, citizen, the negro is his own argument and advocate.*

---

* See Council, Penn, and Spencer, "Voice of Missions" (H. B. Parks, Ed.), Sept., Nov., Dec., 1905. See Booker T. Washington's "Up from Slavery," "Character Building," "Future of the American Negro."

MEMORIAL DAY

Daughters of all the South! Sons of all the South! We, your own old soldiers, pause a moment this day in our march and facing to the front, touching eternity on our right, we stand erect before you as if on dress parade. We know that the day of our personal presence has passed its noon, but we would cast no shadow upon the land we leave to you and yours, nor raise one barrier to your full possession of local and national rights. We are but the living Color Guard of the great army of your Southern fathers, and their history and honor are safely in your keeping. The war flag of precious memory waves peacefully above us, and we ask you for our sakes, and its own sake, to love it forever. The Star-spangled Banner of our country waves over all of us and over all our States and people, commanding the respect of every nation. Let it never be dishonored. With the feeling of pride that we are Confederate soldiers, we salute you, not by presenting arms, but with the salutations of our beating hearts. And now we will march on, march forward in column: and, as we go you will hear from us the echo of the angels' song—Peace on earth, good will to men.—*From an address by General Clement A. Evans, Commander of the Georgia Division, U. C. V., Memorial Day, 1905, Atlanta, Ga.*

CHAPTER XXXIII

Memorial Day and Decoration Day. Confederate Societies

Peculiar interest attaches to the inauguration of Memorial Day in Richmond, in 1866, when Northerners, watching Southerners cover the graves of their dead with flowers, went afterwards and did likewise, thus borrowing of us their "Decoration Day" and with it a custom we gladly share with them.* In Hollywood and Oakwood slept some 36,000 Southern soldiers, representing every Confederate State. On April 19, Oakwood Memorial Association "was founded by a little band in the old Third Presbyterian Church, after prayer by Rev. Dr. Proctor." The morning of May 10 a crowd gathered in St. John's Church,† and after simple exercises led by Dr. Price and Dr. Norwood, "the procession, numbering five hundred people, walking two and two, their arms loaded with spring's sweetest flowers, walked out to Oakwood" and strewed with these the Confederate graves. May 3, the Hollywood Memorial Association was formed, and May 31 was its first Memorial Day. The day before, an extraordinary procession wended its way to the cemetery.

---

* "'Decoration Day,' a legal holiday. The custom of 'Memorial Day,' as it is otherwise called, originated with the Southern States and was copied scatteringly in Northern States. On May 5, 1868, General John A. Logan, then Commander-in-Chief of the Grand Army of the Republic, issued an order appointing May 30."—Encyclopedia Americana.

† In this church, Patrick Henry said: "Give me liberty or give me death!"

405

The young men of Richmond, the flower of the city, marched to Hollywood, armed with picks and spades, and numbering in their long line, moving with the swing of regulars, remnants of famous companies, whose gallantry had made them shining marks on many a desperate battlefield. "It was a striking scene," wrote a witness, "as the long line filed by, not as in days of yore when attired in gray and bearing the glittering muskets, they were wont to step to the strains of martial music while the Stars and Bars of the young Republic floated above them; but in citizens' garbs, bearing the peaceful implements of agriculture, performing a pilgrimage to the shrine of departed valour." It was symbolic. The South sought to honour her past in peaceful ways, and to repair by patient industry the ravages of war, wielding cheerfully weapons of progress to which her hands were as yet unaccustomed. As the soldier-citizens marched along, people old and young, by ones and twos and threes, or in organised bodies, fell into the ever-lengthening line. At the cemetery, the pick-and-spade bearers were divided into squads and companies, and under the direction of commanders, worked all day, raking off rubbish, rounding up graves, planting headboards and otherwise bringing about order. Old men and little boys helped. Negroes faithful to the memory of dead friends and owners were there, busy as the whites in love's labour. Several men in Federal uniform lent brotherly hands. When the sun went down the place was transformed. That first fair Memorial Day looked as though it were both Sabbath and Saints' Day. Over or on doors of business houses was the legend, garlanded with flowers or framed in mourning drapery: "Closed in Honour of the Confederate Dead." Federal soldiers walking the quiet streets would pause and study these symbols of grief and reverence. Carloads

MRS. REBECCA CALHOUN PICKENS BACON
Daughter of Francis W. Pickens, the "Secession Governor" of South
Carolina; organizer of the D. A. R. in her state.

of flowers poured into the city. Every part of the South in touch with Richmond by rail or wagon sent contribution. Grace Church was a floral depot; maids, matrons and children met there early to weave blossoms and greenery into stars, crosses, crowns and flags—their beloved Southern cross. Vehicles lent by express and hotel companies formed floral caravanseries moving towards the cemetery.

Then, another procession wound its way to Hollywood, the military companies and the populace, flower-laden, and a long, long line of children, many orphans. There were few or no carriages. The people had none. Old and young walked. The soldiers' section was soon like one great garden of roses white and red; of gleaming lilies and magnolias; of all things sweet-scented, gay and beautiful. Scattered here and there like forget-me-nots over many a gallant sleeper was the blue badge in ribbon or blossom of the Richmond Blues. Thousands visited the green hillside where General Jeb Stuart lay, a simple wooden board marking the spot; his grave was a mound of flowers. From an improvised niche of evergreens, Valentine's life-like bust of the gay chevalier smiled upon old friends. No hero, great or lowly, was forgotten. What a tale of broken hearts and desolate homes far away the many graves told! Here had the Texas Ranger ended his march; here had brave lads from the Land of Flowers and all the States intervening bivouacked for a long, long night, from whose slumbers no bugle might wake them. What women and children standing in lonely doorways, hands shading their eyes, watched for the coming of these marked "Unknown"!

Little Joe Davis' lonely grave was a shrine on which children heaped offerings as they marched past in procession, each dropping a flower, until one must thrust flowers aside to read the inscriptions that make of that tiny tomb a mile-stone in American history—"Joseph, Son of our Beloved President, Jefferson Davis," "Erected by the little boys and girls of the Southern Capital." As blossoms fell, the hearts of the flower-strewers beat tenderly for little Joe's father, then the Prisoner of Fortress Monroe, and for his troubled mother and her living children.

In freedom to honour the Confederate dead by public parade, Virginia was more fortunate than North Carolina. In Raleigh, the people were not allowed to march in procession to the cemetery for five long years. Yet, even so, the old North State faithfully observed the custom of decorating her graves at fixed seasons, the people going out to the cemetery by twos and threes. Indeed, the claim has been made that Dixie's first Memorial Day was observed in Raleigh rather than in Richmond, and the story of it is too sad for telling. March 12, 1866, Mrs. Mary Williams wrote the "Columbus Times," of Georgia, a letter, from which I quote: "The ladies are engaged in ornamenting and improving that portion of the city cemetery sacred to the memory of our gallant Confederate dead. . . . We beg the assistance of the press and the ladies throughout the South to aid us in the effort to set apart a certain day to be observed, from the Potomac to the Rio Grande, and to be handed down through time as a religious custom of the South, in wreathing the graves of our martyred dead with flowers." All our cities, towns and hamlets shared in the honour of originating Memorial Day, for, throughout the fair land of Dixie, soon as flowers began to bloom, her people began to cover graves with them; and the North did likewise.

In reading the recently published "History of the Confederated Memorial Associations of the South," I am newly impressed with the devotion of Southern women, their promptness, energy and resourcefulness in gathering from hillside and valley their scattered dead and providing marked and sheltered sepulture and monuments when there was so little money in their land. I am impressed, too, with the utter lack of sectional bitterness in this volume, which consists chiefly of unpretentious reports of work done. Here and there is a word of grateful acknowledgment to former foes for aid rendered. The simple records throb with a deep human interest to which the heart of the world might make response.

At a meeting of the Atlanta Memorial Association, May 7, 1897, Mrs. Clement A. Evans offered a resolution providing for concert of action among State Associations on questions relating to objects and purposes in common. Before long, this movement was absorbed in a larger. One of the latest formed local associations was at Fayetteville, Arkansas, where war's end found "homes in ashes, farms waste places" and "every foot of soil, marked by contest, red with blood"; six long years of care and toil passed before the women found time for organised work. Yet from this body, not large in numbers nor rich in treasury, sprang the measures—Miss Garside (afterwards Mrs. Welch) suggesting—which resulted in the organisation, May 30, 1900, in the Galt House, Louisville, Kentucky, of the Confederated Southern Memorial Associations with Mrs. W. J. Behan, of New Orleans, President. In 1903, Mrs. Behan, in the name of the order, thanked Senator Foraker of Ohio for bringing before Congress a bill for an appropriation for marking Confederate graves in the North, a bill Congress passed without delay.

As Ladies' Memorial Associations developed out of the war relief societies, so the United Daughters of the

Confederacy grew out of Memorial Associations and Ladies' Auxiliaries to the United Confederate Veterans. Immediate initiative came from "Mother Goodlett," of Nashville, Tennessee, seconded by Mrs. L. H. Raines, of Savannah, the "Nashville American" aiding the movement by giving it great publicity; the U. D. C. was organized at Nashville in the fall of 1894. Of the United Confederate Veterans, a member of the Association tells me : "The Ku Klux—not the counterfeit, but the real Ku Klux working under the code of Forrest—was the Confederate soldier protecting his home and fireside in the only way possible to him. General Forrest disbanded the order; then, for purely memorial, historical, benevolent and social purposes, Confederate Veteran Camps came into existence, springing up here and there without concert of action; presently they united," the federation being effected in New Orleans, June 16, 1889, by representatives of about fifty camps, General John B. Gordon in command. There are now some 1,600 camps with 30,000 members. Of about 300,000 Confederates at the end of the war, this 30,000 is left—"the thin, gray line."

When our veterans have gone North a-visiting, the North has been unsparing in honour and hospitality. Our old gray-jackets give some illustrations like this. Two, walking into a Boston fruit store, handed the dealer a five-dollar bill to be changed in payment of purchases, and received it back with the words: "It cannot pass here." A veteran laid down silver. "That is no good." Concerned lest all his money be counterfeit, the gray-jacket said to his comrade: "May be you have some good money." The comrade's wealth was refused; but in opening his purse, he revealed a Confederate note. "Now," said the smiling storekeeper, "if I could only change that into the same kind of money, it would pass. That's the only good money in Boston today."

The object and influence of these Confederate orders are primarily "memorial and historical"; they occasionally transcend these—as when, for instance, a few years ago, U. C. V. camps passed resolutions condemning lynching. Their tendency is the reverse of keeping bitter sectional feeling alive. It is their duty and office to see to it that new generations shall not look upon Southern forefathers as "traitors," but as good men and true who fought valiantly for conscience's sake, even as did the good men and true of the North. While the Daughters of the American Revolution, a larger and richer body, are worthily engaged in rescuing Revolutionary history from oblivion, it is the no less patriotic care of the Confederate orders, whose members are active in Revolutionary work also, to preserve to the future landmarks and truths about the War of Secession. Upon Memorial Hall, New Orleans, the Confederate relic rooms at Columbia and Charleston; the "White House," Montgomery; the Mortuary Chapel, "Old Blandford," Petersburg; the Confederate Museum, Richmond; other relic rooms; and monuments and tablets scattered throughout the South; the work of the Confederate Memorial Literary Society; the Battle Abbey to be erected in Richmond for reception of historic treasures;—upon these must American historians rely for records of facts and for object lessons in relics that would have been lost but for the patient and faithful endeavours of these orders.

Mrs. Joseph Thompson, in welcoming the Daughters of the American Revolution to Atlanta during the Exposition of 1895, commended in the name of the South, the "broadening and nationalising influence" of the order. To no other one agency harmonising the sec-

tions does our country owe more than to patriotic societies. In 1866, Northern and Southern women found
their first bond of reunion in the Mount Vernon Association, which began in 1853, as a Southern movement,
when the home and tomb of Washington were for sale
and Ann Pamela Cunningham, of South Carolina, called
upon America's women to save Mount Vernon, won
Edward Everett to lecture for the cause, coaxed legislators, congressmen and John Washington to terms, and
rested not until Mount Vernon belonged to the Nation;
during the war it was the one spot where men of both
armies met as brothers, stacking arms without the gates;
Miss Cunningham held her regency, and Mrs. Eve, of
Georgia, Mme. Le Vert and the other Southern Vice
Regents continued on the Board with women of the
North. In 1889, when the tomb of Washington's
mother was advertised for sale, Margaret Hetzel, of
Virginia, appealed successfully through the "Washington Post" to her countrywomen to save it to the Nation.
The founders, in 1890, of the Daughters of the Amer-
ican Revolution were Eugenia Washington of Virginia,
Mary Desha of Kentucky, Ellen Hardin Walworth of
Virginia and Kentucky ancestry; a most active officer
was Mary Virginia Ellett Cabell, of Virginia. The
First Regent of the New York City Chapter was a Virginian, Mrs. Roger A. Pryor. Flora Adams Darling,
widow of a Confederate officer, had a large hand in
originating the order and founded that of the Daughters
of the Revolution and the Daughters of the United
States, 1812. The daughter of the Secession Governor
of South Carolina, Mrs. Rebecca Calhoun Pickens
Bacon, started the D. A. R. in her State, delivering
seven flourishing chapters to the National society. The
daughter of General Cook, C. S. A., Mrs. Lawson Peel,
of Atlanta, is a power in D. A. R. work. The present

MRS. ROGER A. PRYOR

National Regent, Mrs. Donald McLean, is a Mary-lander and, therefore, a Southerner, as Mrs. Adlai E. Stevenson, one of her predecessors, avowed herself to be in part if her Kentucky and Virginia ancestry counted. In no movement of patriotism, in no measures promoting good feeling, has the South been unrepresented.

"Mary, when I die, bury me in my Confederate uniform. I want to rise a Confederate." So said to his wife Dr. Hunter Maguire, the great Stonewall's Surgeon-in-Chief, a short time before his death. He was no less true to the living Union because he was faithful to the dead Confederacy. Visitors used to love to see General Lee at the Finals of Washington College in his full suit of Confederate gray; it became him to wear it in the midst of the draped flags and stacked arms, for while he was teaching our young men to love our united country and to reverence the Stars and Stripes, he did not want them to fail in reverence to the past. None can want us so to fail. Mrs. Lizzie George Henderson, President of the U. D. C., says in the "Confederate Veteran": "Wherever there is a chapter North or West, our Northern friends are so kind and help so much that it brings us closer together as one people."

The thought of her who was "Daughter of the Confederacy" is inseparable from my text. One afternoon Matoaca and I called on Miss Mason at her quaint old house in Georgetown, D. C., a place of pilgrimage for patriotic Southerners. We sat on the little back porch which is on a level with Miss Emily's flower-garden, and she gave us tea in little old-fashioned cups, pouring it out of a little old-fashioned silver tea-pot that sat on a little old-fashioned table. She and Matoaca fell to talking about Mr. Davis.

"I shall never forget him as I saw him first," said Miss Emily, "a young lieutenant in the United States

Army, straight as an arrow, handsome and elegant. It was at the Governor's Mansion in Detroit; my young brother was Governor of Michigan, the State's first Executive; Lieutenant Davis was our guest; the Black Hawk War, in which he had greatly distinguished himself, was just ended, and he was bringing Black Hawk through the country. I was much impressed with the young Lieutenant. I watched his career with interest. I met him again when he was a member of President Pierce's Cabinet. He made a very able Secretary of War.

"Strange how events turn, that it should have been Mr. Davis who sent General McClellan (then Colonel) and General Lee (then Colonel) to the Crimea to study the art of war as practised by the Russians. General McClellan's son, now Mayor of New York, has said that his father had ample opportunity to form unbiassed opinion of the Secretary, as he spent much time in Washington before and after his mission to Russia and was in close touch with Mr. Davis. He quoted his father as saying: ' Colonel Davis was a man of extraordinary ability. As an executive officer, he was remarkable. He was the best Secretary of War— and I use *best* in its widest sense—I ever had anything to do with.' "

" I like 'Little Mac' for saying that and his son for repeating it. 'Little Mac' fought us like a gentleman. When his son runs for the Presidency perhaps I shall urge everybody to vote for him," said Matoaca.

"Unless a Southerner runs," I suggested.

"Alas! When will a Southerner be President of the United States? I heard Mr. Davis make his famous speech bidding farewell to the Senate when Mississippi seceded. It was the most eloquent thing I ever listened to! All the women—and even men—were in tears.

Senators went up to him and embraced him. I saw Mr. Davis in Richmond as President of the Confederacy. I saw him in prison; His Eminence, the Cardinal, secured me permission. He was very thin and feeble, but he rose in his old graceful manner and offered me his seat, a little wooden box beside his bed, a small iron one. The eyes of the guard were on us all the time. General Miles came and looked in. I asked Mr. Davis if I could do anything for him. He said he would like some reading matter. I had had some newspapers, but had not been permitted to bring them in. I was allowed to remain only a few moments.

"I next saw him in Paris. I am so glad to have that memory of him. So many Southerners came abroad in those days. During reconstruction the procession seemed endless! While in Rome I introduced so many Southerners to Pope Pius IX. that His Holiness used to call me '*L'Ambassadrice du Sud.*' Mr Davis was much fêted in France, as he had been in England. While he was at Mr. Mann's in Chantilly, Judah P. Benjamin came from London to see him. Mr. Benjamin was delightful company. I was at Mr. Charles Carroll's when Mr. Davis was entertained there. I recall one dinner when the Southern colony flocked around him in full force and played a game on him. You know of his wonderful memory and wide reading. We laid our heads together before he came in and studied up puzzling quotations to trip him. But the instant one of us would spring couplet, quatrain or epigram on him, he would answer with the author. He perceived our friendly conspiracy and entered merrily into the spirit of it. I alone tripped him—with something I had read in early childhood. I am glad to have this happy memory of Mr. Davis. Otherwise I should always be seeing him as he looked in prison."

Mr. and Mrs. Davis came to Paris for their young daughter, Winnie, who was under Miss Emily's care. They had left her some years before at school in Carlsruhe. Knowing in the early part of 1881 that Miss Mason was travelling in Germany, they wrote her to bring Winnie to Paris, where the girl was to abide until their arrival, studying music and acquiring Parisian graces. When Miss Mason called at Carlsruhe, Winnie rushed into her arms joyously: "I am so glad," she cried, "to see some one from home!"

She had many questions to ask; no sooner were they alone in their railway compartment than Winnie turned to Miss Mason: "At last I see a Southern woman! Now I can learn all that happened to my parents just after the war, when I was a baby. Miss Em, what did Papa do just after the war—just after Richmond fell? What happened to my papa then?" Miss Emily caught her breath! "Winnie, what your papa did not think best you should know, I must decline to tell you. You will soon see him in France." Winnie took small interest in acquiring Parisian graces. "Miss Em, what are papa's favourite songs?" Miss Mason sought faithfully to turn her attention to *chansons* of the day and to operatic airs in vogue. "But I am only going to sing to papa. I am going to the plantation—to Beauvoir. How shall I need to sing opera airs there? Tell me, dear Miss Em, the songs my father loves!"

"When I met her father," Miss Mason says, "I ventured to question him concerning Winnie's ignorance of his prison life, expressing surprise that he had not claimed the sympathy of his child. 'I was unwilling to prejudice her,' he said, 'against the country to which she is now returning and which must be hers. I thought that but justice to the child. I want her to love her country.'"

THE DAUGHTER OF THE CONFEDERACY

Winnie (Varina Anne), youngest child of Jefferson Davis ; born in
Richmond, Va., June 27, 1864, and died at Narragansett Pier,
R. I., September 18, 1895.   General John B. Gordon
gave her the above title by which she was known.

Years later, in Georgia, Veterans gathered to hear her father speak, greeted Winnie's appearance with ringing cheers. General John B. Gordon, placing his hands on her shoulders as he drew her forward, said: "Comrades! here is our daughter, the Daughter of the Confederacy!" She lived much in the North and died there. An escort from the Grand Army of the Republic bore her remains from the hotel at Narragansett Pier to the railway station; in New York, a Guard of Honour from the Confederate Veterans and the Southern Society received her and brought her to Richmond, and Richmond took her own. North, South, East and West sent flowers to deck the bier of the Daughter of the Confederacy, and the North said: "Let us be brothers today in grief as we were only yesterday brothers-in-arms at Santiago."

Men in blue followed Gordon, Fitzhugh Lee and Joe Wheeler to their graves; Joe Johnston and Buckner were Grant's pall-bearers. Our dead bind us together. The voices of Lee, our Beloved, Davis, our Martyr, Stephens, our Peacemaker, Grady, our Orator, of Hampton, Gordon and all their noble fellowship, have spoken for true Unionism; blending with theirs is the voice of Grant, in his last hours at McGregor, the voice of McKinley in Atlanta, the voice of Abraham Lincoln, as, just before his martyrdom, he stood pityingly amid the ruins of Richmond.

When President McKinley declared that the Confederate as well as the Federal dead should be the Nation's care, he said the right word to "fire the Southern heart," albeit our women were not ready to yield to the government their holy office. The name of Charles Francis Adams, of Massachusetts, is a household word in the South because of his tributes to Lee when Virginia thought to place Lee's statue in Wash-

ington.   The names of Col. W. H. Knauss, of Columbus, and W. H. Harrison, of Cincinnati, and of others
of the North should be, for the pious pains they have
taken to honour our dead who rest in Northern soil.
In Oakwoods Cemetery, Chicago, stands the first Confederate Monument erected in the North; the Grand
Army of the Republic, the Illinois National Guards, the
City Troop, the Black Hussars, took part with the Confederate Veterans in its dedication.   After Katie Cabell
Currie, of Texas, and her aides had consecrated the
historic battery given by the Government, the Guards
paid tribute by musket and bugle to Americans who died
prisoners at Camp Douglas.   A sectional bond exists
in the National Park Military Commission, on which
Confederate Veterans serve with Grand Army men;
General S. D. Lee, Commander-in-Chief of the U. C. V.,
is Chairman of the Vicksburg board of which General
Fred Grant is a member.   When Judge Wilson on
behalf of Bates' Tennesseeans presented the Confederate
Monument at Shiloh to the Commission, General Basil
Duke accepted it in the name of the Nation.

When President Roosevelt and Congress sent Dixie's
captured battle-flags home, the Southern heart was fired
anew.   In all our history no more impressive reception
was given to a President than when on his recent visit
to Richmond, Mr. Roosevelt was conducted by a guard
of Confederate Veterans in gray uniforms to our historic
Capitol Square.   In other Southern cities he found
similar escort.   Earlier, when he visited Louisville, a
Confederate guard attended him, General Basil W.
Duke, who followed Mr. Davis's fortunes so faithfully,
being on conspicuous duty.

True to her past, the South is not living in it.   A
wonderful future is before her.   She is richer than was
the whole United States at the beginning of the War

of Secession; in a quarter of a century her cotton production has doubled, her manufactures quadrupled. In one decade, her farm property increased in value twenty-six per cent, her manufacturing output forty-seven; her farm products nearly one hundred. Her railroad and banking interests give as strong indications of her vigorous new life. Immigrants from East and West and North and over seas are seeking homes within her borders. The South is no decadent land, but a land where "the trees are hung with gold," a land of new orchards and vineyards and market-gardens; of luscious berries and melons; of wheat and corn and tobacco and much cattle and poultry; of tea-gardens; and rice and sugar plantations and of fields white with cotton for the clothing of the nations. She is the land of balm and bloom, of bird-songs, of the warm hand and the open door.

I prefaced this book with words uttered by Jefferson Davis; I close with words uttered by Theodore Roosevelt, in Richmond, which read like their fulfilment:

"Great though the meed of praise which is due the South for the soldierly valor her sons displayed during the four years of war, I think that even greater praise is due for what her people have accomplished in the forty years of peace which have followed. . . . For forty years the South has made not merely a courageous but at times a desperate struggle. Now, the teeming riches of mines and fields and factory attest the prosperity of those who are all the stronger because of the trials and struggles through which this prosperity has come. You stand loyally to your traditions and memories; you stand also loyally for our great common country of today and for our common flag."

THE END.

INDEX

INDEX.